Once you start reading this book, you will be gripped by its powerful and, at times, unbelievable story; you will not be able to put it down. I couldn't. By the time you finish, you will be gripped by the powerful grace of God. It's a story only God could write.

RUTH GRAHAM

Author of *Forgiving My Father, Forgiving Myself: An Invitation to the Miracle of Forgiveness*

Deb and Al Moerke wisely built their house and life on the rock of Jesus Christ. If I had known them at the time, I might have expected God to spare them the steady rain, threatening floods, and repeated battering by the winds of tragedy. They were not spared. Their story rocked and inspired me. *Murder, Motherhood, and Miraculous Grace* is, at its foundation, a story of the undeniable, unexplainable, palpable presence of God who empowers radical obedience and provides miraculous heart-change even when the tragedy remains.

SHAUNA LETELLIER

Author of *Remarkable Hope: When Jesus Revived Hope in Disappointed People*

Murder, Motherhood, and Miraculous Grace is a shocking story of surrender and redemption that will impact the lives of everyone who reads it. Moerke proves herself to be a master storyteller as she causes the reader to fall in love with little Hannah, which creates an intense roller-coaster ride of emotion throughout the rest of the narrative. Prepare for life disruption because this book is impossible to put down once the front cover is cracked. A must-read for fans of redemptive true-crime memoirs.

DARCIE J. GUDGER

Author of the Guarded Trilogy: *Spin, Toss,* and *Catch*

Like a single flickering light in the vast darkness, grace is best seen in the most unexpected places. Debra's story is not one of preservation, but of perseverance in the midst of unspeakable heartache—a grace that only God can give and a story only God can write.

KYLE IDLEMAN

Senior pastor, Southeast Christian Church; author of *Not a fan* and *Don't Give Up*

A terrific story with surprising twists. You will not be able to put it down. It will both break your heart and mend it as you marvel at the power of love to overcome.

ANN SPANGLER
Author of *Women of the Bible*

What a powerful story that touched my heart deeply, moved me to tears, and enlarged my understanding of what surrender and God's amazing grace in action looks like. *Murder, Motherhood, and Miraculous Grace* is a must-read for foster families, adoptive families, birth families, social workers, judicial workers, or anyone who has endured loss of any kind and desires God to transform their pain into purpose. Thank you, Debra Moerke, for your authentic sharing and for opening yourself up to be a willing vessel to be the hands and feet of Jesus to reflect his love, mercy, forgiveness, and grace.

KATHE WUNNENBERG
Author/speaker; president/founder of Hopelifters Unlimited in Phoenix, Arizona

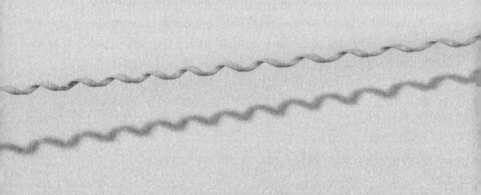

Murder, Motherhood, and Miraculous Grace

DEBRA MOERKE

with Cindy Lambert

TYNDALE
MOMENTUM®

The nonfiction imprint of
Tyndale House Publishers, Inc.

Visit Tyndale online at www.tyndale.com.

Visit Tyndale Momentum online at www.tyndalemomentum.com.

TYNDALE, *Tyndale Momentum,* and Tyndale's quill logo are registered trademarks of Tyndale House Publishers, Inc. The Tyndale Momentum logo is a trademark of Tyndale House Publishers, Inc. Tyndale Momentum is the nonfiction imprint of Tyndale House Publishers, Inc., Carol Stream, Illinois.

Murder, Motherhood, and Miraculous Grace: A True Story

Designed by Julie Chen

The author is represented by Ambassador Literary Agency, Nashville, TN.

For information about special discounts for bulk purchases, please contact Tyndale House Publishers at csresponse@tyndale.com, or call 1-800-323-9400.

ISBN 978-1-4964-3331-2 (hc)
ISBN 978-1-4964-3332-9 (sc)

Printed in the United States of America

25	24	23	22	21	20	19
7	6	5	4	3	2	1

In memory of my sister, Judy,

who not only led me to the Lord,

but was the first to encourage me to write this story.

Blessed is the one who perseveres under
trial because, having stood the test, that
person will receive the crown of life that
the Lord has promised to those who love him.

James 1:12

Contents

Foreword by Carol Kent *ix*
A Note to the Reader *xiii*
Prologue *xv*

part one: The New Arrivals

1. An Easy Yes *3*
2. The Home on Goose Egg Road *13*
3. Clues *27*
4. Inklings of the Past *37*
5. The Bridge *49*
6. The Parting *57*

part two: The Unthinkable

7. Suspicions *73*
8. The Pageant *87*
9. The Yellow Phone *101*
10. The Battleground *109*

part three: The Fallout

11. The Ultimate Question *125*
12. Unexpected Costs *133*

13. Sacred Conversations *145*

14. The Decision *155*

15. Unexpected Standoff *165*

16. The Arrival *173*

17. The Painted Stone *181*

18. The Ruling *193*

19. Obstacle Course *201*

part four: **Going the Distance**

20. A Tender Hello *211*

21. The Garage *217*

22. The Witness Stand *225*

23. New Territories *239*

24. Boots and a Badge *251*

25. Ticking Time Bomb *267*

26. Roots *277*

27. Freedom *287*

28. The Revelation *295*

29. Only God *305*

Interview with Debra Moerke *319*

Acknowledgments *325*

About the Authors *327*

Foreword

THE COVER OF THIS BOOK made my heart stand still. Almost twenty years ago my phone rang in the middle of the night. My only child, a US Naval Academy graduate with an impeccable record, had been arrested for the murder of his wife's first husband. I experienced the nausea, the inability to carry my own weight, and the disbelief that accompanies shocking, unexpected news. My head spun out of control with fear for my child's safety and the welfare of his wife and two stepdaughters. Questions about why a good God could allow such a horrific thing to happen, anxiety over how we would pay for his defense and make a living when the news became public, and sorrow for the family of the deceased surrounded me. One thing was certain: Life would never be the same.

There are defining markers in our lives that change everything. A shocking phone call. A baby—by birth or adoption. An incident that requires a demonstration of character. A devastating personal choice that results in incarceration. An unexpected health problem that brings suffering to someone we love. A crisis of faith when God seems to allow evil to triumph. A soul-stirring decision to help someone who has betrayed us. A willingness to forgive the unforgiveable.

Everything comes to a screeching halt and we feel like an outsider—someone living on the edge of reality, but not really being "in" it. Our thoughts are jumbled and conflicted:

Surely what's just happened isn't real.

I will wake up and find out this was just a bad dream.

If this is truly reality, what am I supposed to do about it?

Could I have done anything to stop this bad thing from happening?

Is God asking me to be personally involved?

How will this impact my family?

How will I be judged by other people?

It takes wisdom for us to fully understand what has taken place, what our role needs to be in the situation, and what God is prompting us to do that may be way outside our comfort zone or far removed from our human abilities.

Debra Moerke faced these challenges as she and her husband, Al, opened their home and their hearts to more than one hundred forty children over sixteen years. Believing she understood God's call on her life, Debra gladly embraced the challenges and pain these wounded children brought with them. Then something unthinkable happened to a precious child they cared for and loved—one they had hoped and prayed to protect.

The mystery of God's ways seemed too incomprehensible to grasp as gut-wrenching tragedy struck this family so dedicated to sharing God's love with powerless children. His ways became even more confounding for Debra when God called her to an even deeper obedience—a sacrificial obedience—that on a human level was impossible for her.

Stretched beyond what seemed the limits of her endurance, Debra took one step after another on this new path that required forgiveness, risk, and a reopening of her wounded heart that seemed unimaginable. Her story is not only about facing fears and fighting giants, not only about inconceivable forgiveness, and not only about the miracles that come with surrender, it's really about what only God can do. Too miraculous to be believed, yet true, the more one reads this story, the bigger God grows.

Throughout my own journey of my son's life-without-parole sentence, I'm learning that God often reveals his purpose through the rearview mirror of time. Just when I think he's busy elsewhere and doesn't see my urgent need, I discover that he's answering my prayers in a different way than what I wanted or expected. Instead of an eventual end-of-sentence date for my son, God opened doors for ministry to inmates and their families through our nonprofit organization, Speak Up for Hope. Personal pain made me sensitive to the needs of others and more willing to give hands-on love and compassion to the families I'm getting to know in long prison visitation lines. I'm watching my son use his education, leadership, and Christianity to teach and mentor his fellow inmates. I, like Deb Moerke, am experiencing miraculous grace in the middle of harsh circumstances.

If you long to believe in love prevailing against all odds and you're ready to see God at work in circumstances that seem to deny his very existence, if you desire to witness the power of fierce forgiveness and you're open to being astonished at what only God can do, keep reading this book. You'll learn how to watch for God's light even in the darkest of times.

This book is Deb Moerke's true story of triumph. As you read *Murder, Motherhood, and Miraculous Grace*, ask yourself who you can encourage with a copy of this remarkable story. You'll be pointing people to an eternal perspective that reveals the blessings on the other side of obedience.

Carol Kent
Speaker and author of
When I Lay My Isaac Down
(NavPress)

A Note to the Reader

THE STORY YOU ARE ABOUT to read is true. Rather than relying on my memory alone, I dug into court transcripts and newspaper reports and interviewed a number of the people involved to ensure accuracy to the best of my ability. I am grateful to each person who participated in that process.

I value accuracy, honesty, and transparency, but I also value courtesy, privacy, and safety. That's why I was determined to find a way to tell my story without violating the privacy of some or putting others at risk of public exposure or danger. After all, this story includes foster children and the Department of Family Services, a murder and a trial, courtroom and prison scenes, and delicate circumstances.

I changed the names and disguised the identities of a number of people in the book as follows:

- Every child mentioned in the book has been given a pseudonym, including one of my own children. The others have given me permission to identify them by name.
- Every legal professional, every Department of Family Services employee, and every public official, if named at all, has been given a pseudonym.

- "Karen," who played a major role in this story, has been given a pseudonym.
- "Karen's" family, friends, associates, and a number of other individuals related to her have had their names changed as well.

Many people whose real names have been used have granted me permission to do so, for which I am grateful.

For private conversations and events that are not part of the public record, I have recreated them to the best of my ability, and I appreciate those who granted me permission to use their words. In some cases, I have made minor adjustments for the sake of the narrative flow, while preserving the integrity of the original text.

Debra Moerke

Prologue

"MOM, CAN I GO TO THE MALL with Katherine?"

It was a warm June morning, and Courtney's 2012 summer vacation had just begun. The temperatures were climbing in Casper, Wyoming, but Alcova Lake would still be too frigid for water activities, so the most exciting social place for young teens to gather was at the local mall.

"Katherine's mom will drop us off . . ."

"And I can pick you up," I said. Now that Courtney was thirteen I allowed her to window-shop and eat lunch with her friends at the food court, unsupervised.

Later that day as I drove to pick up Courtney and Katherine from the mall, I thought a girls' night out, with fast food and a movie, would interest my young teenage daughter. We'd had company to entertain the week before, and I thought we deserved a night for just the two of us.

The mall's parking lot was jam-packed. I maneuvered the car to the main entrance where Courtney and I had agreed to meet. A small crowd of teens clustered near the door. Waving to get Courtney's attention, I noticed a few new faces looking over and pointing toward me. The kids looked familiar.

And then it hit me. Weren't they two of the Bower children? My heart skipped a beat. I couldn't be certain. The last time I'd seen them was almost six years ago in front of our old house.

Despite my momentary unease, I kept smiling and signaling to Courtney. She finally found me in the line of cars and climbed into the front passenger seat of our SUV.

"Hi, honey! Did you have fun? Where's Katherine?" I asked.

"Oh, her mom picked her up a few minutes ago. They were going out to dinner, so she left early." Courtney's voice was soft and her demeanor a little too subdued for someone who had just spent a few hours with friends.

"Who were the kids you were talking to?"

"Oh . . . just some kids. Some from school and others who live in Casper somewhere." She buckled her seat belt and looked straight ahead. Something had happened. Something was said. I sensed it. My mind raced with fear.

"Are you okay?" I asked.

"I'm good. A little tired."

Why isn't Courtney looking at me?

"I thought we could get a bite to eat and then go to a movie since Dad is working late. Would you like that?" I thought my suggestion might perk her up.

"Yes! That sounds fun. Let's do it," she said, sounding more like herself.

After grabbing a burger, we picked a movie we both wanted to see. With popcorn and drinks in hand, we settled into our seats in the back row and waited for the movie to start. Then, out of nowhere, she said, "Mom, what are the names of my biological sisters and brothers?"

This time, my heart skipped two beats.

I knew for certain then. The two teens I had seen with her at the mall were Courtney's biological siblings, Steven and Ally. They had grown up since I'd last seen them, but they looked much the same. Though caught off guard with the question, I answered her with another question. "Are you sure you want to stay at the movie now? We can leave and talk if you want." Resting my popcorn bag on my lap, I looked directly at her.

She paused for a moment before answering. "No. Let's talk after the movie." At that, the lights dimmed, and a preview for an upcoming feature filled the screen.

All through the movie I thought about Courtney's question and wondered if this would be the night she asked me to tell her the whole story behind her adoption.

She may think she is ready, but am I? I'm not sure I know how to tell her. I spent more time praying than paying attention to the movie.

The crescendo of orchestral music indicated the film had come to an end. The lights brightened, and I followed Courtney into the lobby and out the door of the theater. We said nothing to each other as we walked to the parking lot. Still not saying a word, we got into the car and buckled our seat belts.

"Well, did you like the movie?" I asked as I started the car.

Without warning, Courtney burst into tears. I threw my arms around her. "What's going on?" I asked as I held her tightly.

"I'm . . . I'm just really . . ." She sobbed, trying to speak.

"Confused?" I finished her sentence.

"Yes." She wept as if her heart were breaking.

Holding her tight, I whispered, "I think we should go home, get into our jammies, and sit on my bed and talk. What do you think?" I continued to hold her, waiting for her response.

Unable to speak, she nodded as she wiped tears from her eyes. As we headed home, I knew this would be a life-changing night. Was Courtney ready to hear the entire truth? Ready for the answers to all the questions she'd carried in her heart for so many years?

I wanted her to be able to see God's light shining through her story, but she would first need to hear of the darkness.

Was I ready to tell her?

part one

The
New Arrivals

chapter 1

An Easy Yes

DAYS THAT WILL CHANGE your life forever seldom announce themselves.

Only in retrospect can I see how one small yes on a warm June day in 1996 led to a flood of life choices and changes, of crushing pains and unearthly joys. Choices that would not only alter the makeup of our family, but push me above my limits and stretch my faith beyond recognition. I've learned never to underestimate what God will do with a yes.

I had a load of laundry in the washer and was in the kitchen, cleaning to the sounds of children drifting in from the family room, when the phone rang.

"Hi, Deb, this is Ellen." The social worker with the Department of Family Services (DFS) greeted me with her usual friendly tone. My husband, Al, and I had been foster parents for fourteen years and were on a first-name basis with nearly all the caseworkers.

"I know you are fostering two brothers who will be going home soon. Would you be able to take a four-day-old infant, too? The mother is still in the hospital after a C-section. Both she and the baby tested positive for cocaine. We are ordering an investigation and need the baby to be in foster care during that time."

"Sure can!" It was an easy yes. I couldn't wait to tell my twelve-year-old daughter, Helen. She adored babies, and it had been a while since we had cared for an infant.

"Great! When you get to the hospital, go to the nurses' station on the third floor." Ellen knew our history—that we enjoyed fostering infants and toddlers and were successful with "failure to thrive" children. The effects from drugs or alcohol during a mother's pregnancy often left babies with challenging obstacles to overcome. Three of my own five children still lived at home, so these little ones received much love from every direction. Like Helen, fifteen-year-old Sadie and ten-year-old Charles had great childcare skills and big hearts. I was proud of the care my own children gave to the foster children. (Elizabeth, our oldest, was attending college at Texas A&M in College Station, Texas, and our son Jason was in the US Air Force, stationed in Germany.)

A few hours later, after I finished my household tasks and everyone had lunch, Helen and I left for Casper, twenty-five minutes away.

When we arrived at the hospital, Helen made a beeline for the elevator. As soon as the door opened, she was ready. "What floor?" Helen's fingers hovered over the elevator buttons, ready to push all of them if it would get us to the baby sooner. I couldn't help but be excited, too, though I also had concerns. How had the drugs affected this infant's body? What would she need from us?

Why was the elevator taking so long to get to the third floor? Finally the doors slid open.

A nurse met us at the front desk. "We've been waiting for you. Follow me and we'll get everything you need to take the baby home."

In the nursery, lying in a bassinet under warm lights, a tiny baby girl was swaddled in a white and pale green striped receiving blanket. Helen squealed when she saw the pink bow in the infant's black curly hair. She did a little wiggle dance, then stroked the baby's light brown forehead.

The nurse laughed. "You'll have her home in no time and will be able to hold her all you want. She's going to need lots of affection."

The nurse handed me a pile of release forms and instructions and took my driver's license to make a copy. I made quick work of the stack.

"She is sweet, but I need to warn you," the nurse's tone turned serious. "She will be showing some of the effects of the drugs for days, possibly even weeks."

"How severe are her symptoms?" I asked.

"She has been shaking and crying inconsolably at times, but it's best to let her work it out. Keep her swaddled tightly in a blanket and hold her close. She seems comforted by rocking, singing, and hearing a soft voice."

"We can do that," I said.

Helen nodded as if she took personal responsibility to do all that was instructed. Just then, another nurse came into the room.

"The baby's mother would like to meet you," she said.

"You don't have to," the first nurse interjected. "We can relay any information she wants to know."

"No, I'll go. Can I meet her now?" Helen was more than happy to stay with the infant.

I followed the nurse to a hospital room where a young woman with dark wavy hair and ivory skin was lying in bed, drinking a can of soda.

When she saw me, the woman put the can on the tray and tried to straighten up. Locking her jaw, she squeezed her eyes shut as she pushed against the back of the bed. I could see the pain from the C-section on her face.

I stood at the end of the bed. "Hi, I'm Debra. I will be taking care of your baby for a while. Your daughter is beautiful!"

"Thank you," she said tersely, her eyes averted. "I will be staying at my parents' house for a few weeks and plan to freeze my pumped breast milk. Would you be willing to come and pick it up?" She glanced at me, then looked away. "I would really like her to have my breast milk."

I could tell it was hard for her to face me. She probably saw me as part of the system that was taking her baby away—a reaction not uncommon among biological mothers when DFS made the choice to take a child into foster care. I knew I'd feel horrible if I were in her shoes.

"I will talk with the caseworker and ask if it's okay." I smiled, hoping to reassure her that I was not the enemy. "What's your daughter's name?"

"Ally." A soft blush came to the woman's cheeks when she said the name. She lowered her head and her irritated manner melted as tears began to fall onto the sheet covering her lap.

New-mother emotions are tough enough, I thought. *Staying in the hospital while your newborn is being released to strangers has got to be tougher.*

"And what is your name?"

"Uh . . . Karen Bower," she said.

"It's nice to meet you, Karen." The nurse stared at me and began to inch toward the door. I followed her out of the room and back to the nursery where Helen hadn't moved from the baby's side.

"Let's pack up and get ready to go home, you two," I said with a smile. I signed off on a clipboard as the nurse handed me back my driver's license. We placed the baby in the car seat her mother had brought to the hospital and headed for the elevators.

It was well into the afternoon when we pulled out of the hospital parking lot. The maternity staff had given us formula and a bag of lotion, shampoo, and diaper ointment samples, but Helen and

I stopped at Target to buy some newborn sleeper gowns, infant T-shirts, and disposable diapers.

When we got home, Sadie and Charles excitedly took turns holding Ally as I pulled the wicker bassinet from the closet and gathered up the bedding to wash. So many babies had slept comfortably in this bed. Now it was Ally's turn.

Al and I had welcomed the joys and navigated the challenges of being foster parents. When Ally came into our home, we had fostered about 140 children, some for as briefly as one night, some for weeks, months, and even a few for several years.

We first became foster parents in 1982. We'd been married for three years and were a blended family with three children. (We had our other two children in the next several years.) A relationship with God was not part of our adult lives. Growing up, Al was raised with a nominal Catholic influence, as his mother was Catholic and his father had been raised Lutheran. The family seldom attended church. I was raised in a Presbyterian church and as a young child attended often, but as I grew older my family attended less consistently. I have often referred to my family as a churchgoing dysfunctional family. My parents divorced when I was eight, and attending church became a once-a-month event, if that.

When Al and I met and married, we attended a local church on occasions such as weddings, funerals, and special holidays like Christmas Eve and Easter, but in no way was it a part of our weekly routine. We did, however, pray with our children at the dinner table and at bedtime. Then, in 1980, I found myself wanting to get involved with the pro-life movement. Because the church we were attending did not share my views, I sent letters out to churches in our area to see who was supporting the pro-life cause. The only church that responded was a small Baptist church.

I decided to take our children there occasionally, and Al fell off from going to church with us.

One evening in 1982, Al and I were watching TV and saw an advertisement explaining that the community was in real need of families who would take in children—those who had been hurt or neglected by their parents for a number of different reasons. We looked at each other and agreed that we had a nice home, food on the table, and room in our hearts that we could share with such children. The next day, I drove to our local DFS office and filled out an application to become foster parents. After going through interviews and a home check, we received our first child, a little boy.

In our early days of fostering, we were critical of the parents, guardians, and family members who were supposed to be responsible for these innocent children, and we interpreted our role as temporary saviors to these neglected and abused children. We didn't think to question why the abuse occurred. We assumed it was because the adults were on drugs or were alcoholics or they had been abused so they abused others, or they had anger issues that were never addressed. To us, such parents seemed evil with no conscience or boundaries. Ours was a simplistic perspective, and though we didn't comprehend what would cause people to make such choices, we shared a passion to step in and help children who suffered at the hand, or lack of care, of their parents.

One of the first foster babies Al and I received had been rescued from a car when he was five days old. The infant had been abandoned inside the vehicle on a hot day; the mother had grabbed her drugs and run from the car. She was caught and arrested, but the police never knew about the baby until the mother's boyfriend came to bail her out. The baby almost didn't make it and was in the hospital for a month before we were able to bring him home and care for him.

Another infant had suffered skull fractures from abuse. Other children were burned with cigarettes or beaten, leaving their little bodies marked or bruised. Our children could see the abuse suffered by these little helpless children and were outraged. Their reactions gave voice to our own personal thoughts and ranged from "the people who did this should be put in jail for the rest of their lives" to "they should be taken out and whipped, or burned with cigarettes, or shot or electrocuted." There wasn't much grace or forgiveness for such people in their minds. Al and I, in our early years especially, often found ourselves feeling the same way.

But in 1986, four years into foster parenting, our lives changed dramatically. Al had been drinking excessively, and I was overcome with my inability to cope with it. We saw our marriage falling apart and feared divorce. Al decided to put himself into an alcohol treatment center and shortly thereafter, I discovered that I was pregnant.

One Sunday while he was still in treatment, I took the children to church and heard a sermon on Deuteronomy 5 addressing "the sin of the parents." God used that sermon to bring me to my knees and into salvation as I realized how the sins of my parents, grandparents, and previous generations were affecting my life. Sins of bitterness, unforgiveness, lust, greed, and so much more. I saw with fresh eyes that those sins were at work in me and that Al and I, too, would be responsible for generational sin that would be reaped and repeated if there was nothing to stop it. Jesus Christ's sacrifice provided a way to break those curses. If I would confess my sin, I would be cleansed of "all unrighteousness" (1 John 1:9). I chose Jesus and prayed that the sins and curses I was living out would be broken and, through his blood, forgiven and cleansed.

Unbeknownst to me, Al was going through his own journey of discovering faith while in treatment. When he and I shared our newfound faith with one another, we decided to trust God to create a new life in us and a new marriage for us. After Charles was born, Al and I stood and confessed our commitment to Jesus in front of our entire family at a reunion. Al has not touched alcohol since his treatment and lives a life for Christ. Since then, God has brought us into a world of challenges that has grown our faith and called us to serve him fully.

Once we'd learned the truths of sin, confession, forgiveness, and spiritual growth, we realized that the care for our own children and those coming into our home needed to be not only physical and emotional care, but spiritual care as well. That changed everything. We saw that we had the responsibility to minister to these children with the truth that could also set them and even their families free. We could play our part in affecting lives for Christ no matter how much or how little time we had with each child. We were to share life with a future and a hope in Christ in whatever ways we could, so we made Sunday church attendance as a family a commitment, prayer a central part of our lives, and reading Bible stories to our children part of our routine.

Beyond that, we realized that we needed to accept the love God had for us and extend it to those who appeared in our eyes to be unlovely—abusive and neglectful parents. How, I wondered, could I come to love these parents whose children needed foster care? How could I accept that I was not superior to them—that we are all made of the same stuff? I didn't know, but it became my passion that God would work this miracle within me. And I realized that nothing short of a miracle was needed to bring about that love and forgiveness and grace in my heart.

A huge part of my growth in that journey took place as I wrote a Bible study for the crisis pregnancy center I served, to help some of our clients deal with the sexual abuse from which they had suffered. I, personally, had experienced such abuse in my early life and wanted God's truth to transform me. God showed me through the writing of that study that it was he who had the answers, and aside from him there can be little understanding or hope for healing. The self-published Bible study was called *Secret Sins* and was eventually used in a number of ministries by those counseling others and by those who wanted an individual study with biblical answers to the abuse in their lives.

As Al and I experienced our personal encounters with Jesus, his forgiveness, and the Bible, we worked at believing that since God's nature was forgiving, ours needed to become forgiving as well. We challenged each other to seek forgiving hearts toward abusive parents. Not that our conversion immediately altered our natural responses of anger and the desire for retribution. We saw no excuse for such behavior, and though it was a struggle, we sought a change of heart toward such parents through the power of God.

It never got easier to see children hurt, especially by their own parents, and was upsetting every time a child was sent home after a parent fulfilled a list of hoop-jumping steps for the courts. Tragically, children who had been sexually abused were often sent back to the parent who didn't abuse but would probably not protect the child from the next boyfriend or family member who tried to abuse the child. Eventually, however, we realized that though we couldn't change a broken system, we were called to step into the lives of the children and parents for as long as God would allow and show them love and care and another way of living. We learned to explain to our children that this is what goes on in the world and all we can do is play the part we're called to play.

Only later would I learn that when called to play a part that seems impossible, God can make the impossible happen.

The first twenty-four hours with our new guest flew by. When Ally was awake, she was always in somebody's arms.

Fortunately, Ally did not show any signs of failure to thrive. From day one she was active and responsive to attention. She did, however, have withdrawal symptoms—a number of times. Her eyes got wide and she flung her tiny arms out, as if she were scared, and then she would cry. Sometimes she shook and trembled, prompting more tears. We did our best to help calm her with warm bottles, rocking, and singing. When I sang to her, she would look at me and pucker her lips as if she were ready to join in.

The day after we brought Ally home to our modest country house on Goose Egg Road, I received another call from Ellen.

"The baby you are caring for has siblings who need fostering too. Karen's parents are already raising the oldest child, but they are not in a position to take them all."

"How many more are there?" I had four youth beds for foster children, and the two little brothers we'd been caring for had been returned to their mother.

"Four," Ellen answered. "There is a six-year-old boy, two girls, ages four and five, and another boy, age three. If you are willing, you will be receiving them over the next week to ten days. They are scattered with different family members right now. Can you take all four of them?"

I knew I didn't have to check with Al because he would agree with my answer. Long ago we'd agreed that as long as we had room and empty beds, our doors would always be open to more children.

"Absolutely! Bring them all!"

Another seemingly simple yes.

Chapter 2

The Home on
Goose Egg Road

GIGGLES AND HUGS FILLED our living room when the Bower children were reunited over the next week. Andrew, age three, arrived first, two days after we brought Ally home, followed by Kyle (six) and Kyra (five), who arrived together. Then little Hannah, age four, arrived on June 30, completing the family.

As we watched the happy reunion with Hannah unfold, Al and I exchanged a knowing look—it was moments like this that made taking in sibling groups so satisfying. The children were clearly overjoyed at being together once again. Now for the crowning moment. I went to the master bedroom, picked up the sleeping baby, and carried her into the living room.

"This is your new baby sister," I whispered to Hannah, kneeling down so she could see her. "Her name is Ally." Hannah's eyes shone with wonder as she gently stroked her baby sister's tiny hand.

Giving our foster children a warm welcome and a sense of belonging was always our first priority when we brought them into our home. The Bower children were no exception. Just as we had for her siblings earlier that week, we all showed Hannah her new bedroom—the cozy first-floor room with four youth beds that we called the "little room." Andrew pointed out whose bed was whose and in a heartbeat was bouncing on his bed in the corner and needed to be coaxed off. Fortunately, the promise of cookies waiting was enough to entice him to follow us all into the kitchen.

Our own three children still living at home—Sadie, Helen, and Charles—knew the routine well. They understood that this was a time to put the new foster children at ease. Ally was stirring from all the energy in the room, so Helen fixed her bottle and fed her while the rest of us chattered and chowed down on chocolate chip cookies.

That night, as was my practice every night, after everyone was settled in their beds, I went from child to child for bedtime prayers. I saved Hannah for last so she could watch me pray for each of her siblings first. Finally, I knelt by her bed. "Hannah, in our home we pray, and I'd like to pray for you now. Is that okay?"

She nodded.

"Dear Lord, thank you for bringing Hannah into our home so we can show her your love. Help her mommy to come to know you so that she can be the best mommy she can be for her children. We love you, Lord. Amen."

When I was finished, I kissed her on the forehead as I had with each of her siblings. Later that evening I did the same for our own kids before crawling into bed to cuddle with Al.

Before I fell asleep, I silently prayed again and thanked God for bringing the Bower children into our home and asked him to use us to introduce them to his love. That prompted me to remember a little boy we had fostered several years before. His name was Brandon.

When the caseworker first called us about Brandon, she explained that though he was only five, he'd been institutionalized a few times because his mother couldn't handle him. "He is currently on three medications. We are working with a local counselor and doctor, trying to get his meds sorted out so we can get him back home. Would you be willing to take him while we do that?"

"Sure, bring him to us, and we'll see what we can do," I replied.

Brandon looked like he'd stepped right out of a storybook. His blond hair was cut short, parted neatly on the side, and he had freckles across his cute little nose.

"One thing you need to know about Brandon," the caseworker said before leaving. "He does not want anyone touching him. You cannot touch this child."

Brandon had been taught to comb his own hair once it was parted and the first time I parted it for him I was exceedingly careful not to touch him with my hands. A few times when I accidently touched him he recoiled dramatically.

At the time, we had two foster girls in the first floor "little room" with the youth beds, so we placed Brandon's bed upstairs in Charles's room, where we also had two other young boys. We needed to do some furniture rearranging before Brandon got into his bed. He refused to crawl into it until the bed was positioned in the middle of the room, far from anyone else.

On Brandon's first night, he watched as I covered each of the other boys with their blankets, including Charles, then knelt by their bedsides, placed my hand on their forehead or chest or arm, and prayed for them. Then I'd kiss them on the forehead and move on to the next boy. Brandon's eyes watched my every move, and I couldn't help but notice the anxiety on his face. When I'd finished praying for the others, I came to Brandon's side. As I pulled up his covers, he lifted his arms, then laid them stiffly by his sides on top of the blanket, his eyes studying my face.

"Brandon, we pray in our home," I said in a near whisper, standing by his bedside rather than kneeling. "Is it all right if I pray over you? I will not touch you."

He looked at me silently. I held my hand out in the air high above his chest and closed my eyes. "Dear Jesus, thank you for bringing Brandon to our home. Thank you that he is safe. Help him not to be afraid and to know that you love him. Give him sweet dreams tonight. Amen."

When I opened my eyes, his were wide open, locked on mine. "Good night, Brandon." As much as I wanted to kiss his little forehead, I knew better, so I smiled at him and left the room.

I had no idea what Brandon had experienced his first five years of life. I could only surrender him to God and trust that my heavenly Father would help me to love this little boy as he did. Night after night I repeated the same ritual and Brandon watched my every move.

After several nights, I decided to kneel by his bed, still keeping space between us. "I know you see me touch the other children when I pray for them. I want them to feel my love as well as Jesus' love. I will not touch you. I'm going to put my hand over you here."

I placed my hand in the air about a foot above his chest. "Is this okay?" Brandon nodded yes and I prayed.

After another two weeks, I asked him if I could move my hand closer to his chest, and he nodded.

Then one night, while I was praying with my eyes closed and my hand hovering several inches above his chest, I felt his small hand atop mine. He pressed my hand gently toward him until my hand rested on his chest. Tears sprung to my eyes, but I forced myself to maintain my composure and continue to pray in a steady voice. I could feel his little heart pounding as I said, "I pray, Lord, that you would touch Brandon's heart. Let him know how much you love him."

I opened my eyes and said, "Amen." Brandon was looking right at me, his little hand continuing to press against mine. We stared into each other's eyes for a moment, then I took my other hand and patted his. "Goodnight, Brandon."

I wanted to dance, to sing, to wake everyone in the house

and announce this breathtaking breakthrough, but my celebration needed to remain tucked inside my heart as I slipped out of the room.

The following night when I knelt by his side I placed my hand barely a few inches above his chest. This time, before I even closed my eyes to pray, Brandon placed his hand on mine and drew it down to his chest, leaving his hand on mine as I prayed. This happened for the next several nights.

Then, at the end of the week, as I gently pulled my hand away, Brandon touched his forehead, his eyes expectant. At first, I didn't understand.

"What is it, Brandon?"

He touched his forehead again, and I teared up. *He wants me to kiss him.*

"Do I have your permission to kiss you on the forehead?"

He nodded, and so I did. Every night after that, for the next few months that Brandon lived with us, each night's prayer ended with a good-night kiss on the forehead of the little boy who couldn't be touched.

Praying over our own children and our foster children had always been a great honor and responsibility, but Brandon showed me it was also a sacred trust.

Lord, I prayed silently as I lay in Al's embrace reminiscing about Brandon, *show your love, through our family, to Kyle, Kyra, Hannah, Andrew, and Ally. Let them know they are deeply loved.*

July proved to be a wonderful time for the Bower children to settle into our home. With school out for the summer, Helen, Sadie, and Charles were available to help me with the little ones. Over the years, we'd found that contributing to our family by doing small chores, assigned according to a child's age and capability, was a marvelous way to help each child feel a part of the family.

My own kids taught them how to do their special tasks. All the children made their own beds each morning and picked up their rooms. They soon learned that the daily morning routine was to brush their teeth and hair and get dressed. Kyra and Hannah helped Helen and Sadie gather dirty laundry from the rooms and, after I laundered and folded it, they distributed it to each child's bed. Kyle and Andrew assisted Charles with emptying trash throughout the house, sweeping the garage and patio, and vacuuming. Three-year-old Andrew loved to vacuum. Pride was written all over his face as he pushed the wand back and forth. He didn't get very far, but he did a great job in the small area he was given. At mealtimes, all the kids cleared the table, and Helen and Sadie lent me a hand cleaning up the kitchen.

I switched up the chores a little bit each week so the children could learn how to do different jobs that helped keep a home clean and orderly. With everyone working together all week, Saturday morning cleanings went very quickly after our big family breakfast. Each child received an allowance at the end of the week for work done. I could see the sense of pride in the faces of the Bower siblings when I handed them their first "reward" for hard work.

After their first reward, the Bowers took obvious new joy in their jobs. I could see it gave them a sense of pride knowing they each had a job to do like the rest of us. This training applied to all our foster children over the years, unless they were too little to participate. For many foster children, ours was the first home they'd known where everyone, adults and children alike, had responsibilities and learned to take care of themselves.

Al and I explained that our jobs outside the home were part of our grown-up chores. Al worked long hours at the Casper Events Center, where he was the food and catering manager. I worked a few days a week at The Caring Center, a Christian crisis pregnancy center in Casper. I'd been the director for nearly a decade, starting a year after becoming a Christian.

I was also a volunteer lay chaplain at the Natrona County

Detention Center, the local jail about twelve miles from our home. In addition to being on call for inmates who requested a chaplain, I led a biweekly Bible study for inmates before work. A few times each year I also spoke at the Wyoming Women's Center, a women's prison in Lusk, about one hundred miles away. God had given me a heart for prisoners.

At mealtimes, whether at home or at a restaurant, our family joined hands and thanked the Lord for our blessings and for the food. After the first few weeks in our home, it was Andrew who liked to do the "pwaying" whenever given the opportunity. He was usually the first one to put his hands out to whoever sat next to him. Then he'd smile and say, "Let's pway."

I bought some summer dresses for Hannah and Kyra and dressier shirts for the boys to wear to church on Sundays. They sat with our family in the sanctuary for a few Sundays until they felt comfortable to go to Sunday school on their own. Our congregation was full of huggers, and the children responded well to the warmth and affection they received.

Days at the local pool, picnics at Beartrap Meadow on Casper Mountain, running through sprinklers in the yard, cookouts around our backyard grill, and TV movie nights with plenty of popcorn filled the summer. The kids squealed at the July Fourth fireworks that lit up the sky over the whole community, and we all enjoyed the annual Casper parade. Streets were blocked off, and most businesses downtown didn't open until noon on that day. Casper's residents lined the quaint downtown streets with folding chairs and baby strollers, doing their best to beat the heat with cool drinks and mini umbrellas to block the sun.

On the heels of the parade was the annual Central Wyoming Fair and Rodeo in Casper. The Bower children had never been to the fair before and were excited that we went every day. They reveled in carnival rides and cotton candy, and whooped and hollered at the bull- and bronco-riding cowboys and barrel-racing cowgirls competing in the arena. I was the loudest of all, jumping up and down and screaming in my seat, a reaction the Bower children certainly didn't expect from me.

One summer morning while most of us were still at the breakfast table, Kyle came tearing into the kitchen. "There are huge horses in our front yard!" he yelled, causing a stampede from the kitchen to the front door.

Must be the Percherons again.

Sure enough, our neighbors' two draft horses had managed to escape their barn and wander onto our property. While I called the neighbors, the Bower children crept outside to get an up-close look at the magnificent animals. Helen made sure that everyone kept their distance and spoke softly.

Charles loved masterminding imaginative outdoor games of hide-and-seek, cops and robbers, cowboy fun, and leading the gang on an exploration of our ten acres. The children entertained us at mealtime with reports of spotting soaring eagles and watching mule deer and antelope grazing; at night we sat together in the backyard to stargaze and listen to the coyotes howl. I was delighted the children found country living a wondrous adventure.

As with most foster children, the Bowers were on their good behavior for the first few weeks—the honeymoon period—then the time of testing began, but no behaviors were out of the ordinary. Squabbles over toys, occasional temper flare-ups, mean words said to one another or to our children—but years of experience had taught us to take it all in stride. We'd learned to stay calm, quickly correct and communicate what was not acceptable in our home, and move on, expecting the best. Experience had been an effective teacher, and our own children, from years of modeling good behavior, were truly our allies in these efforts. We had dealt with some very challenging and troubled children over the years, and in comparison, the Bower children were a cooperative sibling group and adjusted well.

It helped immensely that the Bowers were all younger than our own children. When we'd first begun fostering we'd naively taken in older children as well, including teenagers. Sadly, we'd learned the hard way that having older troubled kids influencing our own was not workable for our family. One summer we had five teenage girls. One was always causing problems and was disliked by our children, as well as by the other four teens. Al and I thought that sending them all to a Christian camp for a week would be a great idea. We told them that if any of them acted out at the camp and had to be sent home, they would have to go to another foster family. Our reasoning was that it would serve as a serious warning for the other four. Not one of our wisest choices. Unfortunately, the one sent home for bad behavior wasn't the one we thought it would be, and we were sad to see the girl go from our home.

Another time there was a teen who lived with us for several years, and we became very fond of her. One day she decided to run away to another state with some friends from high school. We were crushed. That hurt our children deeply, and we all felt rejection from a girl we loved and thought loved us. In another situation, we had some teenage girls who climbed out the window to see some boys one night. When the police brought them home at 2:00 a.m., the girls told us that there was nothing on our rule list that said they couldn't do such a thing.

Some children fit in well with our family, some did not, and we had to decide how much we were willing to put our family through in helping the children who came to our home. Heartbreak is a very real part of foster parenting. We learned there is a time to show grace but also a time for tough love, but that when showing tough love, it affected all of us, not just the one receiving the discipline. We didn't like seeing our own children suffer as the older children learned their costly lessons. So after a number of such challenging situations in our early fostering years, we made a decision that we'd never take in children older than our own, and that proved to be a very helpful boundary.

Once we had a few years fostering some tough kids in our home and saw them doing better after living with us and experiencing rules, structure, and love, we received training to become specialized therapeutic foster parents. That meant we could take failure to thrive infants as well as fetal alcohol syndrome and drug-born children and were equipped to address some of their special needs. We learned the right way to restrain a child if needed, and when to ask for help when we did not see success with a child.

As the laid-back summer rolled to a close, DFS informed us we'd have the Bowers at least into the fall, so we went shopping for the '96-'97 school year, purchasing school supplies and clothes for everyone. Next came the challenge of working out the plans for our morning routine and transportation to and from school and day care. Sadie was in high school, Helen went to junior high, and Charles was in sixth grade at an elementary school. The two oldest Bower children were in elementary school, too, but in a different one from Charles. Since Kyle and Kyra had undergone enough change in their lives already, we wanted them to return to the same school where they knew teachers and had friends. In the mornings, Hannah went to a Head Start preschool program in downtown Casper, while Andrew and Ally went to the home of Starla, our dearly loved day care provider. Each morning after lunches were packed and backpacks checked, all the kids piled into our blue Toyota Previa van, and I began the morning drive.

Once the kids were dropped off at their various locations, I went to work at The Caring Center. Around noon, I picked up Hannah and took her to Starla's to join her siblings until the end of the day. After work I made the rounds again, picking up all the kids, from day care to high school, and heading home. I had it down to a science—as long as no one got sick.

The early fall months went as smoothly with the Bower children as summer had gone. The occasional sibling squabbles were dealt with quickly, with apologies offered and forgiveness given. On school nights, everyone was busy with homework, and on the weekends we played board games and watched TV together. Elizabeth occasionally came home from college for long weekends and took the children for a wild, vigorous ride in our old pickup over the sage-covered prairie on our property. We could hear them all laugh and scream until after dark as the truck lights flashed up and down with each turn and dirt hill they drove over. Even though Jason was in the air force and Elizabeth was in college, when they came home to visit, all the kids would snuggle under blankets and grab pillows and popcorn and lie across the living room floor watching old movies together. *Anne of Green Gables*, *The Goonies*, and *The Sandlot* were some of their favorites.

As we had discovered over the years with our other foster children, a familiar family routine with clear expectations and healthy doses of lots of love and laughter kept our household running smoothly.

The Bower children were still with us as November moved into December. When the first snowflakes fell, we went shopping again, this time for warm winter coats and snow pants. When the first real winter storm hit, the sunroom became the mudroom with gloves and boots neatly lined up.

On the first Saturday in December, Al retrieved the boxes of Christmas decorations from the garage and brought them into the living room. As the kids opened each one, the spirit of Christmas spilled out.

"Christmas is coming!" Hannah cheered.

I watched joyfully as small hands pulled out shiny bulbs, garland, and lights, and the children danced to "Have a Holly Jolly Christmas" on the radio. We spent the entire day decorating our home for a month of celebration.

"Are we going to have a Christmas tree?" Hannah asked Al.

"We sure are! Let's get it tomorrow," he answered, trying to untangle the lights.

"Will you all help decorate it?" I looked at Hannah and the kids.

They answered in unison, "Yes!"

There is something about children and Christmas that goes hand in hand. As I watched the kids' faces glow with excitement, I asked, "Do you know what Christmas is all about?"

"It's when Santa comes and brings us toys," answered Hannah.

"Yes, that's part of how we celebrate, but it's not the real reason for Christmas. Christmas is someone's birthday. Do you know who that is?"

They looked at me blankly.

"It's Jesus' birthday, the most important birthday in the world. Do you know about Jesus' birthday?"

The Bower kids looked at one another, checking to see if one of them knew about this, but no one answered. My kids remained silent, knowing this was a teaching moment.

"Jesus is God's Son. He was born on earth and came here to show us the way to God and how to live." Four pairs of brown eyes stared at me, as if to say, *Okay. Go on.*

Kneeling on the floor, I opened the box that held our nativity scene and began to unwrap the individual ceramic figures. "Jesus was born in a manger, like this one." I placed baby Jesus on the carpet in front of us. The kids stopped what they were doing and sat around me. As I unwrapped each piece, I told how each one—Mary, Joseph, the shepherds, the angels, the magi, and even the animals were there to welcome baby Jesus.

"So, that is the real reason for Christmas. Jesus came to be the best gift of love we could ever get in our life. We give gifts to show our love to others. Santa is a fun part of the holiday, but Jesus is the real reason for Christmas."

The children looked satisfied with the explanation. They each picked up the ceramic pieces and looked at them. Hannah picked up baby Jesus and studied him intently, as if she would see something different, something special, about that particular piece.

Help them to know you, Lord, I prayed.

A few days later, after all the kids had gone to bed, I snuggled under a throw blanket on the couch. The house was quiet, other than the crackling fire in the wood-burning stove. I watched the flames lap against the logs through the glass door of the stove while Al sat in his chair reading.

My thoughts turned to another group of siblings we had fostered a year before. I had first met their mother when she was hired by our church to provide childcare in the nursery during the services. A few years later, when I was working at The Caring Center, this woman came to my office in tears, disclosing she was pregnant. Her relationship with the father had ended, and she had two other children at home.

"I can't have this baby," she said to me in tears. I prayed for and counseled her, explaining that assistance was available and an abortion was not her only option. Adoption could be an alternative.

"But you have to make your own decision," I said gently.

Months later, my receptionist came into my office and said I had a collect call from Denver. It was the same woman. She wanted me to know she had given birth to twin girls and was coming back to Casper. I told her I would help in any way I could.

A few weeks after the phone call, the woman brought her twins into the center. The babies were beautiful and healthy. I offered her baby clothes and other services that would help her get on her feet. She returned a few more times, and I prayed with her each time, sharing God's love. Then she vanished; I never saw or heard from her again.

Six years later, I was walking in the door after church one Sunday when the phone rang. It was DFS saying they had a family of four children at the police station needing foster care. The mother had been arrested on drug charges and had requested that her children go only to me.

I went to the station and found four dirty, wild little children: twin girls and two younger boys. It didn't click with me who the children could be until their caseworker called me the next morning and told me the mother's name. I looked at the six-year-old twins sitting across from me at my kitchen table.

These are the babies I prayed for in my office.

I didn't know what had become of the two older children, but the two little brothers had clearly come along since the twins were born. God had brought them back into my life for a purpose. A purpose greater than just physical care while their mother got help. *Perhaps I'll have the opportunity to introduce them to the love of Jesus.*

The embers in the fire popped, waking me from my daydream. Then I remembered, this was where I was sitting when the twins came out of their room and said to me, "Debra, we want to ask Jesus into our heart. Will you show us how?"

My friend Marilyn Pipkin, from the Longmont Crisis Pregnancy Center in Colorado, happened to be visiting me that evening. She took one twin in her lap, I took the other, and we explained what it meant to ask Jesus into one's heart, and together we listened to their sweet prayers for salvation.

Would the Bower children do the same? After months of hearing my prayers, would they choose Jesus? I closed my eyes. *Save these children, Lord. Let them and their mother come to know you as I know you. You are love. You are safety. You are their only hope.*

Chapter 3

Clues

RUMMAGING THROUGH CLOSETS and drawers and under beds, I found assorted pieces of clothing, toys, and hair barrettes. I finished organizing and cleaning the little room, returning the treasures I found to their proper places. The Bower children had moved in five months ago, and in a few hours all five siblings would return from their first unchaperoned overnight visit with their mother, Karen.

On this second weekend of December, savoring a rare Saturday afternoon alone with my own family, I moved around the house soaking in the sweet silence and peaceful atmosphere. The scent of pine from the Christmas tree filled the family room. Al was at work, Sadie was at a friend's house, and Helen and Charles were each in their rooms, no doubt enjoying their own space in the peace and quiet before the Bower children returned. There were no little ones running through the living room. No loud shouts or screams of toys being fought over. All the kid-sized plates and cups used for each meal were still stacked neatly in the cupboard.

I prayed their visit was going well, just as I'd been praying since their mom had picked them up the evening before. For months, I had communicated with Karen, inviting her to church, to attend a Bible study where she could meet other women who could befriend and support her, and to The Caring Center to meet one-on-one with me. As a foster mom, whenever a single mom would trust me enough to allow me to step into her world, I tried to be a support.

Karen had taken me up on invitations to church, probably because it gave her an opportunity to see the children. She'd also met with me a few times at The Caring Center so that the two of us could talk about how each of the children was doing. Whenever we got together she offered me an update on her progress in meeting the DFS requirements to get her children back. While I wasn't privy to conversations, updates, or arrangements between her and DFS, she seemed to be making a sincere effort to do what she needed to, to demonstrate that she was trustworthy and responsible. Al had even given Karen a part-time seasonal job at the Casper Events Center in early November so she could get on her feet financially—which she told us was one of those requirements.

I thought back to a few months before when, after having the children for about the first eight weeks, I'd been asked by DFS to attend a hearing that included two caseworkers, Karen, and her parents (who were raising her oldest child, DeAnn). As far as I understood it, I was there for the sole purpose of telling what my experience had been since I met Karen in June, and what my thoughts were as to how she was doing. When asked, I'd spoken highly of her efforts and said I felt she was serious about regaining custody of her children. As I spoke, Karen and I would look at each other and smile. It seemed we had begun a small level of friendship. I relayed to the caseworkers that she had commented to me that the parenting classes she was required to take had been helpful. I was encouraged at what I had seen and learned about Karen in the short time I had known her.

Karen's parents did not seem convinced. They shook their

heads and communicated serious concern for the children and for their daughter. The whole time I was talking, Karen's mother had a troubled look on her face and frequently focused on her hands folded in her lap. She sat very still and made no comment, but her expression spoke volumes. Karen's father was more expressive as he listened. He shifted from side to side in his chair in apparent frustration and would shake his head.

At the time I'd assumed her parents' judgment was clouded by their displeasure over Karen's past behavior and their stated disapproval (according to Karen) that all the children except DeAnn were biracial. But as recent months had passed, I'd been having second thoughts. Perhaps I'd been naive to believe that my first two months of observation should outrank the nearly thirty years her parents had known her. After all, past behavior that had repeated itself could serve as a predictor of future decision making. Maybe her parents had good cause to be leery of Karen's fitness as a parent. I remembered now how the caseworker had smiled as she listened to my statements, in sharp contrast to the weight of sorrow evident in the eyes of Karen's parents as they listened to me and scanned the caseworker's positive written report on the table.

Following that hearing, a preliminary visitation plan had been put into effect in September. Karen complied with the DFS requirement that she move out of her parents' home and get a place of her own. In October she'd rented a little newly refurbished house in Casper. First came brief weekly supervised visits for which I delivered the children to their mom's home when a DFS worker was present. They stayed no longer than about a two-hour playdate. I couldn't help but notice that while Kyle and Kyra eagerly piled into the car for the visits, Andrew seemed hesitant and sober, and little Hannah was downright anxious.

"Please don't make me go, Debwa. I want to stay here with you," Hannah would plead. She'd be especially clingy as the visits approached. I did my best to assure her that the visits would be short, that I'd be close by, and that a nice caseworker would be present.

"I will come pick you up in two hours," I said. She had cooperated, but when we'd arrive at Karen's house, Hannah stayed glued to my side for about fifteen minutes before running off to play with the others.

When I returned later, Hannah and Andrew seemed quiet and withdrawn. I knew from my fostering experience that the transition of visitation was more disconcerting for some children than others, but since I saw no evidence of physical harm, I simply gave the two preschoolers extra cuddles and attention that soothed them both. Still, they reacted the same to each visit.

Karen continued to attend church with us sometimes, where she came across as sweet and shy. She even joined us for an occasional lunch out. What struck me during those visits was her obvious closeness to Kyle and Kyra, and her distance from Hannah and Andrew.

DFS checked in regularly for my observations, and I freely offered them. They saw the visits as a success, though I had mounting misgivings. I discussed them with Al, who confirmed my observations.

In late November, DFS approved brief unsupervised visits. If all went well, they'd permit an overnight visit. If those were successful, the children would spend Christmas Eve and Christmas Day with their mother. Hannah's anxiety grew to the point of tears over the unsupervised visits. Hard as it was, I coaxed and shepherded her to her mother's house. Afterward, when I picked up the children, Hannah seemed happy. The other siblings gave their mother goodbye hugs, but I always had to remind Hannah to do so.

Since Hannah seemed safe at Karen's and she quickly returned to her normal self after spending time there, DFS determined the visits should continue. It was important for Hannah to learn she was safe. As far as I knew, the children had not been removed from Karen's care because of any type of abuse. The investigation had been triggered by the cocaine found in baby Ally's system, raising concerns about Karen's lifestyle, associations, and fitness as a responsible mother.

My concerns for Hannah and Andrew and their apparent uneasy relationship with their mother led me to a conversation one day with Karen at The Caring Center. I was bold enough to ask her why she was less loving to the two of them and often seemed so distant or at odds with them.

Karen explained that she'd had her six children by three men. To put it mildly, there was considerable friction and jealousy between one of the fathers, William, and the father of Hannah and Andrew. The more she explained it to me, the more the word *hatred* seemed to fit William's attitude. She confessed to me that Hannah and Andrew were treated very unkindly by him, yet she still allowed William in her life. Karen admitted that in order to keep the peace in her relationship with him, she had often shunned the two. It was her way of showing loyalty to this man who seemed to have considerable influence over her. Fortunately, one of the DFS requirements was for Karen to have nothing to do with William as he had been in and out of jail or prison for a number of charges. Their concern, of course, was that Karen stay off drugs and away from negative influences.

Hannah and Andrew spoke of this man occasionally, calling him "mean." Whenever I would ask questions about the mean man, they shut down. So, I seldom brought him up but tried to respond with caring concern if they did. By listening and observing over the five months the children had been living with our family, I realized that Karen's unhealthy pattern with her two youngest was not limited to the past when that man had been around. She had adopted the same negative attitude toward them as he had modeled.

I looked at the clock. *A few more hours to go. What has this first overnight visit been like for them? What will be their state of mind when they come home?* I realized I was worrying, so I began praying specifically for Hannah's and Andrew's physical safety and emotional well-being. Then I remembered that Karen's oldest daughter was invited for the overnight. *DeAnn is there, too, so maybe she has added a positive influence.* Still, as the afternoon dragged by, I was haunted with a vague sense of unease.

Headlights finally flashed across the living room windows. The children were home. As the front door flew open, they tumbled in, bubbling with joy. This was a good sign. Karen, carrying baby Ally, followed behind them all with a bright smile on her face. She appeared as happy as her children.

Hannah pushed through the other children to get to me first. Her hair was beautifully combed in a tight ponytail that curled into a ringlet, accented with a large bow in her hairband. Her outfit was new and she was carrying a doll I had never seen before. She came right to my knees, anxious to share something. I bent down close to her sweet face. That was when I saw it—her forehead and left eye were black-and-blue.

Before I could ask what happened, Hannah blurted, "Debwa! I slipped in the bathtub last night. There were bubbles and I slipped when I was getting out." Her eyes were dramatically opened wide. Her jaw was tightened, and she showed her teeth with a forced smile.

"Mommy bought me this new doll because I was so brave. I got to pick it out myself," Hannah said, holding her doll up for my inspection.

"Wow! You sure did fall. That must have hurt." I returned a forced smile as I looked up at Karen, who had moved quickly behind Hannah.

"Yeah. The kids all wanted to play in the tub, and Hannah was trying to get out of the tub by herself. I told her to wait, but she didn't listen, and she fell against the side." Karen's smile was big. *Were Karen and Hannah glancing at each other to confirm their story?*

Karen caught my questioning look and said, "Well, bubbles

can be slippery." I was sure Karen could read the incredulity in my expression. The story was presented with a bit too much drama and sounded a little too practiced. If the whole bathtub-and-black-eye story proved to be true, the presentation certainly warranted suspicion.

After hurriedly hugging each child, Karen left and drove off into the dark.

"It's so good to have you home. Go put on your pajamas, then come to the kitchen for milk and cookies before bedtime."

Five minutes later, the kids were sitting at the table, eager for their snack. "So what did you do with your mom?" I kept an upbeat happy tone to encourage the children to talk, but they all became quiet as they drank their milk and nibbled their cookies.

"Did you go anywhere? Did you have visitors?" They grew even quieter as they glanced at each other. Hannah stared at the cookie crumbs on her plate. Her shoulders drooped. Andrew, still nibbling on his cookie, quickly looked at his sisters and brother. Kyle and Kyra stared at Hannah. *It's wise not to push for answers.* I suspected from their responses that they had been given firm instruction to say nothing. Good or bad, they were obeying their mother.

"Okay, time for a story. Everyone in bed!" They knew the routine, but I felt they needed to hear it announced, to help them adjust to being back in our home again. For a child, even one night away from familiar surroundings can be a disruptive change. Everyone climbed into bed, and I began to read. Prayer time followed story time. I went from bed to bed, kneeling and praying with each child, ending with a kiss on each forehead.

When I got to Hannah's bed, I tucked the blanket around her and prayed God would help her to be able to share what was in her heart and that he would take good care of her. I prayed for Karen as well. When I opened my eyes, I could tell Hannah had been staring wide-eyed at me during the prayer. I lingered a minute more in case she had something to say, but she was silent.

I smiled, gently kissed her forehead, and whispered, "I love you, and Jesus loves you even more."

Monday morning was cold, so I started the fire in the wood-burning stove. Al had needed to work late Sunday night and was still in bed. As I waited for the household to come to life, I poured myself a mug of steaming-hot coffee, holding it closely to warm my chilled hands. Alarms would start going off and hungry children would soon be rushing to get dressed, make beds, and then pile around the table for breakfast. Once everyone was fed, lunches would be packed and backpacks placed at the front door. The Moerke caravan would be ready to roll on its weekday route to get everyone to school and day care.

That morning as I walked Hannah into her Head Start class, her teacher immediately asked about the black eye. It appeared more swollen, more black-and-blue. Hannah stiffened at the question, then quickly repeated her bubbles and bathtub story. Her teacher looked at me with a wrinkled brow. I shook my head slightly, indicating I wasn't so sure about the truthfulness of the story either.

After saying good-bye to Hannah, I drove to the pregnancy center. As soon as I walked in the door, I turned up the heat, started the coffee, and put three cups on the counter. My receptionist and counselor would be arriving soon.

I couldn't get the image of Hannah's bruised forehead and black eye out of my mind. Should I call the caseworker? I knew every bump and bruise didn't need reporting. Yet, since this had been the children's first overnight stay with Karen, I decided to call and leave the rest up to Ellen, the caseworker. She always seemed to care about the families she worked with, yet she stayed professional enough to keep an emotional distance.

I dialed her number. "Hi, Ellen. It's Deb Moerke. I called

because I'm a little concerned about the Bower kids' overnight visit with Karen. Hannah came back with a bruised forehead and black eye. Karen and Hannah said she slipped getting out of the tub. I doubt them both. I can't tell if it is actually true and they're afraid that it will look bad, or if it's not what happened and they're trying to cover it up with a well-rehearsed story. I thought you needed to know."

Ellen said what I thought she would say. "Can you bring Hannah to my office this morning? Once I look at her, I can let you know if I believe a doctor should see her. What do you think?"

Reporting my suspicions made them seem more real, and my heart began to race. "I will pick her up from Head Start shortly. I don't want her to be scared, though, wondering why she is the only one of her siblings coming to see you." I didn't want Hannah to distrust me. She and I had become close, and I wanted her to believe she was safe with me.

"I will play it down. You can tell her you need to stop by my office to pick up a paper from me. I will be cool about it. We may put her in the playroom with the two-way mirror. How quickly can you be here?" I knew she wanted it to be soon.

"As soon as a staff member comes in." I hung up the phone, put on my coat, and grabbed my purse. While I waited, flutters of anxiety rose in my chest.

I hope Hannah's story is true. I want Karen to be the mother Hannah needs her to be.

My spirit was arguing with my heart and my mind. Tears pooled in my eyes and my hands became sweaty. *What's going to happen?*

The moment the morning receptionist arrived, I flew past her. "Sorry, I have to run!" I didn't even say good morning.

In the car, I fumbled with my keys to find the right one. My tears made everything blurry. Now that I was acting on my suspicions, I realized how strong they were. *What's happened to Hannah? Is she afraid, vulnerable, and alone?* I closed my eyes and prayed,

"Lord, help me to be calm. Don't let me make Hannah worried or anxious. I want her to trust me. I want her to trust *you*! Calm my heart and prepare hers for the visit with Ellen."

I opened my eyes and took a deep breath, then exhaled. "I am entrusting Hannah, Ellen, and myself into your hands, Lord." I hoped that the black eye was an accident. But my instincts told me it wasn't.

Chapter 4

Inklings of the Past

"YOU'RE *IT*!" I heard Kyle declaring his victory, followed by Kyra's giggles.

"Come out, come out, wherever you are," Helen's voice rang through the house. She had organized a game of hide-and-seek to keep some of the children occupied on this frigid Friday afternoon in January 1997. From the kitchen where I was preparing dinner, I heard the stampede of little feet running toward the family room. After dinner, Karen would be picking them up for another overnighter.

"Kyra is *It* now," Helen announced. "Kyra, count to twenty while everyone hides again. Don't count so fast this time."

Then I heard Hannah's familiar giggles coming from Sadie's room. "That's perfect, Hannah. Now smile!" Sadie had set up a pretend photo shoot in her bedroom for Hannah in dress-up clothes—a favorite pastime.

Charles wandered into the kitchen and opened the fridge.

"What's for dinner?"

"Hamburgers. Are you hungry?"

He nodded as he poured himself a glass of milk, then blurted out what he must have been struggling with for weeks.

"Mom, why is Karen still allowed to have unsupervised visits with her kids after Hannah got that black eye? I don't get it."

"Well, it could have been an accident. We only know what Hannah and Karen told us." Charles looked at me doubtfully, but I continued my less-than-convincing reasoning. "Ellen made a note of the injury, questioned Karen, and seemed reasonably convinced Hannah slipped in the tub. And Hannah did go willingly to the Christmas overnight at her mother's. Our responsibility is to observe and listen to the children after their visits. Hopefully, nothing like that will happen again."

Charles couldn't hide his frustration. "It isn't right, Mom. Why do these bad parents always get second chances? How many hurt kids have we seen over the years go back to these parents? How come they get away with it? It isn't fair!"

I looked at my son's troubled face. We'd had this conversation before, and I knew we'd have it again. In fact, I'd had many similar conversations with all my kids. Charles was very protective of the foster kids who moved through our home. He'd seen a lot in his ten years, as had all of my kids—children with cigarette burns, bruised bodies, and traumatized psyches. He wanted justice for each one, demanding punishment for abusive and neglectful parents and instant, permanent removal of the kids from their homes. Visitations and counseling and the complexities of rehabilitating and reuniting families were beyond his comprehension. I was proud of my son for caring so deeply and for his strong sense of right and wrong.

"The reason such kids wind up with us is because their parents are *not* getting away with it," I tried to explain. "When the authorities discover a child has been abused or isn't in a safe environment, they do intervene. That's why they need families like ours who will welcome these kids and love and care for them while DFS tries to figure out the truth, what the problems are, if they can be fixed or helped, or if children need to be adopted by new families. It takes time and a lot of work for them to discover what's really going in in these homes and what the best solutions are. It's a difficult, messy process, isn't it?"

"Do *you* think the Bower kids are safe with Karen?"

"That's what their time with us is all about," I said, aware that I was avoiding the question that was worrying me. "While DFS is figuring that out, we'll keep doing our part. We report what we see and hear. And we show the children what a healthy family looks like. We love them and care for them and make sure they know they are special to us and to God. And as hard as it is sometimes, all we can do is play our part the best we know how."

Apparently satisfied for the moment, Charles finished his glass of milk and left the kitchen, leaving me to ponder the Bower kids while I defrosted the ground beef.

In the nearly seven months since the Bower siblings had arrived, I'd come to love them all. It hadn't taken long to decipher their family dynamics. Kyle and Kyra were buddies, doing most things together. At six and five they were both well-mannered and obedient. They were doing well in school and got along with everyone in the family, although I always sensed they had a strong filter in place, carefully choosing their words to make a good impression.

Kyle clearly held some sway over Kyra, Hannah, and Andrew. He had "the look" down and could often stop the other three in their tracks if their behavior disturbed him. He was the most serious and clearly felt responsible for what they all did—a heavy weight for a six-year-old to bear.

Kyra always wanted to be seen in a positive light. She flashed her "perfect child" smile often. In so many ways she reminded me of Karen. She could be soft-spoken and sweet, but she, too, used "the look" on her younger sister and brother when they got out of line. Sometimes, if Hannah cried or whined, Kyra would stand silently in front of her, her presence and demeanor communicating disapproval. Immediately, Hannah would go quiet. Kyra also had a defiant side, and would stand her ground if she felt she was being treated unjustly.

Hannah was by far the most affectionate, freely giving hugs. She loved holding hands, cuddling with us, and being tickled. Her giggles always made me smile. She had bonded deeply with each of us from the start, and that bond was growing deeper each day.

The night before, when Al was sitting in his recliner, Hannah had walked over with a book.

"Would you read to me?" she asked. When he pulled her up into his lap and started reading, she snuggled into him like a little teddy bear.

For all the ways that Kyle and Kyra seemed to have strong filters in place, Hannah had none. She was the most emotional of the siblings, easily hurt and brought to tears. Whatever she felt was evident for all to see—anxiety and excitement, fear and delight, joy and sadness.

Andrew was a bundle of playful energy. He always seemed to bounce through a room rather than walk—when he wasn't bouncing on a bed. That morning I'd had to intervene in a tiff between him and Hannah because after she'd made her bed, he'd crawled up and bounced on it, messing it up to her dismay. But he was so adorable and smiley it was hard to be stern with him for more than a minute. He definitely had a mischievous and sneaky side. I'd catch him sneaking cookies from the cupboard or find crackers, cookies, even cheese stashed under his pillow or his bed. I wasn't surprised. Many foster children hoard food, sometimes a symptom of having grown up with too little to eat, but often a sign of unmet emotional needs. They stock and hide things they find soothing, demonstrating their fear that their needs won't be met unless they take matters into their own hands.

Baby Ally's personality was still developing, but so far she was all cuddles and smiles.

Yes, these five unique children have worked their way into the fabric of our lives.

When dinner was ready I called everyone to the table.

After taking his first bite, Andrew announced, "Mmm-mmm.

Debwa, you sure are a good cooker!" This was one of his favorite phrases at the table.

"I love cooking for you, Andrew, because you appreciate it more than anybody I know," I said. He beamed.

After dinner, Sadie and Helen helped me make sure that each child had packed his or her toothbrushes, pajamas, and a fresh change of clothes in anticipation of Karen's arrival. As usual, Kyle and Kyra were excited about their visit with their mom. Andrew grew quieter than normal but was compliant. Hannah, though she didn't protest this time, moved slowly and was withdrawn. After she finished packing she attached herself to me, literally, by wrapping her arms around my legs as I finished wiping down the kitchen counter. I picked her up and hugged her close, and she buried her face in my neck.

"Mom's here!" Kyra called out from the front door where she'd been keeping watch.

Hannah and I both stiffened. I set her down, knelt down to be eye-to-eye with her, and whispered, "I will see you tomorrow after dinner. I will come to pick you up, okay? Remember that I love you, and Jesus loves you more."

I took her face in my hands and kissed both cheeks. She didn't respond—just sadly looked into my eyes.

Kyle opened the door for Karen, and he and Kyra hugged her waist. Andrew followed their example. I took Hannah's hand and walked her over to the door as Helen handed Ally to Karen. "Okay, everybody grab your bags," I instructed. "Have fun!" I let go of Hannah's hand as the family headed out the door, Hannah trailing last in line.

The children continued their unsupervised visits during February and March. While there were no additional "accidents" that raised suspicions, Andrew and especially Hannah continued to demonstrate reluctance before the visits and moodiness after them. Sometimes Hannah would plead tearfully, asking if she could stay home with me. It was agonizing to send her on those days, wondering what was behind her distress. Was she being mistreated? What was happening during these visits? Or was it the past that Hannah was responding to?

Several times when the children returned from the visits, the younger ones would start to blurt out something that was said or done and were immediately silenced by the older two's threatening looks.

One evening while I was bathing Hannah, she chattered nonstop about all sorts of things. My ears perked up when she mentioned going to Mommy's house. Suddenly, she clammed up.

"Did something happen at Mommy's house?" I asked.

"I'll be in big, big trouble if I tell," she said.

I never pressured any of them to talk, not wanting to encourage them to go against something their mother may have told them. There is such a fine line for a foster parent between seeking the truth and disrupting the birth parent's authority. There is a time to speak up and a time to be silent. I wouldn't place the weight of pressure on them. I did discuss, however, each observation with the caseworker.

Though the children were mum about their visits, Karen had continued to open up to me about the past, especially her past with William—the man with whom, by the court instructions, she was not to associate. Karen had recently admitted to me that this man so hated the father of Hannah and Andrew, and so resented that Karen ever had a relationship with him, that far worse than shunning them, he'd usually been harsh and unkind to them, often screaming at them and wanting them sent to another room when he visited. She'd even revealed that he had an explosive temper, not only toward the children but toward Karen as well. Yet Karen had been so deeply enmeshed with him that rather than cut off her relationship with him she had worked hard to appease him, wanting him to be a part of her life. I couldn't help but wonder if she was defying DFS and seeing him now.

———————

One day when I was at the mall picking up a few things I ran into a friend of Karen's named Lisa. I'd met Lisa a few times at Karen's home when I'd dropped the children off for visits. I liked her. She seemed levelheaded and appeared to care about the children.

"How are things going with the Bower children?" she asked.

Not wanting to betray any confidences, I kept my answer light. "Just fine. How do you think they are going?"

Lisa's face darkened. "Debra, to be honest, I've been relieved they are with you and that DFS is telling Karen to stay clear of William. He's a wretched influence on Karen and has been cruel to Hannah and Andrew. He's bad news."

"Sounds like he's been a real source of trouble. If you don't mind me asking, how was he cruel to Hannah and Andrew?"

Maybe I'll finally get some answers.

Lisa described a grotesque picture of abuse. If Hannah or Andrew would whine or fuss or irritate William, he would grab them, put duct tape over their mouths, bind their hands together, and put them into a closet and close the door, leaving them there, sometimes for hours at a time.

"Karen wouldn't intervene," she told me. "Her relationship with this man is so dysfunctional, so tragically misguided, that she'd rather placate him than protect her own children. I'd talk to her 'til I was blue in the face, but she'd never stand up to him. Recently, I warned her that she'd better not let anything like that happen again. I hope she is staying away from him."

I wasn't shocked. I'd heard much worse over the years and seen the results on tiny bodies. I hadn't become desensitized to cruelty to children—I still felt a shudder deep in my soul—but I didn't gasp or rage or rant. I closed my eyes for a moment and let the ugly truth sink in.

"Thank you for telling me," I said. "This answers some big questions."

I called Ellen later that day and told her what I'd learned. She didn't sound surprised, which made me wonder if perhaps DFS had already known. Maybe this was one of the reasons they'd mandated that Karen not associate with William and not expose the children to him.

"William is trouble all around," Ellen said. "It's good that Karen seems to be keeping her word about not seeing him. Have the children reported any encounters with him?"

"No. The children say nothing about what goes on during home visits," I said. "I heard this from a friend of Karen's."

"I'll make sure it's noted in the file," she assured me.

Several days later, I drove the children to Karen's house for their half-day visit, hoping for a chance to talk with Karen. Once the children were off playing in the living room, I had a few minutes alone with Karen in the kitchen.

"I have a question for you," I said. "It's about William and the kids."

"Okay," Karen said cautiously.

"Were there times when William would bind Hannah and Andrew with duct tape and put them in the closet?"

Karen looked away, then said in a quiet voice, "Yeah. . . well . . . that happened . . . sometimes." She looked down at the kitchen floor. "That was something that William started. I wasn't in favor of it, but you don't argue with William."

Her response confirmed my fears. This wasn't an isolated instance. This was a pattern—something that had happened repeatedly.

"Who told you?" Karen asked.

"I'm not at liberty to say," I said, "but it wasn't any of the children."

She didn't push me to know more. Just then, Kyra came into the kitchen, so we changed the subject. I left a few minutes later, wondering what other secrets this family was keeping.

Now that I realized how severely Hannah and Andrew had suffered before being removed from their mother, I understood why their relationship with her was broken. This family's secrets were far more sinister and dark than I'd first imagined.

The trust that should exist between mother and child had been shattered. Karen had violated her role as protector and nurturer of Hannah and Andrew. And because Kyle and Kyra had witnessed abuse of the younger children with the willing compliance of their mother, Karen had severely damaged their understanding of the value of their siblings. All four children had repeatedly seen their mother welcome this threatening, menacing, and vengeful man into their home, tolerate his behavior, and silently go along with it.

I was weighed down by so many questions now. If William's control over Karen had been so powerful, was she being successful now at staying away from him? When the children were with their mother, did they worry that William would show up unexpectedly? Was this what frightened Hannah and Andrew? Could this be why they came home moody and sullen? How had William's influence twisted and damaged Karen's ability to love and nurture them? Was she capable of treating Hannah and Andrew in a healthy, loving way?

I recalled several times when Karen initially acted with kindness to all of the children, but then changed her treatment of Hannah. Karen would first make Hannah laugh, but then her expression would become intimidating. Hannah's smile would vanish, and she would become reserved with her head down. I never knew what was going on between the two of them, but it wasn't good.

All four children were well behaved, but guarded with their

mother. It was as if they didn't know where the line of true affection and indifference was drawn. The unspoken clues to figure that out appeared to be different for Hannah and Andrew than for Kyle and Kyra.

I now had a much clearer understanding of how to pray for the Bower kids. Hannah and Andrew needed healing from their past abuse and courage during the unsupervised visits with their mother. They needed Karen to develop a consistent bond of trust with them that they could count on. Kyle and Kyra needed to realize that their mother's treatment of their younger siblings was wrong; instead, they should show empathy and treat Hannah and Andrew lovingly. It was important that our family model this for them in every way that we could.

My prayers for Karen included new requests as well—that God would keep her away from William and any other evil influence, that she would recognize the wrongness of her past actions, and that she would develop a nurturing heart. I decided to invite Karen to church again, not just as a way for her to see her children, but also so she might learn of Jesus and his love for her.

I was grateful to the Lord that he had shown me long ago how to handle my bedtime prayers for the children we fostered. When I became a new Christian, I heard a powerful sermon on "honor thy mother and thy father." As a result, Al and I had committed to teach our own children to honor us as their parents, but meditating on that sermon made me realize there was some work I needed to do in my own heart. There were things for which I had not forgiven my parents. They may not have been big, horrendous things, but they were unresolved in my heart. Over time and with much prayer I'd learned to forgive and honor them.

Al and I believed we had a spiritual responsibility to teach our foster children how to honor their parents, but early on we struggled with that. How could these children who had been neglected or abused honor their parents? After much soul-searching, we decided we could explain that abuse is wrong and that parents aren't supposed to hurt their children, but we could also ask God to change them. When I prayed with each child at night, whichever children we had, I would name their parents, asking God to watch over them and to turn their hearts to him, to work in their lives and help them to be better parents. I prayed for the children to want to honor and respect their parents.

Committing our foster children and their parents to God and giving up any control I may have thought I had in their lives was often a wrestling match I would have with God. I knew, just like with my own family, I had to surrender them into the Father's hands. Only he knew their hearts. Only he knew their needs. My power to protect any of them was limited.

One night, soon after learning about William's abuse of Hannah and Andrew, I said these words at Hannah's bedside. "Dear Jesus, thank you that you love Hannah and want only the best for her. We pray for her mommy, Karen. Watch over her and help her to be a better mommy. Help her make sure that no one ever hurts Hannah again. And help Hannah to be able to tell someone if anything bad or scary happens to her. Let Hannah know that you are always with her and that you love her. Amen."

Chapter 5

The Bridge

KYRA AND HANNAH SAT next to me in the front seat of the pickup truck as I turned onto the highway, still wet from the early morning April snow. I was driving them to a friend's house to play. The sun sparkled on the road ahead as I approached the bridge. The dreaded bridge. It always reminded me of the accident. We had to cross it in order to reach the rural, sage-covered land where their friend lived.

In spite of the traumatic memory, I smiled, knowing that the bridge story was a favorite of all the kids. I loved to tell a good family story, and I certainly didn't have to embellish this one to capture their imaginations. I expected to be asked to retell it now and was not disappointed. But I wasn't expecting the profound exchange it sparked—an exchange that would take on far deeper meaning in the months to come.

"Show us where you hit the bridge," six-year-old Kyra said with a sense of mystery and excitement when the rusty old structure came into view.

"Yeah. Show us Debwa," added Hannah, now five. Both the girls had had their birthdays in late March.

I stopped a few feet before the bridge. "It was there." I pointed to the spot of first impact, surprised that my stomach still churned at the memory. It had been a little over a year since my accident, and though I'd crossed the bridge many times since, it seemed like only yesterday.

———————————

Helen, eleven when the accident occurred, had been packed and ready to go for thirty minutes and was pacing the living room floor waiting for me to drive her to a friend's slumber party. Al had offered to drive, but knowing he was exhausted from his long work hours that week I'd insisted he stay home. Besides, he'd hardly seen the kids all week, and this would give him a chance to relax with them. Minutes before Helen and I headed out the door, however, Al leaned against the doorframe, hands in his jeans pockets, filling the kitchen doorway. "I know the snow has stopped, but the roads will be bad. You're not taking Bessemer Bend Bridge, are you?" he asked.

I laid the dish towel on the counter and peered out the window over the sink. True, the snow had stopped falling, but the temperature hadn't. I knew this was no evening to be out, but Helen had been anticipating the party for days. "I'll be fine. Taking Bessemer is so much shorter."

"The bridge will be slick. It's not a good idea."

"I'll be careful. If I don't take it, I'll have to drive twice as far, all the way to Robertson Road Bridge. The shorter the drive, the better. I can handle the bridge, Al."

Al approached me from behind, his slippers flopping noisily against the linoleum. I turned to face the concerned look in his eyes. "Really, I'll be fine. I'll take it slow. I just don't want to be out there all evening."

"You know I don't feel good about you going that way. You have no control on ice." His hands rested on my shoulders as he looked directly into my eyes. After a long pause, he pulled me into the fold of his arms and whispered, "You can be so stubborn."

"I . . . will . . . be . . . careful," I whispered with confidence.

After wrestling on coats, mittens, and crocheted hats, Helen and I gathered her sleeping bag, pillow, and backpack.

"Don't worry!" My closing assurance to Al echoed through the mudroom before I headed for the van, surrounded by a mound of snow in the driveway.

Helen helped me brush the snow off the front and side windows of the van, and then we climbed inside. Knowing the engine would take a few minutes to warm up, I tucked my hands between my knees and waited. Helen pushed her sleeping bag to the floorboard to cover her feet, then wrapped her pillow across her pink cheeks, creating a warm mask by breathing into it.

"How much below zero is it, Mom?"

My teeth chattering, I pointed to the minus seven on the dashboard thermometer.

Finally, we were on our way. We followed our split rail fence down Goose Egg Road as far as our ten acres extended. Once the dirt road met up with the blacktop, I turned right, crossed the slick pipes of the cattle guard, then turned left onto Highway 220. Slushy snow mixed with sand beat against the tires until we took the Bessemer exit. Rumbling across the pipes of another cattle crossing, I slowed to a snail's pace until we rolled onto the packed snow on Bessemer Road.

Finally, the heater began to warm what felt like a freezer on wheels. Slivers of brilliant orange now peeked over the horizon as the moon ascended above the prairie. I could see the silhouettes of livestock following us along the road, and chimney smoke drifting from the tops of the little country houses spread across the range. The steel trusses of the bridge loomed ahead over the North Platte River. I tapped my brakes lightly and gripped the steering wheel, Al's words of caution in my mind. The van glided over the bridge's wooden planks with a soft rumbling sound. Within seconds we were on snow-covered gravel once again.

"No problem." I grinned, pleased at my safe crossing and how much time I'd saved by choosing this route.

A halfmile from her friend's home, Helen began folding her sleeping bag, now cozy and warm from the heat. The crossing at Poison Spider Road where Helen's friend lived was dark and deserted. Only a dim yellow porch light flickered as we pulled up to the front door.

"Love you, Mom." Helen leaned toward me to receive my kiss on her forehead. I chuckled as I watched her make her way toward the front door, her boots sinking into the deep snow as she wrestled with her sleeping bag that had unfolded and was dragging behind her. Her friend greeted Helen at the door and waved at me, signaling I could leave.

"See you tomorrow," I mouthed through the glass.

Only a whisper of wind responded. The van's tires crunched on the snow-covered road as I began to retrace my route toward home. I was pleased with myself. I'd made it across both the bridge and the prairie the first time without mishap. The van was toasty, so I relaxed in the leather seat.

Al will have a cozy fire waiting for me. I can't wait to get home and chat with him. I hope the children have been behaving.

Mesmerized by the moon's reflection on the water, my thoughts drifted as I rounded the river and headed back toward the bridge, paying little attention to the road.

Approaching the bridge from the north now, I had to maneuver a curve along the twisted river bend. Coming off the curve, I tapped my brakes and rolled forward. The front wheels touched the bridge, then whisshh . . . from out of nowhere blowing snow swirled across the windshield, temporarily blinding me. I tensed and tightened my grip on the wheel.

The front wheels of the van refused to go the direction I steered.

A sudden unexpected oomph grabbed at the rear of the vehicle, swaying it back and forth. Then the van whipped sideways.

Ice!

My grip on the wheel intensified. My knees locked.

The van started to spin, and my foot slid off the accelerator. Hurtling uncontrollably toward the guardrail, I braced for impact.

Oh God, don't let me go into the river, I thought, seeing the icy waters rush below me.

I only had time for one quick breath before the van slammed headlong into the rusty steel framework of the bridge. I screamed as I heard the glass of the headlights break with the crashing blow. The sound of metal cracked and crunched around me like a pop can being crushed. The van bounced off the guardrail into a spin that propelled me toward the opposite side. The bridge, with its steel arms towering over me, looked threatening as I careened into the other rail with a wretched blow. My head slammed into the side window.

Time seemed to slow down, but the van did not. My body lurched against my seat belt with each thrash, and it tightened, cutting into my abdomen and hips. The van jerked me violently upward, and my knees banged the steering wheel. Once again the van slid across the bridge and collided with the opposite side. The bridge wrestled me, twisted me, thrashed me about, and again threatened to toss me into the icy river below. With each spin and collision, I could see the moon's reflection on the frigid swirling waters not far below.

"Dear Jesus, please don't let the side rails break. Don't let my van go into the river. Please, please, please." There was a horrible screeching sound, and sparks flew as the side of the van scraped the guardrail. I let go of the wheel and covered my eyes.

If I don't watch, maybe it will all end.

The van hurled sideways again, then jerked to an abrupt stop. I spread my fingers enough to peer through them to see where I had landed. My vision blurry, I shook my head and blinked a few times.

I was free from the bridge, having been spit out the south side onto Bessemer Road, finally out of danger of being propelled into the water. Though the van had stopped, my insides continued to spin as nausea flooded over me. I gasped to breathe. My heart hammered, clawing to escape my chest.

When my eyes focused, I saw a flickering light on the ground ahead of me—a dislodged headlight was swaying back and forth. Other than the thudding of my heart and a dull hissing from under the hood, the van was silent. "Thank you, Lord. Thank you, Jesus." I rested my face in the palms of my sweaty, trembling hands.

"Al warned me." I took a deep breath, and with gentle caution pressed the accelerator, hoping the van would roll forward. The engine revved. Metal groaned and . . . movement! I coaxed the van away from the bridge.

"Thank you for saving me, Lord."

Part of me wanted to sit and wait until my hands stopped trembling and my heart stopped thundering, but home was less than half a mile away and I was afraid the van would die, leaving me stranded, so I kept moving. As the Toyota inched its way to Highway 220, spasms climbed my spine. My legs were in pain and my head throbbed.

What has my pride cost us?

Had I totaled the van? Even if it was reparable (which seemed unlikely) and the insurance covered most of the repairs, we'd have added expenses to pay. While the van was in the body shop, Al would need to help carpool the kids in the pickup, interrupting his workday. I'd be stuck with the older banged-up pickup we called the Skunk Truck. That alone would be humbling.

I crept along at twenty miles per hour. When I reached the house, I sat for a moment before turning off the engine. I couldn't go back and change what had happened. I could only hope I would find grace ahead. Shifting into park, I turned the key. The engine whined and sputtered to a pathetic stop.

As I pushed against the battered door, the hinges creaked. Closing the door cautiously, I took a deep breath and let myself into the house. I heard the TV in the family room.

Al was sitting in his overstuffed leather recliner; the wood-burning stove was ablaze.

"Hey, hon! How were the roads?"

I stood in the middle of the family room.

"So . . . what's up? Everything okay?"

"No. Not really." Sucking in a corner of my bottom lip, I bit down, then mumbled, "Uh . . . you need to come see."

I took Al's hand and led him to the door. The garage light illuminated the wreckage, its wounds accentuated by an array of fluids leaking from the undercarriage.

Al stared. "Are you all right?"

"Yes. Banged up, but I'm okay."

"You took Bessemer Bridge, didn't you?"

I rested my head against his shoulder. "I am so sorry. Please forgive me for not listening to you." The tears flowed uncontrollably down my cheeks.

Still holding my hand, Al wiped my tears with his free hand. "I am thankful that you're safe. That's what matters." He then pulled me to his chest and wrapped his arms around me.

As I finished telling the girls the story, my heart full of the thoughts of the gentle grace of my husband, Kyra and Hannah pushed up against their seat belts to see over the dashboard. Kyra stretched as far as she could to study the rushing water below. After peeking, Hannah, however, quickly sat back in her seat with a pensive, worried expression on her face.

"What if the bridge broke and your car went into the water?" Hannah asked.

"Jesus would have taken care of me, Hannah."

The name *Jesus* was by now familiar to all the Bower children. They'd grown accustomed to bedtime prayers, praying together at meals, and attending our church. The love of Jesus was shared in our home and we spoke of him often. He was a part of our family.

Hannah seemed to study my face for a more convincing answer. "But Debwa, what if your car went in the water and the water started to come in through the windows?"

"Jesus would have been there with me and would have taken care of me."

Hannah pushed up against her seat belt again to see the river. As her eyes teared up, her voice began to crack. "But Debwa, what if the water came in and you drowneded?"

I looked directly into Hannah's searching eyes and with conviction whispered, "Jesus . . . would have . . . taken care of me. I love Jesus and I trust him to take care of me, even if I drowned."

Hannah and I locked eyes for the longest time, and it seemed the soul behind those large brown eyes was far older than a mere five years. Kyra watched our silent conversation. It was a teachable moment. *Will the girls understand?* It seemed as if Hannah wanted to understand. Studying my face, she squinted and bit her bottom lip as if by looking hard enough and deep enough, she would be able to mirror my thoughts. She sat very still and was especially quiet the rest of the way.

What is going through that little five-year-old mind? I pray it is you, Jesus. Lead her to call out to you in times of danger and come to trust you.

I had no way of knowing then how significant that little conversation would be. Where once I'd left pieces of my vehicle strewn about, now I'd left seeds of faith sown.

Chapter 6

The Parting

ON A WET AND SLUSHY MORNING in early April, I took Ally and Andrew to Starla's, then dropped Hannah at Head Start and the others at each of their schools before heading into town for a meeting at DFS. With wipers frantically swiping across my windshield, I fought the sprays of sludge thrown against my car from other vehicles. The road conditions were not good and traffic moved slowly.

I don't want to be late for this meeting.

DFS had invited me to participate in planning the steps toward moving Karen's children home, and I appreciated being asked to be a part of the plan. I pulled into the parking lot of the office with a few minutes to spare.

For the next hour and a half, Karen, Ellen, and I developed a six-month, week-by-week schedule. It included home checks, visitations, overnight stays, parenting classes, counseling, and random drug testing for Karen. When we finished, I was encouraged. The plan was solid and Karen's attitude was positive. Ellen would present the plan to the juvenile court judge for approval. In my years as a foster parent, I had never known a judge to reject what a caseworker recommended. If Karen wasn't fit to parent, I expected evidence to turn up during this intensively supervised period. If she was fit, these six months could help the children ease back into being parented by her.

A few days later I invited Karen to meet me at the crisis pregnancy center. I hoped I was continuing to build a relationship of trust so I could support her if and when she regained custody of her children. Also, I couldn't help but notice that Karen had put on some weight recently. *Was it possible she was pregnant again?* I certainly wasn't going to ask her, but maybe she'd bring it up. If so, I wanted her to know how The Caring Center could help.

We talked for more than an hour, and I was thankful for her openness with me.

"I really want to raise my youngest children. DeAnn is doing well living with my parents, so I think that's the best place for her. But the other five should be with me."

"It won't be easy for you as a single mom," I said quietly.

I had lingering unsaid doubts. When she got frustrated, stressed, and tired, how would she handle it all? Would she allow others to help her? When she felt trapped or lonely, would she call William? Would she go back to the lifestyle she was living with this man who'd been cruel to her children and have more children with him? She didn't appear interested in returning to her former life. I hoped for a positive change and had been praying she would let God get hold of her heart and show her another way.

Karen would still have to jump through DFS's hoops for at least six more months in order to get her children back. That included getting a job (the seasonal job Al had given her had ended in December), finding a larger place to live, and getting counseling. The plan called for her to continue to stay away from the people in her life who used drugs, including William. Such people could hurt her chances of being credible and serious about wanting to parent.

Now that the caseworker wasn't present, Karen appeared to be a little impatient and indignant with all the rules and regulations she would have to follow, yet she said she was ready to do it all. I talked about how it could be a blessing. She didn't seem too interested in seeing it as a blessing but knew it was their way or no way.

I asked Karen how she felt her relationship with Hannah and Andrew was progressing. She admitted that she and Hannah often butted heads and that she saw Hannah as being responsible for many of her own problems. She resented the fact that Hannah didn't want to come visit her. She mentioned the one time in January when Hannah had put up such a fuss about going to an unsupervised visit that the caseworker allowed her to stay home with me. Karen had agreed to that arrangement though she wasn't happy about it, and obviously, it still bothered her.

I explained to Karen that Hannah needed to feel she was okay to go to her mother's without having problems or getting into trouble.

Karen told me she felt Hannah was acting like she was special and manipulating all of us so she could have more attention.

I was disappointed to hear her thoughts. I'd come to know Hannah intimately and knew that her anxiety over being with her mother was real, not an act of manipulation. In fact, Hannah's anxiety had been worsening lately rather than getting better.

I asked Karen if she thought it would help for the other kids to go home and for me to keep Hannah with us for a while longer.

"I'll think about it," Karen said.

"Karen, do you want to raise Hannah?" I asked.

"I would let my parents raise her or her father take her, but my parents can't handle another grandchild, and her father has said he couldn't work and take care of her."

To me, these comments meant that Karen would be willing to give her up if she had someplace for her to go.

The longer we talked, the more Karen demonstrated such resentment toward Hannah that I felt it would be unhealthy and unsafe for them to be together. Fear for Hannah stirred my heart. I couldn't rest with the thought of her returning to such a toxic environment.

"If you don't want Hannah to come home, would you consider letting us take guardianship or even adopting her?" I would never have made such a suggestion if I didn't feel Karen was thinking about what she would do with Hannah. I was afraid that Karen might not care where Hannah went or who took her. But then again . . . who was I? Did I even have the right to ask Karen this question?

Lately, during Hannah's bedtime prayers, when I would pray for her mommy, Hannah would whisper, "Can't you be my mommy?"

I would kiss her sweet forehead and whisper back, "I would love to, but you have a mommy, and I am sure she loves you and wants you to come home." Hannah would look at me wide-eyed and shake her head. It would make my heart sad.

I adore each of my children. Each one is a gift. I could never look at them with such disgust or disregard.

But I was not Karen, and I had not been in her situation. I cautioned myself not to judge her.

I could only pray Karen would consider letting us take Hannah. Maybe in the next six months, she would make that decision.

That evening Al and I discussed the six-month plan again in light of the conversation I'd had with Karen.

"I'd be open to guardianship of Hannah after the other kids go home," Al told me. "We could see how that goes and how Karen feels about not having Hannah in her home. I wouldn't move toward adoption until we tested the situation first."

"I'll talk more to Karen and see if she would consider it," I told Al.

But in the meantime, the Bower kids would be in our home until August or September. For now, we had a workable routine with our temporary family of ten. We could do it for another six months.

One evening, a week after my conversation with Karen, I walked into Helen's room carrying clean laundry. To my surprise I found Hannah, alone, lying on Helen's bed playing with two dolls. It was rare to find her alone, so I decided to make the most of the opportunity.

Hannah was changing the dolls' clothes.

"That's a cute outfit," I said, stroking the dress on one of the dolls.

"It's my favorite," she said, lighting up as I stretched out on the bed next to her. For the next few minutes we played with the dolls.

My concerns about Hannah had not eased. I had assumed the visits with her mom would grow easier over time, but she had put up a considerable fuss before the past weekend's visit and had come home quite anxious. Clearly, something was troubling her, and I had my suspicions.

"Did you have a good visit with your mom this weekend?" I asked. Her face fell, and she turned to make sure no one else was within earshot. She shook her head no very slowly.

"I'm so sorry to hear that," I said. "Do you want to tell me what happened?" Again, she shook her head no as a tear slipped down her cheek.

"How about I ask you some questions, and you can nod yes or shake your head no. Would that be okay? It's only the two of us, and no one else can hear."

She turned over on her back, nudging closer to me, and cuddled her baby doll to her chest. Then she nodded yes. I knew I had to tread lightly. I wanted her to feel safe.

"Was anybody mean to you?"

She nodded.

"Did you have any visitors?"

Another nod. Dare I ask the question haunting me?

"Was it the mean man? Did William come?"

For a moment she just stared sadly at me. Then she gave a tiny nod. She started to tremble, and I realized I'd probably taken this as far as I should. I reached over and stroked her cheek.

"Were you afraid?" I asked.

She didn't answer but continued to stare at me with big eyes. She was starting to shut down. I picked up the other doll. "I think she likes this pink dress you put on her. These two dolls look like best friends. My doll is going to hug your doll."

Just then, Helen came bouncing into her room, and that was the end of our one-on-one visit. While I couldn't be certain that William had made an appearance at Karen's, I decided I'd give the caseworker a call in the morning.

"Hi, Ellen," I said. "I'm calling because I am a little worried and have a feeling that William is going over to Karen's." I explained my interaction with Hannah the night before.

"Well, I wouldn't put it past her, but if she is caught, her reintegration plan will be set way back."

I'm not sure what I expected, but somehow this response fell short of my hopes. I wanted assurances that they would investigate. I realized that DFS couldn't watch Karen's house 24-7 and had to rely on what she reported to them. And I wasn't a DFS worker. I was a foster parent. All I could do was make my observations and concerns known and advocate for the children. At least, I assured myself, Karen would remain under DFS scrutiny for another six months before the children were returned. I'd pray that the truth would be revealed. But what could I do for Hannah in the meantime? I wasn't yet sure.

On April 16, my phone rang at The Caring Center.

"Debra, I don't even know how to tell you this," Ellen said. "I have news. I went to the judge's office to present the six-month plan but was told that he was not going to meet with me. He, along with some attorneys, made the decision that the five Bower children should be returned home—immediately."

I was speechless. *Did I hear Ellen correctly? How can this be? What is the judge thinking?* Ellen and I both knew Karen wasn't ready to take all the kids yet, nor were they ready to be thrust back into her home.

Trying to catch my breath I blurted out, "Ellen, you've got to be kidding. Why wouldn't he meet with you? Why weren't you allowed to present the plan? I don't understand!" I was holding back tears.

"I don't understand either. Nothing like this has ever happened to me before. I had everything ready, file in hand, but I was asked to remain outside his chamber; then someone came to tell me a decision had been made. I was as shocked as you. I don't get it. I left and went back to my office and contacted my supervisor."

She stumbled over her words. "That's all I can tell you. You have to pack up the kids and take them home. Today. I'm getting their paperwork ready now. I have to go." She sounded frustrated and in a hurry.

"Wait!" I cried into the phone. "What about Hannah? Can we work something out for us to keep her until Karen gets settled with the other children? You know it's not a good situation for her."

"All of the children are ordered back. Today! You need to do it, Deb."

A lump rose in my throat and my mouth went dry, but I had no time to process my shock. It was time to pick up the children. I got my three kids first. As each one climbed into the car, I told them about the judge's decision. The first response out of each of their mouths was, "What about Hannah? They're not making her go home now, are they?" When I told them she would have to go as well, the looks on their faces mirrored the fear in my heart.

"Please don't say anything to the Bower children. I want to tell them all together at home." My throat tightened as each of Karen's children got in the van, but I tried to act as natural as possible.

When we pulled into our driveway, I instructed the kids, "When we get inside, hang up your coats and set your backpacks on the seat in the mudroom. Put your boots along the wall, neatly, and then come into the kitchen for snacks. I want to talk to all of you. And no . . . you are not in trouble." I forced myself to give them a big smile to reassure them. I could see their faces relax, knowing there would be snacks and a talk, but not a lecture.

Within a few minutes, the children were seated in their usual places at the table. "What you gonna to talk to us about, Debwa?" Andrew mumbled with chocolate chip cookie crumbs falling from his lips onto the kitchen table.

"I got a call today from Ellen at DFS. She said that you are all going home today."

I stopped for a moment to see the children's reactions. They all stopped chewing and looked up at me. With their little brows furrowed and eyes squinting, I could tell they were as confused as I had been at the news. Kyle was the first to speak up.

"Today?" His eyes brightened as he sat up tall in his chair. Kyra watched her older brother's reaction and began to smile along with him.

"Yes. Today." I repeated.

Hannah's eyes widened. She put her cookie down and swallowed hard. She stared at me a moment and then asked, "Me too?"

Andrew sat, almost as frozen as Hannah, watching his sister's face change from smiles to terror. Ally, being a ten-month-old in a high chair, was more interested in her pile of Cheerios and sippy cup of milk. She had no understanding of where she was going.

"After you finish your snack, we need to get some boxes and pack up as much as we can to take with you today. I can bring the rest of your things on another day."

My children watched as each child responded to the news. Then they looked over at me as if I were going to say something to Hannah that would make her feel better. I didn't know what to say. There wasn't anything I could say that would make her feel comfortable about going home to her mother. I knew my kids had been looking forward to downsizing the family back to the five of us for a while, but they, too, had serious concerns for Hannah.

When the cookies were gone, the table was wiped clean from crumbs and milk, and I sent my children off with Ally, Kyle, Kyra, and Andrew to begin gathering clothes and toys.

"Hannah, let's go sit on the couch."

I sat down close to her and spoke quietly. "I talked to the case-worker about you going home to your mother. She said you had to go with the other kids. I have no choice. I can't keep you with us. But I promise to check on you, and DFS will check on you to make sure you are okay."

My whispered conversation with Hannah was drawing more attention than if I had spoken out loud. Kyle and Kyra peeked curiously out the bedroom door. I sensed they were more con-cerned with what Hannah was saying to me than what I was saying to her. Their mother would hold them accountable for what any of them said to a caseworker or to me. Fortunately, they couldn't hear us.

"But I want to stay with you. I want to live here. I don't want to go." Hannah's eyes filled with tears.

"I know. We don't want you to go. But I have no power to keep you. Maybe your mommy will let you come back to visit. You'll be okay." I could see she was not believing my words of reassurance any more than I was.

The packing was finished in a half hour, and Sadie, Helen, and Charles loaded the boxes into the car. After giving each of the Bower children a good-bye hug, they helped get everyone fastened in their seat belts. Hannah sat stiffly in the front seat next to me. I kept looking over at her, but she wouldn't look at me.

I can't do this.

Hannah began to weep as we drove the bumpy dirt road from our home. Her heartrending cry gave voice to the grief locked in my own soul. Her siblings—even Ally—sat quietly in the back seat. As we turned onto the highway, Hannah started to plead, "Please don't make me go!" She whispered as if she didn't want her siblings to hear her. She was trembling. Her fists, clenched, rested on either side of her little body on the seat.

I had the radio on, so I adjusted the volume to be louder in the back of the van to muffle what I was about to say to Hannah. "I will come see you. I will come see all of you. Often. You will be fine," I whispered.

Lord, what do I do?

The closer we got to town, the harder Hannah sobbed.

The judge's decision made me boil. I couldn't go through with this. I had to do something. I turned down a side street that headed to the DFS office instead of Karen's home.

I could take the kids in with me and ask to meet with Ellen. We need to come up with a plan B for Hannah.

I pulled over to the side of the road near the DFS office and got out. The children looked concerned. I told them I would be back in a minute. I walked to the shoulder of the road and dialed DFS.

While I was waiting for Ellen to answer, Hannah got out of the car.

"Hannah, what are you doing? You need to stay in the car."

She was sobbing as she ran to me. I picked her up, and she wrapped her legs around my waist, threw her arms around my neck, and buried her face against my chest. I could barely hold on to her and the phone. She wept relentlessly.

"Hello, this is Ellen." I could hardly hear her over Hannah's wails.

"Ellen, this is Deb Moerke. I am with the kids. I was driving them to Karen's, but Hannah is hysterical. She is terrified." My voice cracked as tears streamed down my face. "I can't take her back like this. Please, can we work something out for her?"

"It's out of my hands now. The judge has ordered it, and you have to take them all home. Take her back, and we will keep an eye on things. I know it's not good for Hannah, but I will make sure there are home checks and that she is okay. You have to do it, Deb."

Hannah was squeezing me so tightly I could hardly breathe. The other children stared at us through the car windows.

Panic hit my heart like it had never done before. I had thought I was a reasonable person. Levelheaded. Focused. But now I felt as if I was caught in a desperate life-and-death situation. I said the craziest thing. "What if I take her out-of-state, or out of the country? What would happen?"

Ellen spoke slowly. "Debra, you would be brought up on kidnapping charges. Think of your family. Don't do something crazy." It was the slap I needed to bring me back to reality. *What could I do?* No one was on Hannah's side. No one was there for either of us. No one had the authority to change the course we were doomed to take.

"All right. But you have to promise you will keep an eye on things and make sure she is okay." I had never talked to a caseworker like that before. I knew Ellen understood how serious I was. But I didn't think she understood how afraid I was for Hannah.

When the call ended, I struggled to peel Hannah off me. I had scratch marks on my neck from pulling her hands away. I held her tightly. "I love you, Hannah. I love you and Jesus loves you."

Fifteen minutes must have passed before Hannah calmed down enough to listen to me. I told her she had to go to her mother's and I couldn't do anything to change that. I reminded her that I would come to visit her and make sure she was doing okay. Her eyes glazed over with a look of defeat and surrender. *She is shutting down.* She had learned how to do it when she was scared. The crying stopped. Her breathing slowed. She wouldn't look at me and wiggled to get down from our embrace.

I walked her to the car door and buckled her in. She refused to look at me.

Suddenly, the silence in the car was broken by Ally's fussing. She whined until I pulled a bottle from my purse and gave it to her. Kyle and Kyra exchanged looks. Were they sad for Hannah, or were they planning to tell their mother how Hannah had acted and get her in trouble? My experience with them told me that their loyalty was always to their mother, not to Hannah. That was how Karen had trained them.

I pulled away from the curb and drove across town to Karen's new rental home. It was nice—a bi-level with an attached garage. It was newer and larger than the previous house, and the backyard had a nice swing set. But all the nice and new wouldn't change the fear Hannah and I both felt in our hearts.

Kyle and Kyra bolted from the car, excited to run into the house to their mother. Andrew was slower, and I had to get Ally out of the car seat. Hannah didn't move. She didn't undo her seat belt or look out the window. She sat staring at the glove compartment with the white of dried tears covering her precious dark cheeks.

When I looked up toward the house, the first thing I noticed was Karen's pronounced baby bump—she was clearly pregnant. This was the worst possible day to absorb this new information, so I pretended not to notice. Karen's face was lit up with joy as she hugged Kyle and Kyra. Andrew tagged along behind.

Carrying Ally on one hip, I grabbed the open package of diapers from the car and headed to the front door. The other three children had already disappeared.

"They found the swing set in the backyard," Karen said.

As I handed Ally to Karen, I said. "Are you ready for all of them to come home on such short notice?"

Karen laughed and shook her head. "I don't know. I was surprised when Ellen called me. I'm a little overwhelmed." Her honesty accentuated one of my fears. Would she be so overwhelmed that she would fall right back into her old ways? Especially with a new child on the way? I smiled and excused myself to retrieve more boxes and get Hannah.

She hadn't moved an inch. Her stare was still locked on the glove compartment.

I unfastened her seat belt. "You need to get out, honey," I said as tenderly as I could. I slid her legs to the side of the seat and tucked my hands under her arms. She was dead weight, almost lifeless. When I tried to look into her eyes, she turned her head away.

Side by side we walked slowly up the driveway to the house. Karen had gone in with Ally and was upstairs when we reached the front door. I offered my hand to Hannah. She didn't take it; she walked alone up the stairs. She went straight to the couch and sat on the edge of it.

I could hear the other children laughing in the backyard. Karen was watching them through the glass patio door in the dining room, smiling. I took advantage of Karen's momentary distraction and knelt down next to Hannah.

I wrapped my hands around hers. "I know you cannot trust big people. We have all failed you. But you *can* trust Jesus. When you need him, call out to him. He will never fail you." For a split second, Hannah looked me in the eyes and then looked down again.

I sensed God was telling me I had to surrender her to him. I had to trust him as much as I was encouraging Hannah to trust him. My heart twisted with pain. Surrender was never easy, but this surrender felt beyond me. Yet surely, God loved Hannah more than I did. *Lord, I entrust her to you.*

Out of the corner of my eye, I could see Karen turning and heading our way. I kissed Hannah on her forehead and stood quickly, not wanting to bring much attention to her. It was too late.

Karen looked at me and then at Hannah. "What's wrong, Hannah? Are you okay?"

Playing down our tender and emotional few seconds together, I smiled at Karen and said, "She'll be fine. She's a little tired today."

Hannah never looked up as I went out to the car for more boxes.

"I'll bring the rest of their things in the next few days. There just wasn't time . . ."

I went to the patio door and waved good-bye to the kids. "Please don't hesitate to call me if you need anything."

Hannah still had not moved from her spot on the couch. My heart was heavier than I could bear. I got into my car, pulled away from the curb, and sobbed all the way home.

Part Two

The
Unthinkable

Chapter 7

Suspicions

"HI, KAREN, THIS IS DEB," I said on the phone a few days later. "I made a dinner I know the kids will like—lasagna with garlic bread and a salad. Would it be okay if I brought it with me today when I drop off some of the things the kids left behind?"

Karen welcomed the offer, and we set a time for me to come. The few days since returning the children to Karen had been emotionally brutal. I couldn't get the image out of my mind of Hannah clinging to me and sobbing. I felt guilty for leaving her, and I wept more than once from worry. Was she safe? Was she traumatized? What must she be feeling? It was all I could do each day to resist driving over and rescuing her. So I did the only thing within my power to do—I prayed for her. Repeatedly.

I wanted to trust God with my whole heart through this trial, yet I struggled to understand why he'd allow Hannah to be put in what seemed to me harm's way. As a foster mom I'd come to terms with the fact that we live in a very broken world—a world where abuse and evil happen on a regular basis, even to children, the most innocent among us. I'd grown to realize that God is not to blame for that evil—it is the enemy's doing. God's solution for evil is an eternal solution—only salvation through Christ will bring an eternity where evil is banished. But knowing that didn't stop the ache in my heart for Hannah's well-being. All I could do was entrust her to his care.

As I pulled up in front of Karen's house, I was excited that I'd soon be seeing Hannah and all her siblings. I'd missed them all. Karen came to the door.

"All the children are at a friend's house," she said. I was incredibly disappointed. It helped a bit to think of Hannah playing with her sisters and brothers.

I hope that means she is adjusting and discovering that she is safe. At least this gives me a private moment with Karen.

"I see that you are expecting! Congratulations. When are you due?"

"September," she answered, without much emotion. She made no mention of who the father was, so I didn't ask. It wasn't my business. We chitchatted for a few minutes, and then I left the meal and boxes, promising to return in a couple of days to pick up the dishes.

Feeling uneasy that I was not able to make good on my promise to Hannah that I would see her soon, I anxiously waited a few days, then called Karen and went back. This time only Andrew and Ally were home with their mother.

With a friendly tone to mask my anxiety, I asked, "Where are all the other kids? I seem to keep missing them. I brought presents for Andrew and Kyle. I know they will both be having birthdays soon."

Karen picked up Ally, who had crawled across the carpet to her. "Andrew and Ally are the only two here," she said. "Andrew had to stay home because he wasn't behaving." Standing near his mother, Andrew looked up at me with wet eyes and a pouty mouth. I gave him a warm smile and then made my own pouty face, trying to keep the mood light.

I didn't ask anything further. Karen thanked me for the meal as I placed the gifts on the dining room table and picked up the clean glass casserole and salad dish. As I turned to leave, I changed my mind. I went back to the table, picked up the gifts, and said, "I'll bring the birthday presents back for Kyle and Andrew in a day or two, if that's okay." I was glad for another reason to stop by.

Every little thing of the Bowers I could find in our home gave me a reason to visit them again to see how they were doing. Each time I went, however, either none or only one or two of the kids were at the house. Karen said they were at a friend's house playing or visiting family for the day. I didn't see Hannah at any of the visits and trusted she was with her other siblings. I felt better if I imagined her joining the others in an afternoon of play and told Karen I hoped to see them when I came to visit next time.

School ended in May. The needed break from foster care allowed us to enjoy our own children and give them undivided attention. Taking our boat out to Alcova Lake to fish, water ski, and go tubing provided lots of laughter and fun. Warm-weather activities were something to cherish in Wyoming, and I enjoyed running the kids from swimming pools to slumber parties, and from afternoon movies to parks. Hannah, however, was never off my mind or out of my heart. I prayed for her, her siblings, and Karen as well. "Please keep them safe, Lord. Protect them from harm and help Karen to be a loving mom to her children—*all* of her children."

Several weeks into the summer we welcomed three little sisters, ages five, four, and one, and a two-year-old boy with his six-month-old sister. The six-month-old was a failure-to-thrive baby. She had been left in a bed or infant seat with little to no attention. When we received her, she was dirty and had a terrible diaper rash. Her little body felt rubbery and squishy, like a baby doll filled with water. She didn't respond when we talked to her.

I asked the caseworker if she could be evaluated at our local child development center. The woman who tested her said that lots of love, affection, and stimulating activity would help her improve. *Stimulating activity?* That described our home most of the time.

As I watched my kids and our foster kids sprawled across the living room floor, with pillows, blankets, and snacks for an evening of family fun, I hoped that the Bower children carried wonderful memories of such times in our home and remembered that we loved them. Was DFS checking on Hannah, as the caseworker had said they would? Did she remain the center of Karen's negative attention? Was the man who scared Andrew and Hannah staying away and not hurting or being mean to them? I asked the questions over and over in my mind, trying to entrust the kids into God's hands and not interfere.

One Sunday in June, nearly six weeks after returning the children to Karen, I was grocery shopping at Walmart. As I turned down a main aisle, I saw Karen and all her children heading toward me. My heart fluttered in excitement. Karen saw me and hesitated for a moment, but when she realized I had picked up my pace, she stopped and waited. Kyle, Kyra, and Andrew stood next to their mother. Ally was in the children's seat of the shopping cart, and Hannah was sitting inside the main basket. My heart leapt at the sight of her.

I smiled and said hello. Karen returned the smile, but the kids moved closer to their mother and stared at me with serious faces. They didn't say a word. All the children looked well kempt . . . except for Hannah. Her hair was messy and her skin ashen.

"Hello, Hannah," I said.

She didn't respond. She sat in the basket with the same distant look on her face as the day I had left her at her mother's home. I didn't want to act differently toward Hannah, showing her any more attention than the other children. I was afraid it would make things difficult for her when she got home.

"It's so good to see all of you. We miss you!" Hannah peeked up at me, then immediately dropped her head again. I desperately wanted to grab her out of the basket and run.

It will be okay, I told myself. *DFS knows the situation and is doing home checks.* But I didn't believe my own reassurances. I made a mental note to call DFS and report what I'd just seen.

It would prove to be my first call of many.

On Monday morning, I dialed DFS and asked for Ellen. "I saw the Bower kids at the store yesterday. They all looked good . . . except for Hannah." I described her physical condition, her demeanor, and that she was riding in the basket instead of walking. I found it strange that Andrew, a year and a half younger than Hannah, was not the one inside the basket.

Ellen's response seemed a little cool. "I'll document it. Thanks for letting me know."

Maybe there wasn't much more for her to say. I expected more than simple documentation, though what I'm not sure. I wrestled with playing down what I had seen, but I simply couldn't. I decided to start calling DFS to report anything I felt or saw that was questionable. Over the years I had never called DFS after children we had fostered had gone home. I'd never felt a need to. But there was something wrong about the Bower case. Something I couldn't shake or let rest. I couldn't give up on it. Hannah needed an advocate. I sensed the Lord stirring in my spirit saying, *"Pay attention."*

———

July gave me another reason to visit—Karen's birthday. I made a meal and a sheet cake and bought ice cream. After I phoned Karen about bringing it to her, Helen and I loaded the food up and headed into town. Helen hadn't seen the kids since they left. She was looking forward to it as much as I was. She also knew I had concerns.

We arrived late in the day, hoping the whole family would be there to celebrate their mother's birthday. Only Andrew and Ally were at home with Karen.

"Where are all the other kids?" Helen asked.

"Playing at a friend's house. They won't be home for an hour or so," Karen said.

Helen went up to Andrew and gave him a hug. His arms rested limp at his sides. I watched him look at his mother as if he didn't know if he would be in trouble for letting Helen hug him. Ally clung to her mother. Their bond appeared to have developed, which was a good sign. But Andrew's behavior left an awkward silence between Helen, Karen, and me.

"Tell the kids hello for us!" I broke the uncomfortable moment with a cheery, almost obvious icebreaker. Helen's eyes shifted toward me, then to Karen, ending with a smile for Andrew. She felt the tension too. She squinted at Andrew and gave a little wave good-bye. She dropped her smile quickly as she turned back toward me, where Karen couldn't see her face. Andrew was not the same Andrew for whom she'd felt such a sisterly affection. She and he would tease each other in fun when the Bower children lived with us. He'd always loved to wrestle with Helen as she tickled and laughed with him. This little boy appeared frightened, unsure, and uneasy.

Moments after we got into our car and drove away, Helen burst into tears.

"Something is really wrong there, Mom. Andrew acts like he hardly knows me." I pulled over to the curb so we could wrap our arms around each other and cry.

"I know. I am concerned, too."

"What about Hannah?" Helen asked. "You said you never see her at the house. Do you think she is okay?" Helen settled back into her seat, still wiping away tears.

"I don't know. DFS said they are doing home visits and keeping an eye on all of them. Each time I have called they say everything is going fine and for me not to worry. They tell me that I don't need to keep calling. They have a caseworker who does home visits, and if there was any concern about any of the children, they would step in and do something."

I looked at the Bower home in the rearview mirror. The house looked still, quiet, almost peaceful on the outside. But my spirit said there was great turmoil going on inside.

I waited until August to call Karen and ask if Helen and I could stop by with a few more of the kids' things.

All the children were home—except Hannah. Karen said she was visiting her daddy and grandma for the weekend. Helen was excited to see Kyle and Kyra.

As we stood in the middle of Karen's living room chatting about nothing of importance, Ally, now fourteen months old, worked her way around the couch, showing off her new ability to walk almost on her own. Helen and I chuckled as Ally toddled from the couch to a chair. The other children stared at Helen and me with fake eerie smiles, watching our every move. They didn't talk or move toward us to give or receive a hug. They were like plastic statues with painted smiles, seemingly holding their breath until we left.

Once again, when Helen and I got into the car after this ten-minute visit, we agreed that something was not right. We both believed the children must have been instructed to be still and not talk to us. Karen acted as she always had—friendly, hospitable. It was as if she knew she had to act normal so we wouldn't question anything. Still, it felt that we were being viewed suspiciously. Had Karen convinced her children that we were untrustworthy, even enemies? That was a heavy burden for any child to take on.

I wondered if they behaved the same way when a caseworker came to their home. Their silence and forced smiles could be charming to an inexperienced DFS worker. Was a seasoned caseworker conducting the visits, one who could pick up on the manipulation and control going on in the home?

The next morning, I made another pesky phone call to Ellen. "I was at the Bower house again, and everyone but Hannah was there. Karen said Hannah was visiting her daddy. I know you can't tell me anything since they are not in my home anymore, but . . . can you tell me how often home visits are being done?"

Ellen sighed, then said, "Since you and I have known each other for so long I will say that visits are happening, and all seems to be going fine. You have to stop stressing over Hannah, Deb. You have other foster children to be concentrating on."

She's right, I told myself, yet my heart screamed that something was wrong.

Summer activities were drawing to a close for our family and foster children. The three little girls were having overnight visits with their grandparents, and the plan was for the siblings to eventually go live with them. School would be starting within weeks, and shopping for clothes, shoes, backpacks, and supplies was, as always, a major event. Al watched the little ones while I took my teens to the mall. It allowed me to give my own kids the attention they needed and deserved. School got off to a good start for all.

As we neared the end of September 1997, I remembered that Karen's due date was quickly approaching. I had bought a baby gift for her and some small gifts for each of the other children to make them feel special. I called Karen but she didn't answer, so I left a message asking her to call me back. I didn't hear from her. After a few more calls and recorded messages she contacted me.

"Hi, Karen! I haven't seen you in a while. How are you feeling?" We chatted for a few minutes about the last stage of pregnancy. Then I asked about bringing the gifts.

She sounded hesitant at first. "Maybe next week. We are really busy with school and the kids' activities."

"How about if I just drop them off? You don't have to be there." Even if I couldn't see the kids, I wanted Karen to know we were thinking of her. I still hoped to build a supportive relationship, though my hopes were waning. Normally, I would not have brought gifts or food or stayed in touch with past foster children or birth parents, but since I had begun a relationship with Karen and had her children for so long, I felt the situation was different.

"Sure. Uh . . . just leave it by the front door. Thanks!" Karen was softer spoken than usual. She had never hesitated to allow me to visit before. My mind ran the gamut. The kids starting school could add more stress. Especially with the baby due any day. Maybe she was involved with William again. Was he the father of the child she was carrying?

Karen gave birth to Steven on September 26. The second weekend in October, I decided to take the gifts to Karen. Helen asked if she could go too.

As I drove, a soft rain began to fall.

"Are we going to leave the gifts at the door if it's raining?" Helen asked.

"We'll see when we get there," I said over the rhythm of the wipers.

Once we reached the house, the sky was looking clearer. We felt only a few drops as we walked up to the front door, but the ground was wet. I knocked a few times and rang the bell, but there was no answer.

"Should we leave them here, Mom?"

"I don't think so. It might rain again after we leave." I looked for a dry place to tuck the gifts. I didn't see any possibilities on the front step.

As we turned to walk back to the car with the gifts, I noticed a side door to the garage. If the door was unlocked, we could set them inside. I tried the door and it opened. Helen and I started to go in, but an overpowering odor hit us like a tidal wave. It was so strong our eyes began to burn. I could hardly breathe as I set the gifts on the floor.

The garage appeared half empty. A large rubber trash can on wheels sat next to the garage door.

Helen and I quickly stepped outside, gasping for fresh air. "What is that horrible smell?" Helen asked, covering her mouth and nose with her hand. Her eyes were watering.

"It smells like rotting meat," I said. "Maybe Karen's freezer went out. I have never smelled anything so horrific." I followed Helen with my hand over my nose as I continued to talk to my daughter.

"Let's get to the car. I can't breathe." I shooed her to move quickly, and with my other hand I reached back to the side door of the garage and closed it tightly.

Just before reaching the car, Helen and I both turned back to look at the garage as if we were expecting an explosion or some-thing gross to emerge, explaining the smell. Nothing happened. We both turned and stared into each other's eyes.

"What are you thinking, Mom?" We looked at each other for a long moment.

"Nothing. I'm not thinking anything," I said, but we both knew that wasn't true. For a split second, I let my imagination get away from me, thinking unthinkable things. I immediately dismissed the bizarre fears circling in my mind. *My concern has driven me to crazy thinking*, I rationalized. *I will call Karen and ask her about the odor. I am sure she is aware of it and has a logical explanation.*

Helen and I discussed the foul odor all the way home. Maybe an animal had slipped into the garage and died. Or . . . the freezer theory. The smell so lingered that when we got home, we brushed our teeth trying to rid the taste of spoiled meat in our mouths. We put on lotion and sprayed ourselves with perfume.

It didn't help.

I called Karen that evening to tell her where we left the gifts. I explained about the rain that brushed over Casper just long enough to get everything wet. Then I asked her about the smell in the garage.

"Oh. Yeah. I had to throw out a bunch of food that was spoiling. I know. It's bad, isn't it?" Her voice sounded a little hesitant but calm. I dismissed my irrational thoughts and believed Karen's explanation.

———

The following weekend Charles and I stopped by the Bower home. I didn't call first this time. I told Charles I wanted to pick up a dish I forgot. He wanted to go in and see the kids with me.

I knocked on the door, and Kyra opened it slightly and peeked through. Her eyes widened when she saw us. She closed the door a few inches without saying a word. I could hear her talking to someone. A moment later she opened the door, pressing her head between it and the frame, and said, "Just a minute." She then slowly shut the door until it latched. Standing on the cement step, we waited to see if we were going to be invited in.

Suddenly the door opened wide and Karen waved us in. She led the way to the living room where Ally was playing on the floor and Andrew and Kyra stood, almost side by side, by a wooden cradle. Like little soldiers, they stood in formation, only no plastic smiles greeted us this time. Just serious faces.

"I stopped by to pick up the casserole dish I forgot on my last trip and to see the new arrival. Charles wanted to say hi to the children."

Karen smiled warmly as she turned toward the kitchen. I caught her giving Kyra and Andrew a stern look as if to say, *Don't say anything while my back is turned.* She quickly returned and handed the dish to me. Charles looked at the Bower children as seriously as they were looking at us.

I moved toward the cradle that Kyra was rocking and peeked in. "He's beautiful like your other children," I said.

I looked at Kyra. "What's his name?" She didn't answer.

"Steven," Karen said, returning from the kitchen.

"Where are Hannah and Kyle today?' I asked.

Andrew, stiff as he was, answered. "Kyle's playing at a friend's house, and Hannah was sent away."

Karen looked as if she were going to leap at Andrew. Her jaw tightened, and her eyes almost bulged out of their sockets as she fought to contain herself.

"Ah . . . yeah . . . Hannah went to live with a friend of ours for a while. She couldn't behave and was causing too many problems. Kyle is usually over at his friend's house." Karen chuckled. The room fell silent as Andrew glared angrily at his mother and clenched his little fist. Then a glaze came over his beautiful brown eyes and he looked as if was going to cry.

My body tightened as I watched Andrew and Karen locked in a combative glare. Something was terribly wrong, not only between them, but with Hannah as well.

I broke the silence. "Well, we have to get going." We all seemed to exhale with relief. As Charles and I left, I feared what wrath might come down on Andrew. I decided I would call DFS on Monday.

Monday morning, after dropping the children off at school and day care, I went straight to my office. Walking through the reception area, I prayed as I flicked on the lights, turned up the heat, and hung up my coat before reaching for my phone. I determined to be bolder when the caseworker answered. Something was very wrong, and someone with authority needed to do something.

"Department of Family Services, how may I help you?"

The familiar greeting frustrated me. *That is the point for my call. I need someone to help. Will anyone listen?*

"I need to talk to a caseworker for the Bower children," I replied.

"I'll transfer you."

"Hello, this is Kim. How may I help you?" I had spoken to Kim a few times. I knew she had been at DFS for many years. *Maybe I can get somewhere with her.*

"Hi, Kim. This is Deb Moerke."

"Hi, Deb. How are you?"

"Well, not so good. I am calling again about the Bower children. Mostly concerning Hannah. I have called a number of times, and each caseworker I speak to tells me everything is fine. I don't think that's the case."

"Why do you feel that way?" Kim asked.

I explained Andrew's comment about Hannah being sent away and how many times I had gone to the house and Hannah was never there. I told her about what I saw at Walmart and that there was not a good history between Hannah and her mother. I asked if home visits were being conducted by DFS and if someone had seen Hannah at those visits.

"Yes. A new caseworker has gone to the home several times and seen all the children." The information should have reassured me, but a thought came to my mind.

"I know the mother. She is very manipulative and good at it. I wouldn't doubt that she would use a friend's child and say she was Hannah to satisfy the caseworker. I saw pictures of all the children when they first went back home, but I've noticed there are no pictures of the children in the house anymore. If the new caseworker didn't know what Hannah looked like, she wouldn't know the difference." Words poured out of my mouth as the whole idea came to my mind. I realized it sounded crazy, but it was possible.

"Deb, I don't think that could have happened. The caseworker said she saw all the children during her visit. I will check with her and ask if she had any concerns. Thanks for calling."

I was put off again. Would Kim actually follow up?

I'd made the call. I could do no more. My hands were tied, and I was becoming an annoyance to Karen and to DFS. Was it time to give it a rest and let God deal with it?

Chapter 8

The Pageant

I STEPPED INTO 1998 knowing it would bring some major changes. First, I would stop visiting Karen's home. Though my concerns for Hannah plagued me and I still felt guilty for not finding a way to be in touch with her, I realized I'd done all I could for now. Since she was, according to Karen, no longer living with her, I had to stop my attempts to see her and trust that DFS would do their job and follow up as needed. It was agonizing, but I did my best to surrender her to the Lord.

Second, for the past year I'd felt that it was time to draw my leadership of the crisis pregnancy center to a close, not so much because I had tired of it, but more because I felt an inner nudge to do so. I'd invested ten years in The Caring Center and was confident it would be in good hands with the current team. So I passed on the baton with a profound sense that in God's perfect timing, he'd lead me to my next area of ministry.

I couldn't help but be a little nostalgic about my early days at The Caring Center. I had been a believer for less than a year when I'd become director. All the counselors were more mature Christians than I, yet the board wanted me for the position.

Soon after I began, I attended a seminar on discerning one's spiritual gifts. The day after the class I excitedly told three of my counselors, "I know what my spiritual gifts are now!"

"That's great," they said. "What are they?"

"Well, there are two," I said. "The first is the gift of prophecy. I am such a black-and-white thinker, so the bottom line for me is what God's Word says is true. And the second is that I'm an extortionist!"

The three women's mouths dropped open. Then very graciously one of them said, "No, honey. It's not *extortionist*. I think you mean *exhorter*. You have the gift of exhortation."

"Oh, yeah. That's what it was." To this day some of my close friends still tease me about my spiritual gift of "extortion."

When I first took the position, I'd thought all Christians were pro-life, but I quickly learned otherwise. To my dismay, when I would go to churches or Christian organizations to speak and raise support, I began to feel that more than a few in the audiences had rotten tomatoes ready to fling at me when I brought up the gut-wrenching topic of abortion. It was painful to realize how naive I was, and I hit a low point in my new faith.

What am I doing in Christian ministry? I wondered. *I may be a Christian, but who am I to think I can serve and lead?* I wanted to crawl off into a cave and lick my wounds. One day after a particularly hurtful encounter, I was driving along, bitterly discouraged, and decided to pull off into a parking lot and go before the Lord right then.

I wept as I spoke to him. "Lord, I don't get it. What is my job? I'm obviously not doing it well right now." I thought I must not be doing God's will because I was uncomfortable, hurting, and suffering. Oh, how little I knew! I have since learned that sometimes we are totally on track when we're suffering and hurting and miserable.

I'm not one to claim supernatural visions on a regular basis, but right then I sensed God saying, *"Okay. You want a good picture of your job? This is your job."*

I pictured a vast underground sewer system in a city. I was there in the sewer pipe, standing ankle deep in raw sewage. I trudged through the filth in the dark, the only bit of light filtering down from the slits in the occasional manhole above. The vision was so vivid I could smell the stench.

I came to a metal ladder that went up to a manhole. God said, *"This is your job. Freedom and life in me are through that manhole. Your job is to stand here, and when someone comes by, you are to put them on this ladder. You are to do whatever it takes. Fold your fingers together and hoist them up by their foot. Kneel down in the sewage and let them climb up on your shoulders. You do whatever it takes to get them on that ladder, get that manhole cover moved, and get them into the light. That is your job."*

Then God asked, *"Are you willing?"* It sounded like mission impossible. *"Even though it can be a stinky job? Even when you are alone? Even when you are ankle deep in poop? Are you willing to man the manhole? Are you willing to serve me by serving others?"*

I knew I was making a major life decision right there on the spot. "Yes, Lord, I am willing. I will surrender to what you call me to do."

Ever since that day, when I fight depression or worthlessness, helplessness or hopelessness, and wonder why I'm here on this earth, that vision comes to mind. My job is simply to man this manhole. It stinks sometimes. And it's lonely at times. There are some people who pass by me who don't want help. Sometimes they'll even pick up some poop and throw it at me. But in spite of all that, God says, *"I have called you to a special calling. It may not look pretty to anybody else, but you've answered the call."*

My understanding of that vision became the common thread of my work at the crisis pregnancy center, the prison ministry, and as a foster parent. I understood my purpose, and I realized that there were many ways to man the manhole. It was time to seek God's wisdom regarding the next place I was to serve in that capacity.

Meanwhile, I continued my lay chaplaincy work at the local jail with leading biweekly Bible studies and serving as an on-call chaplain. My heart was still tender for prisoners, the time investment was manageable, and the work was extremely gratifying.

Nothing could have prepared me for the next service opportunity that sprang up in February. In truth, it didn't look like service at all from the outside looking in. It looked downright frivolous.

I was at Starla's to pick up one of my foster children. In addition to being a childcare provider, Starla was the state coordinator for the Mrs. International pageant. She was a real champion for this pageant because it showcased married women involved in community service who exemplified high moral values. Unlike the Miss America pageant, this one didn't include a swimsuit or talent competition. Instead, contestants were judged on public speaking, leadership, poise, and the platform that each woman championed as her own.

"The Mrs. Wyoming pageant is coming up again," Starla said casually.

"That's great, Starla. I know you have fun with that."

"There are some representatives for other parts of the state," she said, "but I don't have anyone for Casper."

Even with that lead-in, I didn't see it coming.

"Deb, would you consider representing Casper?"

I laughed. "Starla, that is so not me. I'm in women's ministry. I do things like crisis pregnancy, jail ministry, and foster parenting. I don't know anything about pageants. Besides, I can't walk across a room in heels, much less cross a stage in them."

But Starla wasn't taking no for an answer. "Yes, Deb, it's because of all the things you do that you'd be an ideal candidate." She pushed an application into my hands. "Just think about it."

At the dinner table that night I said, "You guys will not believe what happened to me today." When I told them about the pageant, we all started laughing at the idea. Suddenly, my kids shifted gears, all of them talking at once.

"Mom! You should do it!"

"Yeah, go for it."

"Do it, Mom."

"Are you kidding me?" I was taken aback. "You know this is not me."

Then Al chimed in, "I think you should do it! Everything you get involved with is heavy, serious stuff. You're saying this pageant is fluff and frivolous. That's exactly what you need. You need to lighten up and have fun."

"You guys are crazy. I don't know how to glide across a stage. I'm no beauty queen!"

Everyone talked at once. "You need to go have fun." "You can do it." "You've got all kinds of community involvement." "At least give it a try and apply."

Reluctantly, I filled out the application, and the next day I handed it to Starla, barely believing I was following through with the crazy idea.

"So . . . what's next?" I asked Starla.

"The deadline is tomorrow. Since you are the only Casper applicant, you will compete in May for the state title of Mrs. Wyoming. Liz, a former pageant contestant, can help you with hair, makeup, how to walk, what to wear, questions the judges may ask, everything."

Though filled with doubts about proceeding, I reassured myself that Starla knew what she was doing. I'd have to have confidence in her, even if I had little in myself.

Starla kept me informed of each step I needed to take until she handed me over to Liz, who filled me in on all I'd need to do over the next few months to get ready for the competition. We had two foster children at the time, so my hands were full. Feeling stressed, I again questioned my participation. *What will people think? How will other Christians see me?* I felt unsure, insecure, and foolish. *I'm no beauty, and I'm more comfortable in one-inch pumps, calf-length skirts, and entering and exiting through a side door unnoticed when I speak to a group of people.*

I wondered how I could get out of the contest. So I made an appointment with my pastor. Surely Pastor Bergie would counsel me not to do it.

The next day, I climbed the steps of the old white stucco church. *What will he think when I tell him what I've gotten myself into? I'm sure he'll say I shouldn't participate, and that will be my out.*

"I'm almost embarrassed to tell you what I have agreed to do," I told him when I entered his office. "You know as a leader in a parachurch ministry and as a Sunday school teacher, I need to be very careful how I appear to people in our community and in our church."

"My goodness. Sit down and tell me what's wrong." Pastor Bergie focused on me, his hands folded, serious and ready for my confession.

"I was approached to enter a Mrs. Wyoming International Pageant, and I agreed to do it." I winced and braced for his response.

He said nothing for a moment. "And . . . ?"

"And I don't think I should do it."

"Why not?"

"I don't know if it's something a Christian leader should do."

"I think it would be wonderful."

I was stunned. How could he say that? I'm sure my puzzled look prompted him to go on.

"Years ago, my wife and I were asked to judge two pageants. We realized what a great platform pageants were for women to have a voice in the community. There isn't anything wrong with it. You have been given an opportunity that can influence many people, to inspire other women to get involved in service. You should jump at the chance!"

Really? I sighed.

"Everything you have ever been involved in is pretty serious ministry. You need to lighten up. Have fun. God can use this new venture, and I am sure he will. You have my blessing."

That's not what I'd come to hear, but it was the same message my family had delivered.

Now how do I get out of it?

For the next few weeks, I had appointments with Liz at her salon. While highlighting my hair, doing my nails, and waxing my eyebrows, she educated me on what I could expect. Attitude, poise, clothes—all were important. I would have three wardrobe changes: sportswear, casual dress, and a formal gown. She posed questions I might be asked: *What do you like to do in your spare time? What are your greatest concerns about the world today? What are your favorite hobbies and why?*

In the midst of all my doubts, I began to believe that God actually wanted me to enter the pageant to prepare me for something to come. I couldn't stop speculating as to what could relate to such an experience. Was it going to help me with speaking at women's retreats? Addressing church congregations? Or just stretching me beyond my comfort? Maybe God was blessing me with busyness to take my mind and concerns off of Hannah and let DFS do their job without me bugging them.

Not everyone was supportive of my involvement. A woman at church told me she thought it was inappropriate. A friend said she was shocked I'd even consider such a thing. A woman at the grocery store said she was surprised at me. A few others also expressed their disappointment.

Still uncomfortable with my participation, I wondered again if I should bow out and try not to hurt Starla's feelings. But the more

I wanted out, the more I sensed God urging me forward—through my family, my pastor, and an inner voice that wouldn't quit.

I did what I thought was the reasonable thing to do and made an appointment with my good friend, Ron Kirkegaard, a Christian counselor. I knew I could trust him and his counsel.

After our usual hug and a casual question about the family, Ron said, "So what are you here to talk to me about?"

"I have an issue I don't know how to handle, and I need your advice," I blurted. I felt heat move up my face. I was actually embarrassed that I was embarrassed. Ron's smile faded. He settled deeper into his chair, readying himself for the announcement I was about to make.

"I have entered a pageant, but that just isn't me, and I feel foolish and caught between my family and friends wanting me to do it and some Christian friends who disapprove. They say my decision to participate has led them to question their understanding of me." Tears began to flow. "I know it must seem stupid to you, but I am really wrestling with it."

"I don't think it's stupid. But why shouldn't you be in a pageant? Are they asking you to do something against God? Or your faith? Or your morals? I think it's great! I'll be one of your best supporters. Look, Deb, you cannot please everyone, especially Christians. Do it and have fun. I think you're just lacking confidence in yourself in this new and different realm."

I sighed. I hadn't gotten what I wanted. Instead, I had the go-ahead from those I felt knew me best and were looking out for my best interest.

It looked like I was in the Mrs. Wyoming pageant to stay. I needed to stop whining, accept it, and follow through, embracing the experience and keeping my eyes open for what God planned to do.

March and April sped by. Following Starla's and Liz's leads, I exercised, watched my weight, practiced my walk, and even rehearsed quick dress changes. It all felt so silly, but it sure was a change of pace after my year with the Bower children and my fears over Hannah.

I also worked on the written statement I would submit and the topic I would address for my public speaking portion of the program. I chose *Making a Difference* as my platform and wrote about the difference I saw in the lives of foster children our family cared for. My encouragement was to not wait for government agencies to do the work of caring for people around us. We can be a part of changing lives by showing we care and demonstrating that with love and action.

Pageant day arrived in mid-May. I was one of five women vying for Mrs. Wyoming. The event was being held at an old historical building on Wolcott Street in Casper. I would say it was charming, but it was just old.

Wide-eyed and dazed, I caught Starla out of the corner of my eye, coming through the dressing room door. "You're ready!" She wrapped her arms around me and swayed back and forth. "You've got this!" She was much more excited than I was.

The crowded dressing room was full of dresses and gowns. An array of women's shoes lined one wall. Makeshift dressing tables were spaced only feet from one another. One dusty overstuffed chair was tucked in a corner, and dated dark oak paneling surrounded us. The only full-length mirror hung on the back of a closet door. The dim lighting and few table lamps scattered around the room cast unattractive shadows, making it difficult to apply makeup, but we all made do with the room we had been given.

I enjoyed each of the four women as we got to know a little about one another. I scanned the dressing room. *Who would win?* Surely it would be Mrs. Star Valley. She was poised, beautiful, had the perfect figure, and gave a smile that welcomed any stranger.

Her gown and sports clothes complemented everything about her. Yep. She would take the state crown.

As I slipped into my gown, I thought of my dearest friends, Lauree and Dale. A month earlier, they had flown from their homes in Texas, and we had met up in Denver on a mission to find the perfect pageant dress. We found it at Lord and Taylor's at an affordable price. Lauree and Dale said that God had helped us find the dress he wanted me to wear, and they came up with the line, "The dress is from the Lord's Tailor!" We laughed, but we all believed it was *the* dress. I love evening dresses from the twenties and thirties, and this one fit the image. Padded shoulders, an almost fitted but straight-line bodice, round collar at the neck; it was beautiful and modest. With each step, the brass beading that covered the entire dress glistened and danced across the black fabric.

I had family and friends in the audience to support me, and I now believed God had placed me here for a purpose, though what it could be was still a mystery. I still couldn't understand why he put me in a position that would cause division among some of my friends, but I decided to stand firm in the knowledge that there are times when God calls us to do something that others won't like. My job was to please God, not others.

The music began. The master of ceremonies welcomed the guests, and the pageant was underway. The judges asked us a number of questions, but one was especially memorable. "If there was a vehicle that described you, what would your husband say it would be and why?" I looked at Al, who was smiling.

"A Rolls-Royce," one contestant said. "A race car," another answered. "An SUV," said a third.

When the emcee came to me I said, "A bus. I believe a bus fits me the best. Sometimes I'm wider than I want to be, but my husband loves me just the same. I am always loading up people who have needs, and I try to help them get to where they need to be, emotionally, physically, or spiritually. A bus has so many windows, and you can see right through it. That describes me as well. It was between a bus and a convertible. Sometimes I do go into a situation with my brain blowing in the wind. But I would have to say mostly, a bus."

Laughter filled the room. Al nodded and laughed along with the others. The judges laughed, too, and marked their papers.

After the walking, talking, and judging took place, we were escorted backstage, where we laughed and shared what we believed were our weakest or most embarrassing moments in the pageant. Our chatter exposed our nervousness and anticipation. Then the signal came, and we were led out to the stage for the big announcement.

"Before we see who will be crowned Mrs. Wyoming International this evening, we will present the individual recognitions," the master of ceremonies said loudly into the microphone. "The women participating in the pageant have had the opportunity to vote for one another in the following categories: Mrs. Congeniality, Mrs. Photogenic, and Mrs. Community. And the winners are . . . Mrs. Casper for Mrs. Congeniality and Mrs. Community. The Mrs. Photogenic award goes to Mrs. Star Valley." Applause broke out as Mrs. Star Valley and I stepped forward to receive our awards.

I was shocked and touched that the other ladies had voted for me in two categories. I could have gone home happy at that point, but there was no escape. I laugh today when I picture Sandra Bullock in the hilarious movie *Miss Congeniality*, especially how the director of that pageant continually refers to it as a "scholarship program" and not a beauty pageant.

I stepped back into the lineup. We all held hands as the presiding Mrs. Wyoming International 1997 came onstage with the winner's envelope. I squeezed Mrs. Star Valley's fingers and scooted closer, knowing she would be the winner. She squeezed back and nudged me with her hip.

"And the new . . . Mrs. Wyoming International . . . for 1998 is . . . Mrs. Casper, Debra Moerke!" My smile slowly began to droop. Mrs. Star Valley and I looked at each other, both stunned. It couldn't be.

This is not what I do or who I am. What are they thinking?

My family and friends jumped to their feet, clapping heartily with others in the crowd.

The acting Mrs. Wyoming took my hand and led me to the front of the stage to retrieve a huge crown atop a satin pillow. She lifted the purple and white satin Mrs. Casper sash over my head and replaced it with a rhinestone-trimmed purple and white sash that read "Mrs. Wyoming International." Then she pinned the crown to my head above my French roll, while someone else laid a bouquet of long-stemmed red roses in my arms.

"Take your walk," Mrs. Wyoming 1997 instructed with a huge smile. She kissed my cheek and nudged me forward. I was in shock. And then it dawned on me. Now that I'd won, I'd have to compete in the national Mrs. International Pageant in Tyler, Texas, in August. *What could God possibly be doing with all of this?*

Later that month I got a call from the director of the Central Wyoming Rescue Mission in Casper. Carl and I had crossed paths many times over the years. He'd been part of the spiritual support team for The Caring Center, and he and I both served on the local ministerial organization. I had tremendous respect for him and the work of the rescue mission, which provided much-needed housing and meals for those in need.

"Debra, as you know, over the years the rescue mission has served mostly men. However, we've had more women and children to serve this past year. We've never had a female in a leadership role here to focus on the women and children. We'd like you to consider joining us as the chaplain of women's and children's ministries. Will you give it some thought?"

My heart leapt. I knew immediately that was right where God wanted me. By June, I was serving in my role three days a week.

I still wasn't sure why God had filled my time between The Caring Center and the rescue mission with the pageant, but it certainly had distracted me from my concern over Hannah. Now I felt refreshed and ready for this new assignment.

I'd always loved to tackle fresh challenges and be stretched in new directions, so I looked forward to pioneering the women's and children's ministry at the mission, helping them through crises in their lives. But I never could have imagined that while I was serving in this new ministry, God would allow a devastating crisis of my own, touching nearly every aspect of my life. I was about to be stretched not only far beyond my comfort zone, but to the very edges of my capacity, beyond what I'd ever dreamed I could endure.

Chapter 9

The Yellow Phone

THE LARGE YELLOW ROTARY phone mounted on our kitchen wall was as essential a fixture as the sink, and many days it seemed to get as much use. Maybe more. Its best feature was the four-foot-long cord that could reach every corner of the kitchen, plus a good portion of the dining room. Its ring was loud enough to be heard in every corner of the house. It fit our home perfectly—dated but comfy.

On this day in late June 1998, I heard its ring from the downstairs bathroom where I was scouring the tub. I peeled off my rubber gloves on my way to answer the phone.

"Hi, Deb, this is Jill from DFS."

It had been a good while since I'd received a call from Jill. She was a young, fairly new caseworker whom I had worked with not too long before. I felt a kindred connection between us. We were comfortable sharing our mutual faith in Jesus, and I always enjoyed running into her at the DFS office.

"I received a file today for some children who I learned had been in your care in the past—the children of Karen Bower." This took me by surprise—DFS calling me about Karen. For so long it had been the other way around. It had been fourteen months since I'd been forced to return the Bower children to their mother.

"Their mother was recently arrested for grand larceny and has just been sentenced to two years at the women's prison in Lusk," Jill continued. "We are trying to gather up her children to place them in foster care. We have located most of them but are missing two. I thought maybe you could give me an idea of where they might be." Her voice was calm and professional.

"Their mom is in prison?" I was taken aback by the information. "I haven't seen Karen in quite a while. Which children are missing?"

"Andrew and Hannah."

My pulse quickened.

"Andrew might be with one of the mom's friends who lives in Denver," I said. "When Karen ran out of patience with him, she would send him there for a while. I don't know anything about the friend or where they live. As far as Hannah, I have called DFS many times over the past year asking if they have had a visual on her. I was worried because whenever I would go to visit the family, Hannah was never there. Her mother always had an excuse—she was at a birthday party, visiting her daddy or grandma, or off playing with a friend. I thought it was strange because I saw all the other children at home, but never Hannah.

"After calling DFS so many times to express concern I was, uh, nicely told by one of the caseworkers to . . . well . . . butt out and let them do their job. I felt something was wrong, but they said the caseworker had gone to the house and had seen Hannah. I often wondered if her mother had a friend's child sit in for Hannah when she knew there would be a home visit. When I told that to the caseworker, she said they didn't think that would happen. I can't help you with where she could be. I have been concerned for a very long time." I could hear myself sounding anxious as I unloaded on poor Jill. I paused.

There was only silence.

"Jill, you still there?"

"I realize I've known you only a short time, Deb, but I trust your judgment and your gut feelings. What are you trying to tell me? I'm listening." I could tell she was being sincere.

"I believe there has been foul play, Jill. I never use those words, but that is what my gut and my heart tell me." Anger rose within me as my eyes filled with tears. My voice cracked. "I have felt that way for a long time. But no one would listen . . . before now."

Again . . . silence.

"I'm going to take a chance on what you are telling me. I trust your instincts. I am going to file a missing person report with the police." Her strong tone gave me assurance.

"Thank heaven. Please let me know when you hear something." I didn't know if I should be scared or happy with her decision. That conversation was on a Friday. I didn't hear anything for the next four days and did my best to take my worry to the Lord in prayer.

A warm July breeze streamed through the kitchen window, providing refreshing relief from the heat as I prepared dinner. Al was on the computer in the little room off the dining area. The kids, two of our own and one foster child, lay sprawled in front of the TV. Only the muffled sound of cartoons and the soft whistle of the wind outside could be heard.

Pulling out a frying pan from under the stove, I turned up the heat and crumbled ground beef into the pan for tacos. As the meat began to sizzle, the wall phone started ringing. "I'll get it!" I hollered.

"Hey, Jill," I said, recognizing her voice. "What are you doing calling at 5:30 in the evening?" I teased. "I thought the time clock ended at 5:00 for all of you at DFS."

"What are you doing right now?" Jill's tone was soft, low.

"Cooking dinner," I answered, now curious.

"I think you need to sit down."

"Okay." I lowered the heat under the pan and took a few steps back. I felt my stomach tighten. "What's up?"

"I wanted to call and tell you personally before you saw it on the evening news. They found Hannah . . ."

"Where?" I jumped in excitedly.

"Deb . . . they found her body in the garage of the home where they were living. She's clearly been dead for some time, and her body was placed inside a black garbage bag. I am so, so sorry."

All the air seemed sucked out of the room. I couldn't catch my breath. I paced in circles, wrapping myself in the long cord of the yellow phone like a cord tightening around my heart, strangling its ability to pump blood to my brain.

"No. No. No," I whispered.

I couldn't think. I could only feel pain everywhere, clawing at my stomach and ripping up through my chest, squeezing breath and life out of me. I stopped in the middle of the kitchen. Frozen, I couldn't speak another word.

"I have to go." Jill's voice cracked. "Out of care and respect for you, I wanted you to know first."

"Thank you." I could only choke out those two words. I held the phone to my ear long after Jill had hung up. If I didn't put the receiver back in its cradle, maybe I could put off the reality of the news a bit longer. Maybe Jill would come back on the line and tell me she had made a mistake.

Dear Jesus, can this be real? Hannah dead? How do I tell Al? The kids? What do I say? My mind raced, even though my body seemed to be moving in slow motion.

Returning the phone to its base, I held on to it, bracing myself against the wall with my other hand. I was stinging. Breathless. Voiceless.

Managing a short breath, I called out, "Al! I need you! I need you now." My cry was weak but desperate. "Al!"

"What is it?" His response indicated he was slightly irritated for being interrupted, but as soon as he saw me, his scowl softened to concern and tenderness as he approached me. "What is it?" he whispered.

"They found Hannah's body. She's dead. Our sweet little Hannah." I began to sob. Al wrapped his arms around me. I could feel his body shake, and then I heard his sobs and felt his tears as he held his cheek tight against mine.

The crying drew the kids from the living room. They stood with eyes wide. They had never seen us like this, falling apart in tears with arms clasped desperately around each other. I turned toward them and cried, "They found Hannah." That was all I needed to say. Our sobs told them the news was bad. They all started crying and wrapped their arms around us. We stood as a family, broken, devastated, our hearts and souls torn, grieving and mourning as we had never done before. Our legs gave way, and still embracing each other, we dropped to our knees on the carpet, drowning in our loss. This could not be true. This could not have happened.

As I hugged my children, I looked into the living room at Al's recliner. I could see Hannah there as Al read to her. I could see her smiling and lying back against his chest as he turned the pages. I could see her. She couldn't be gone.

Helen was staying the night at a friend's house. I would have to call and tell her the terrible news. She would be heartbroken. She loved Hannah.

We all loved Hannah.

Through the tormented night I wrestled with God. Why? Why had he allowed Karen to regain guardianship of Hannah, only to allow her to be murdered? It made no sense, especially since we fought to hold on to her, to keep her safe. Why had I been unable to arouse the concern of DFS for Hannah's safety—before and after her return to Karen? Was this my fault?

My mind replayed the agonizing day I had to take Hannah back to her mother. Overwhelmed by the judge's decision and full of fear for Hannah, I knew she was not returning to a safe place. There would be no love shown to her there.

Though Al slept fitfully at my side, sleep would not come for me. I punched my pillow as I tossed and turned. My mind refused to rest. *I should have just taken her out of there.* But the law had not been on my side. Now, the law *had* stepped in—when it was too late. The news report announced that the mother, already in prison on another charge, had been charged with the murder. Karen was behind bars this night, but I was imprisoned as well—by unspeakable grief and relentless pain. I lay in the darkness of my room trapped in the darkness of my soul.

I was surprised when the sun broke through the opening of the bedroom curtains. Somehow, I hadn't expected light to ever come again. While the rest of the family remained asleep, I slipped out of bed, grabbed my bathrobe, and headed downstairs to start the coffee. Since it was summer, the house would remain quiet for a little longer.

I sat at the kitchen table, my chin resting on my folded arms as I watched the coffee fill to the ten-cup mark. Pulling a mug from the cupboard, I poured half a cup of the steamy brew and topped it off with cool water from the faucet. As I took my first sip, the phone rang.

I stared at the yellow phone for a moment, nearly afraid to pick it up for all the bad news it had brought me in such a short time. I couldn't think who might be calling so early. Then, I raced to grab it before it woke everyone in the house.

"Hello. Moerkes'." My voice was low and lifeless.

"Hello. This is the Natrona County Detention Center,"

a recording announced. "You have a collect call from an inmate. If you wish to accept the charges, say yes now. If not, simply hang up."

An inmate? The word ripped at my stomach and wrenched my body. I could think of only one inmate—the one on my mind all night. Pressure began building behind my eyes as my jaw tightened. I couldn't swallow.

Are you kidding me? Aghast at the thought of Karen calling me, I gripped the phone tighter. *You have to be kidding me!* I turned toward the wall to hang up. *Does she really think I would accept the charges and take her call? What is she thinking? Is she crazy?* My mind raced as my hand, gripping the receiver, moved from my ear toward the phone base. "No way," I whispered, about to hang up.

In that very second, a voice swept through my mind. *"If she were to call me, would I take her call?"* My heart recognized the voice—Jesus. I froze. *"You are my hands and feet and voice. Do you represent me or not?"*

I knew I had to take the call. "Lord, be with me. I cannot do this alone," I whispered. Raising my eyes toward heaven, I heard myself say clearly, "Yes" to the recording and to Jesus.

"Debra? Debra, are you there?" Karen's familiar voice was on the other end.

"Yes, I'm here." I could hardly get the words out. My shoulders dropped. My jaw relaxed. I had given up. My voice and my body demonstrated it. Had I? Or was I simply submitting to my Lord?

"Will you come see me?" Karen asked in a desperate whine. "I really need to see you."

At those words it seemed as if the world stopped spinning for a moment—time stood still. I tried to absorb her audacious request. Would I come see her? An unearthly rage surged up from some dark place inside of me. *See* her? I wanted to reach right through the phone and down her throat and rip her heart out of her body. I wanted to slam her up against the kitchen wall and scream at her, "What is wrong with you?" Then, just that quickly, the rage was gone, replaced by the echo of the words, *"You are my hands and feet and voice. Do you represent me or not?"*

"I don't know. I'll see." With those blatantly honest words, I hung up the phone. I didn't know what else to say. The decision to go would not be mine alone. What would Al say? What would the kids say? Yet somehow, in that moment, I already knew I'd go. But what would I say once I got there?

Chapter 10

The Battleground

IT HAD BEEN ABOUT TWENTY-FOUR HOURS since we'd heard the news about Hannah; maybe twelve since Karen had called me early in the morning. Silent grief tore at our hearts as we sat around the dinner table. Sadie, Helen, Charles, and even our foster daughter picked at their dinner. Al had hardly touched his, and I could barely swallow. No one wanted to eat, and yet no one seemed ready to leave the comfort and presence of the family.

I looked at the clock. Visitation at the detention center ended at 9:00 p.m. If I was going to go see Karen, I would need to leave by 8:00 p.m. That gave me thirty minutes to finish eating and clean up the dishes. I moved at a relaxed pace and tried not to appear anxious. I'd arrive in plenty of time for a brief visit.

Al and I had talked in the late afternoon about me visiting Karen. When I asked him about it, he'd winced and then looked sternly at me. He appeared shocked that I would even consider such a thing.

"Deb, haven't you been through enough? What could she possibly have to say to you? What would you say to her? I don't want to see you bearing any more pain just so Karen can feel better."

His argument was sensible. I was feeling the same way. I'd spent the entire day torn by inner conflict. On the one hand, when my rage surged, I wanted nothing to do with her. *Let her rot all alone. She deserves far worse.* On the other hand, I wanted to be who God wanted me to be. I wanted to be a living example of grace. In the end, I could not deny the message from the Lord. I didn't like it, but I couldn't deny it.

"All I can say is that during my phone conversation with Karen I felt the Holy Spirit challenging me to go."

He shook his head as if he didn't want to hear what I was saying. He didn't seem to doubt what I'd heard, but out of his protection for me and anger toward Karen, he wrestled with agreeing that I should go. He asked for time to think about it. I understood. Moments before dinner Al gave me a reluctant yes.

As the last of the dishes were put in the cupboard and the counter was wiped clean, I took off my apron and hung it on the wall. The kids had already completed their kitchen chores and gone into the family room to watch TV. Al joined them and settled into his recliner.

"Hey, guys! I'm running out to see someone. I'll try to be back in time to watch the end of the movie with you." My announcement was upbeat and lively as I reached for my keys and purse, hoping to hear only "Okay . . . bye, Mom."

"Who are you seeing?" Charles called out as I reached for the knob of the front door. I froze.

"Just a friend. I'll be back soon." I hoped to get out of the house before there were any more questions.

"Are you going to the jail?" Helen asked. Her tone sounded accusatory.

I wanted to avoid a straight answer. *How should I respond?* My hesitation drew more attention.

"Are you going to see Karen?" Charles sat up sharply. Suddenly, all the kids looked at me.

"Yes. I am."

Sadie shook her head and marched to her bedroom, closing the door hard behind her. Charles and Helen continued to stare at me. Their faces flushed, and their bodies stiffened.

"Why?" Helen asked, raising her voice a bit.

"I believe God wants me to." What else could I say? That was the truth.

Charles shook his head and lay back down on the carpet. Helen continued to stare at me in disbelief. Al looked on in silence.

Their anger was justified. How could their mother spend time with someone who had done something so unthinkable? I knew that now wasn't the time to try to counsel them through their anger and pain. I was dealing with my own. I could only pray for them and for Al.

Though I did my best to explain that as a Christian I needed to go and do what God wanted me to do, they didn't understand. My children's faith was still young. They had not experienced the tests God allows in our lives that give us opportunity to trust him more and build our faith.

It was hard knowing that Al didn't support the visit either. He did support *me*, though. He always had. And that meant the world to me. He didn't doubt God had called me. I was sure this was a test of faith for both of us.

I left my family stinging and angry. I was not the one who could bring understanding or calm their hearts. Only God could do that. I had to go.

"I love you all. I'll be back soon."

As I drove the car down the bumpy dirt road from our house to the highway, I was confident I was doing the right thing, yet tormented over how much I didn't want to go. "I am ready to do this," I spoke aloud as I attempted to convince myself. I felt a strength come over me—until I reached the end of the dirt road and turned to head to town.

Suddenly, I felt like someone had punched my stomach and I was going to throw up. A woozy wave of confusion filled my head, and I could barely see the speeding cars around me. I needed to get off the road and calm myself before I caused an accident.

As I pulled over, heavy sorrow flooded my chest. Putting the car into park, I rested my forehead on the steering wheel. Tears drenched my cheeks. I felt as if a giant vacuum was sucking the life out of me, and I struggled to breathe.

Maybe the devil is trying to use my pain to discourage me from seeing Karen. Yes, I'm experiencing understandable turmoil considering what has happened to Hannah, but there is a spiritual side to this as well. I slowly regained my composure. I was not one to side with the devil, but his ways could easily be justified if they felt like an easier way out. *Isn't this what we battle every day? A tug-of-war between what God would have us do and the temptation to take Satan's easy way out?* I wouldn't let him win. I would get myself together and go.

"God, give me what I need to do your will," I prayed.

I thought back to the years I had spent facilitating the Wednesday morning Bible study with the women at the jail. I thought of the many inmates I had gone to visit, those who requested to see a chaplain. I relished those visits. But this one would be different. This one was personal—a visit I never could have dreamed I would be called to make. What did she want? What would I say to her? How would I behave? What if I lost my temper?

I felt a tumultuous war within—anger, grief, the desire to be obedient to God, and the fear I wasn't up to the challenge.

Desperate for air, I rolled down my window and stuck my head out. I felt as if I was coming up out of a deep body of water, gasping for oxygen. I inhaled and exhaled two or three times, and my heart rate slowed and my focus returned. The hum of the evening traffic and the sound of chirping crickets gradually became louder than the pounding of my heart. I rested my head against the frame of the open window, closed my eyes, and whispered, "Thank you, Jesus."

When I opened my eyes, I knew it was time to go. I feared that someone might think I was having car trouble and stop to offer help. I didn't want to have to explain anything to a stranger. I put the car into drive. "Don't let my anger and fear keep me from doing what you want me to do, Lord," I said aloud.

All my senses seemed suddenly alive. The stars appeared unusually brilliant against the darkening evening sky, and the moon was brightly defined. I welcomed the kind face of the moon as it escorted me past the bridge, across town, and up the hill to the parking lot of the jail.

I pulled into the visitors parking area and turned off the engine, giving myself a few minutes before going into the gray brick building. Huge circles of razor wire lined the top of the inmate recreation wall, and they sparkled like glistening diamonds as the parking lot lights shone down on them. Everything appeared so much more vivid. I felt as if something dark had been pursuing me ever since I left home, and yet now I was safe in the familiar parking lot of the jail. The Lord was near.

Drawing in one more deep breath, and exhaling slowly, I forced myself to get out of the car and walk across the parking lot to the jail entrance. The empty lobby had seen many visitors; the vinyl floor was well worn. Centered in the lobby, a glass security window with a short laminated countertop served as the only introduction to the detention center. There was a sterile feel to the almost colorless decor. No one was present except the woman behind the glass window.

"Hi, Deb! What are you doing here so late? Visitation time is almost over. I assume you are here for a clergy visit." Jean had worked at the detention center for a long time. She and I would often spend a few minutes visiting with each other before I'd go in.

"Hi, Jean. Yeah . . . I'm here to see Karen Bower. I know I don't have much time, but she requested the visit." I knew I wasn't my usual friendly, lighthearted self but hoped Jean would not ask me questions or want to chat. I wanted to fill out the visitor form, hand over my car keys and driver's license, and get this visit over with as quickly as possible.

"Do you know her personally?" Jean asked. "It's all over the newspaper, you know."

"Yes. I know her," I answered softly. Jean looked at me for a moment. I was sure she could tell I had been crying.

"Okay, honey. You're cleared to go in. Take care, okay?" I appreciated Jean's attempt to be tender but didn't have the emotional energy to respond. I smiled at her and walked outside to the visitation entrance.

My legs seemed so heavy I could barely shuffle to the door. Every step felt like a battle. Tears streamed down my face as the door to the lobby closed tightly behind me. I had only one tissue, and it wasn't enough to soak up the tears drenching my face. I knew the lock on the visitation door would click open as soon as I was in the security camera's view. I desperately needed to be able to go into the visit calm and with some sense of control.

"Help me, Lord," I prayed.

Suddenly, an unseen, gentle hug of warmth wrapped itself around me. From head to toe, peace filled me, calming my heart and body. It reminded me of my cozy bed comforter on a cold snowy night. But this warmth didn't just cover me—it actually filled me. The anxious weight in my chest dissipated. My shaky hands became still. I not only stopped crying, but my eyes were dry. I knew the Lord was giving me a direct and instant answer to my prayer.

Was this *grace* being given to me? Grace to be like Jesus to Karen Bower? Was God preparing me to be the hands and feet and mouthpiece of the one true lover of our souls? What was God planning to do with this supernatural grace of his? I knew, somehow, it was not given for me alone, but for Karen as well. I was in awe that God was using me in an extraordinary way.

The security door unlocked, and I pulled it toward me. As I walked down the short hall, I heard the next door click open before I reached it. An officer waited for me.

"Good evening," the officer greeted me with little expression.

"Good evening."

When I reached the special visitation area for attorneys and chaplains, the officer offered me any room I wanted. No one else was there.

"You're here to see Bower, correct?" the officer asked.

"Yes, sir."

The officer disappeared through the visitation security door, and I watched him through the glass window as he walked to the next interior door. I dragged one of the plastic chairs from behind a small table and moved it to where I could see him coming with Karen. I thought I might be better prepared if I could see her before the door opened. The smell of bleach and sweat assaulted my senses. The jail often smelled of it, but it seemed especially strong that evening.

"The officer is getting Karen now, Deb." Jean's voice came over the speaker. "It will be a few minutes. He has to get her from the infirmary." I waved at the camera in the corner of the hallway ceiling, indicating a thank-you. *Why the infirmary? Is Karen sick?*

Minutes passed before I heard the sound of several metal doors unlocking through the hallways. Then, through the glass window of the security door, Karen appeared, dressed in navy blue jail scrubs. She peered through the glass as she came closer, and our eyes locked. Her eyebrows shot up at the sight of me. We each gave a quick smile, and the escorting officer radioed to security control to unlock the door of the special visits area.

Why did I smile at her? She murdered Hannah!

Was I here as a chaplain, an ambassador of grace, or as the foster mother whose precious foster child had been murdered?

Pulling the heavy door open, the officer directed Karen to walk through. Then, nodding at me, he pulled the door closed behind him.

"Inmate Bower is secure in visitation for a clergy visit." The officer radioed the control center before disappearing through the door.

Clergy visit? Is that really what this is? I wasn't sure what this visit felt like, but my frame of mind certainly wasn't typical of my chaplain visits. Turmoil waged in my soul.

I found myself extending my arms to hug Karen. We usually gave hugs, so it seemed the natural thing to do. It would have felt more awkward not to hug. It could have indicated hardness in my heart. *Jesus would hug her,* I thought.

"You came!" I could hear the surprise and relief in her voice. I realized she'd had no idea who was waiting to see her. She'd had no idea if I would come or not.

"Thank you for coming." Karen spoke softly.

I gave a slight smile but said nothing. We each grabbed a plastic chair and set them on either side of the small Formica table in one of the visitation cells.

"Do you know where my kids are?"

"Four are in foster homes. I'm not sure if they've located Andrew yet. And DeAnn is still at your parents," I said soberly.

A few seconds ticked by with no eye contact and no words spoken between us.

"I guess you know by now what happened." Karen opened the conversation.

"I know only a little." I folded my hands on my lap.

Silence.

Karen looked down at the floor, then up at me. She appeared nervous but not necessarily emotional. No tears. No signs of distress or remorse. I held a steady stare with her and waited. I could feel God's presence in the room. I knew he was there because I felt an unexplainable sense of peace and a sound mind. Perhaps the emotions would come later, once I left the jail. But for this moment, I was given a calm spirit.

"What happened?" I whispered.

Karen looked at me for a moment and, after a long sigh, began describing the terrible evening Hannah died.

"I was angry at her for something. I can't remember what it

was now. We were standing at the top of the stairs and I told her to go downstairs. She was crying and arguing with me and wouldn't move. I pushed her toward the stairs, but she fell down the stairs to the landing by the front door. She started to scream, and I got madder and went down to her and yelled for her to shut up and stop screaming. She kept crying and screaming, and I started kicking her with my shoes; they had hard wood soles, and I kept kicking her harder and harder until I heard her head crack and her face became distorted. I could tell I had cracked her skull. Then she stopped screaming and just lay there moaning."

I listened in horror, yet didn't flinch or move. Karen was reporting this all so matter-of-factly. No tears, no apparent anguish or trauma. Just a straight, apparently unfeeling telling of events. It was surreal.

"I didn't know what to do," she continued flatly. "I watched her for a minute, and I could tell she was seriously hurt. I yelled at the other kids to stay upstairs and not come down. Then I picked up Hannah and carried her to the bedroom on the bottom floor and laid her on the bed. I ran upstairs to see where the kids were and told them to stay in their rooms. Then I went back and checked on Hannah. She was hardly making a sound, and blood was coming out of her ear. I could tell she was in a bad condition." Karen paused for a second.

I knew the layout of the home. I could visualize the tragic scene as she described it all—the violence and the insanity.

"If you knew she was in such bad shape, why didn't you call an ambulance?" I knew the answer before I asked it.

"I was afraid. I could tell she was probably not going to make it or there would be so much damage that, well . . . I panicked."

"What did you do then?" I asked, not knowing if I really wanted to know.

"I grabbed a yellow blanket and wrapped her in it and left her on the bed until the kids went to sleep." Karen rubbed her fingers nervously as she spoke, looking at them as if she would find some sort of comfort in them.

"What did you tell the kids?" I asked. I couldn't believe how calm I was.

"I told them that Hannah was in big trouble and had to go to bed early. I told them that they were not to go downstairs; all of them were to sleep upstairs that night." Karen looked at the floor, then at the cinder block wall next to her, then up at me as she waited for my next question. Was she trying to focus, or was she scanning the cell to distract her from mentally replaying the attack on Hannah?

"What did you do then?"

"I checked on Hannah again. I could tell she was dead. I didn't know what to do. I couldn't leave her there on the bed. Where could I take her? I couldn't take her anywhere. And I didn't want her to be far from me. I wanted her to be near. So I got a large black trash bag, curled her up, and put her in it. Then I carried her to the garage and tucked her under a desk out there." Karen looked down, then sat back in her chair as if telling me had somehow lifted the heavy weight she had been carrying for a long time. She let out a deep sigh, then looked at me.

I didn't want her to feel any relief from that weight. I wanted her crushed by it.

We sat silently for a moment as I stared at her pale face and thought, *Oh, dear God, this is real. This is really happening.*

"Why did you leave her there all this time and not bury her or . . . something?" My mind was boggled by the questions I was asking. A voice inside me wanted to scream, wanted to come unleashed and scream something, anything. But the Holy Spirit kept me calm. I knew it had to be him. I wasn't in denial. I knew the gruesome story I was hearing was all true.

Karen continued. "I couldn't bring myself to move her. I would go out into the garage for weeks after, once the kids went to bed, and I would sit on a folding chair in the garage and talk to her.

I don't know why. I just needed to do that. After a while, I couldn't imagine her not being there. I knew where she was by keeping her close." Karen shook her head slightly. She appeared to be still reasoning why she kept Hannah in the garage.

"And what did you tell the kids? Where did you say she was?" I knew our time was running out. Visiting hours were almost over, and the officer would come to get Karen soon.

"In the morning, I told them she had behaved badly and had to go live with a friend."

"And they never asked about her after that?" I questioned.

"No. Not really. If they did, I would remind them she was living somewhere else." Karen picked at her fingernails.

"And you told the police all of this?" I asked.

"Yes. They came to the Lusk prison and taped my confession."

Karen needed to purge her thoughts and her memories of what she had done nearly ten months before. I didn't believe she was emptying her heart, though. She didn't cry, tremble, or wring her hands. It was as if she was relieved it was all out in the open. But I saw no remorse. Had she become so numb, so hardened over the past months? How could she commit such a terrible crime, hide the body for so long, and keep the secret from so many?

As difficult and shocking as it was to hear the gory details of what had happened, I didn't cry or yell or walk out. I couldn't have walked out if I had wanted to—I was in a secured room and would have to wait five to ten minutes for an officer. It was not a situation that I could run away from. I had to stay and hear Karen out. Hear about the terrible nightmare that she would never be able to wake from.

"I know I'm in big trouble," she blurted.

I thought it strange that she would be thinking of how much trouble *she* was in, rather than the fact that she had taken the life of her child. Had the years of abuse she had inflicted on Hannah while under the influence of drugs and alcohol and bad company meant nothing to her? Had murdering her daughter meant nothing more than that she was "in trouble"? It all seemed so bizarre. We were talking evil, abuse, and murder, and all Karen could think of was that she was in "big trouble."

Over a year before I had told the caseworkers at DFS that I was afraid for Hannah's safety. They had reminded me that I was not the foster parent of the Bower children anymore and that they were taking care of watching over the children in their mother's care. Now my greatest fear had happened. Devastated, I shook my head in disbelief. *This cannot be happening. I am not with Karen Bower hearing about the murder of her little five-year-old daughter. The precious girl our family loved. It is all too big. It is all too crazy. This atrocious event should not be in my life.* Yet here I was.

Karen asked if I knew anything else about her other children. I told her I didn't. Then she told me she'd just been sentenced to the women's prison in Lusk for two years for grand larceny. Suddenly it occurred to me that it was not a good thing that Karen had confessed everything to me. It may have made Karen feel better, but I knew attorneys would soon be involved, and they would not be happy that a full confession was given to a lay chaplain who was a previous foster parent to Karen's children. I knew the visit should end.

"Karen, it's time for me to leave and get home to my family."

"Will you come back to visit me again?" Karen asked with a crack in her voice. "It's hard to be here, and no one is willing to visit me. Not my parents or any friends."

What friends? I knew that many of the people she had associated with were involved with drugs and would want nothing to do with visiting a jail. Others surely were so angry at what she had done. Who would visit her? *Me. Why, Lord, have you called me to be the one? Who am I?*

"Yes, I will try to visit again. It is not easy for me. My family does not want me to, but I will try."

I pushed the intercom button on the wall and requested that an officer come to get Karen. We only had a few minutes more alone. Though I believed Karen's heart was hard, I also saw relief in her eyes that she didn't have to hide the truth anymore. I asked if I could pray with her. She nodded, and I held her hands. I prayed for truth to be revealed and that God would show his grace and love to Karen as she sought him. I knew the Holy Spirit led my prayer. As we were praying, I was struck by the horror that I was holding the hands of the murderer who had taken Hannah's life.

My voice cracked a little, and I knew I needed to get to the safety of my car where I would be free to cry out to God. My heart was swelling, and I could take in no more. I felt queasy, as if I had taken a toxic poison. I needed to find a bucket quick. That bucket would have to be the Lord. Only he could handle something so vile.

After I said, "Amen," Karen and I stood up and walked silently to the door. We could hear the security doors unlock one by one as the officer made his way through the maze of hallways to us. As the door to the visitation room unlocked, we gave each other another hug.

As she stepped through the door, I spoke up. "Oh! One more question."

"What's that?"

"Why do they have you in the infirmary?"

Pausing for a moment, she turned her eyes away and then answered.

"Because I am considered a high-profile case and . . . I'm five months pregnant."

Part Three

The
Fallout

Chapter 11

The Ultimate Question

SILENTLY, Al, Sadie, Helen, Charles, and I filed out the front door of our home to the van. The usually annoying Wyoming wind whooshed around us, but this morning it felt like a warm soothing blanket. My heart, frozen in crushing grief, needed the comfort.

Belting ourselves in, we braced ourselves for a somber drive to Hannah's funeral. We drove the highway along the North Platte River toward Natrona Memorial Gardens in silence. None of us was ready to accept the reality of the dark deed that had taken Hannah's life. The twenty-minute ride would be too short. We needed more time.

Twelve days had passed since I'd visited Karen in jail where she made her shocking revelations to me. Was she sitting in her cell right now, imagining her daughter's funeral service? Was she grieving the child she didn't have anymore because of her own violent actions? And what of the child she now carried in her womb—one she would never be able to mother?

I reflected back to when I was the director of the crisis pregnancy center. I'd been driving home one evening along a less-traveled backcountry road when I stopped at a crossroads surrounded by sagebrush, dirt, and dried grass. It was almost dusk as I gazed up at the sky. Gray clouds were forming.

At that moment I experienced what I would call a vision. Captivated, I saw a long staircase going up to heaven toward Jesus, who was standing next to a short pillar. On top of the pillar lay the limp, lifeless body of a newborn baby. My heart began to pound as I watched an image of myself climbing the staircase. When I reached Jesus, he lifted the lifeless infant from the pillar and held it out as if presenting the child to me.

Suddenly, a second vision appeared next to the first. The same stairs, the same pillar, the same lifeless infant. But now, I saw myself climbing up to the pillar, lifting the infant in my arms, and humbly presenting the child to Jesus. He held it to his chest and smiled at me. The visions faded.

I didn't need anyone to interpret the vision. I knew exactly what Jesus was saying. I had been given a choice. I could deny that I had taken the life of my unborn child through abortion when I was seventeen, or lay that truth, in confession, at Jesus' feet and receive forgiveness. I chose confession and forgiveness by presenting my sin to him. Because of that forgiveness, he would then use me to show others the road to forgiveness. That had been my confirmation for my call to be the director of the crisis pregnancy center.

Now on the way to Hannah's funeral, I had to acknowledge that my sin was no different from Karen's. We had both taken the lives of our children. Could there be forgiveness waiting for her as well? I knew the answer was yes. God will always forgive if we ask. Would I forgive her as Jesus had forgiven me? As much as I wanted to believe I could, I was acutely aware that I harbored judgment toward her. There in the car I asked the Lord to help me forgive her, just as I'd been forgiven.

We entered the cemetery grounds and parked behind a line of cars. The dank smell of moist dirt and the fresh scent of cut grass swept over me as I got out of the car. Forty feet away, a canopy of soft cream-colored canvas flapped in the wind. Under it lay a small white casket. Two pastors I recognized from the community stood side by side near the canopy, holding Bibles in their hands. A modest crowd gathered around, laying flowers on the grass. The sight of such a tiny casket pierced my heart. For some, today might bring closure to this nightmare. But I wasn't ready for closure. My heart was torn wide open.

As Al led us toward the gravesite, a man broke away from the crowd and approached us. With the sun reflecting off his sunglasses I couldn't make out who he was until, as he drew nearer, he removed the glasses. It was Karen's brother. I'd first met him the day I met Hannah, as she'd been staying with him and his wife and children while Karen was in the hospital giving birth to Ally. I'd also taken Hannah to his place a few times to visit. He was marching toward me with such fervency that Al moved protectively to my side. Then, a few steps away from me, he opened his arms for an embrace. As he squeezed me tightly, he began to sob. "I am so sorry. I know you tried."

His words grabbed my heart, and I answered through tears, "We all tried. I am so sorry for your loss."

He looked at Al and our children. "I want to thank all of you." Then, wiping tears from his face, he turned and walked back to the small crowd. We followed slowly behind.

In the distance, I spotted three DFS employees standing back, away from the crowd. I was sure their attendance was out of respect. Many in the community were angry and felt DFS was responsible for the tragedy. I recognized one of them as the caseworker, Ellen. I thought back to when she, Karen, and I had set up the six-month plan to work the children back into their mother's care. It was she who, when about to present the plan to the court, was told the judge had ordered the children to be sent home that day.

I looked at Al, knowing he'd understand my desire to go speak to them, then walked toward Ellen. We wrapped our arms around each other and wept.

Her voice choked with emotion as she whispered, "We tried. You tried."

I then looked at her supervisor next to her. As a foster mom I had known him through many years of service. I cared about and respected him. As I moved closer, he lowered his head to avoid my eyes and began to cry.

"Don't do this," I whispered, wiping tears from my own eyes. "We have known each other too long. You have to look at me." He raised his head enough for me to see his face covered with tears.

"We will all get through this and it will never happen again," I said. He gave a slight nod as I embraced him. With his face buried against my shoulder, he sobbed, his body shaking, but he wouldn't bring his arms up to respond with a hug. He was broken, heart and soul. I held him for a moment. Then, hearing one of the pastors begin to speak, I returned to my family.

I couldn't keep the image of Hannah's little body stuffed inside a black plastic trash bag for months from invading my thoughts. I stared at the white casket. *Darkness always wants to overtake the light. I won't let it.* When the tsunami of sorrow shredded my soul, I closed my eyes and asked God to replace those images with a picture of him embracing Hannah. I believed that she was in his arms the moment she took her last breath. She was with him—the best place she could possibly be. No more fear. No more pain.

The service ended in prayer. The final words from the pastor were "Go in peace."

As the mourners dispersed, Hannah's father made his way to us. I recognized him from the few times he'd dropped Hannah off after a visit. "Thank you for everything you did for Hannah," he said, his voice breaking. He turned and left.

Al, the children, and I then sought out the Bower children to give each of them comforting hugs. (Andrew had been located at the home of one of Karen's friends.) It broke my heart to see their grief-filled faces. We shook the pastors' hands and thanked them for their messages of hope and salvation. Then, lagging behind many of the others, we headed for our van.

Karen would be transported from the detention center to the prison within a few days. I had promised to tell her about the funeral, so I planned to visit her the next day.

Once again, I sat in a visiting cell, waiting for Karen. My mind flashed through a reel of events—the phone call notifying me of Hannah's death, the first visit with Karen and the revelation of her being pregnant with her eighth child, and scenes from the funeral. So much to digest in such a short time. The sound of the security doors unlocking down the hall pulled me back to the present.

We were nearly face-to-face again. Was I ready? At least I was less anxious than I had been during the first visit.

Karen moved through the door and shuffled toward me. She looked pale. I gave her a hug as the officer left, locking us in.

"How are you doing?"

Karen shrugged. "I'm okay, but I didn't sleep at all last night. My back is bothering me, and it's cold in the infirmary. They don't let you have much in the way of a blanket when you're on suicide watch."

"Are you suicidal?"

"I don't think so, but it's their policy due to my crime and hormonal changes from the pregnancy." Karen's tone was flat, almost lifeless.

"Maybe you can get some rest this afternoon." My comment sounded so normal in this abnormal setting.

"Did you make it to the funeral yesterday?" Karen asked, shifting in her chair.

"Yes, I did." A fresh wave of grief washed over me, and for a moment I couldn't speak.

She tapped her fingers lightly on the table. "Will you tell me about it? Who was there? Were all my kids there? Who were they with? How are they doing?" Her eyes teared up as she probed for information. I knew she wanted me to paint the whole picture. I took a deep breath.

"It was windy, but beautiful." We both smiled since Casper is almost always windy. "The service was at the cemetery. There were many people there—your children, your parents and brother, two pastors, DFS representatives, our family, Hannah's daddy, and I believe his family and relatives. The pastors gave a nice message. Someone donated a lovely little white casket for Hannah." I paused when I saw tears rolling down her cheeks.

"Good. That was nice." I sensed she had desperately wanted Hannah laid to rest with a proper burial and meaningful service. I sensed Karen was also ready to rest. Though Hannah's death was a shock to everyone else, it wasn't to her. It was a heavy burden she'd carried for almost a year. Dark circles outlined her eyes, which told me she was done. Done, and ready to give it all up.

The murder. The lies. The hiding.

I leaned toward her. We were both ready to talk. Our safe corners were not needed anymore.

I told her that the children were all dressed up and looked good, and that I gave each of them a hug. She smiled. Then we sat in silence again. Reflections of Hannah danced through my mind. Her bright smile and shining eyes. Her expressions of wonder and her love of being cuddled. I realized that Karen never mentioned Hannah's name. I felt grief beginning to crawl up through my heart. My throat ached with a stifled sob. I wiped my tears away before they could run down my face. I could not let the floodgate open. Not now. Not here.

Finally, Karen broke the silence. "You know, I wanted to go but they wouldn't let me."

I couldn't believe what she had said. "Did you really think they would let you go? Do you think the authorities would let you out of here, even cuffed with police security around you? You are the one who took her life. There would have been an emotional riot at the gravesite if you were there." I could hear myself getting louder and more agitated, my tone accusatory, so I stopped to get control of myself.

"I didn't mean I wanted to be at the gravesite. I was hoping I could be in a police car and watch from far away."

I stared at her for a moment, then looked away, too baffled to respond.

Silence again.

Karen cleared her throat. "There isn't any forgiveness for what I have done, is there?"

Her words jolted me. Forgiveness? I wasn't ready to talk about that yet. I was still in shock and grief. How should I answer her? Forgiveness for killing Hannah? Whose forgiveness did she want?

"Whose forgiveness?"

"God's."

I leaned back and waited for the Lord to give me the words. They had to come from him. They had to be his truth, not my judgment.

"Yes. There is forgiveness . . . even for what you have done." Even as I spoke the words I marveled at their truth. "I'm sure God is grieved right now because he loved Hannah. He loves Hannah now. But he loves you as well." I knew the Holy Spirit was speaking because all I wanted to do was lash out and hurt her.

"God tells us in his Word that for those who love him and humble themselves, any sin can be forgiven. Before his conversion, the apostle Paul hated people who believed Jesus was the Son of God, hunting them down to imprison, torture, and put them to death. God had to allow a crisis in Paul's life in order to get his attention. I would say you are in the same place. For Paul, there was forgiveness waiting for him. Not only forgiveness, but then he was used tremendously to spread the gospel of Jesus. Taking another person's life is not an unforgivable sin if a person is truly sorry and genuinely turns to God. First John 1:9 says, 'If we confess our sins, he is faithful and just to forgive us our sins and to cleanse us from all unrighteousness' (ESV). Yes, Karen, there is forgiveness for what you have done, but only through Jesus."

She nodded as tears ran down her cheeks.

My heart raced. We said nothing more. Only God could speak to her at that point. I had no more words of hope for her other than what I had shared. She had no more questions. She'd asked the ultimate question. I'd shared the ultimate truth.

I felt my heart of grief and anger changing as I sat in the cold visitation cell, inviting God to speak to both of us. "Do you want to find that forgiveness and hope in Jesus?" I heard myself asking. My heart swelled as the Holy Spirit moved in and took over. It was only by God's power that I could share such hope. It was only by his grace that I could tell her the truth about her sin.

"Yes. I want him in my life. I want him in my heart, and I pray for his forgiveness."

I reached for her hands, and she gripped mine firmly. Her hands were warm and moist with sweat. We both bowed our heads, and I said I would lead her in a simple prayer. It wasn't anything memorized or fancy. I told Karen that we are all sinners who need a Savior. We must accept Jesus as God's Son, who came to earth so that we might find salvation, hope, and forgiveness in him. Then I prayed, "Come into my heart, Lord. Save me and forgive me of my sins. I love you and want to follow you. Amen."

Karen repeated my words, and it seemed that she truly sought God's forgiveness for herself. Did I doubt her sincerity? I wondered about it, but I knew God well enough to know that wasn't a question for me to ask or answer. That was between Karen and God alone. I didn't doubt God had heard her prayer. I didn't doubt he could save her and forgive her. I had done my part. I had shared the gospel and prayed with Karen. Was I able to forgive as freely as God? That was the question between God and me. And I hated facing the truth that I didn't yet know the answer. All I knew for certain was that I was still hurting. I was still angry.

Chapter 12

Unexpected Costs

IN THE DAYS FOLLOWING THE FUNERAL, a solemn silence hovered over our home. Scenes from the gravesite flickered through my mind. The driveway into the cemetery, the fresh mound of dirt on the grass, the Bower children weeping, the caseworkers isolated on the edge of the crowd—it all circled around in my head as if each picture were on a slow-moving carousel that never stopped. Tears often came when I was alone.

Each day I hoped for healing that would bring my family to a place of normalcy. At night, I could hear muffled weeping from my children's bedrooms. For some, the funeral may have brought closure. But not for me. And not for my family. Would we ever move on? It was as if our whole family had been hit by a Mack truck. Lying on the road, we were all bleeding, all hurting. We couldn't help each other. I knew we needed someone to help us address our pain. Someone we could trust, who could guide us in expressing our hearts.

I called my friend and Christian counselor, Ron, who invited us all to his office after hours. He would give us all the time we needed. The kids did not want to go but agreed. Ron placed folding chairs in a small circle, opened in prayer, and then invited us each to share how we felt. It was painful but good for each of us to hear what the others were feeling and thinking. Ron's gentle spirit and soft voice helped to lessen the uncomfortable meeting. After an hour and a half and many tears, our family left Ron's kind embrace and drove home in silence.

The days dragged, and then one morning on cleaning day, the yellow wall phone rang. Charles was vacuuming, and over the noise I could hear him yell, "Mom! Phone!" I headed for the kitchen. As I lifted the receiver I hollered over the vacuum. "Hello!"

The soft voice on the other end was barely audible. I dragged the four-foot spiral cord across the kitchen to a corner where the roar of the vacuum would be less intrusive.

"Hello!" I repeated. "I'm sorry, I couldn't hear you."

"Hi. This is Renee. Karen's friend." I had met Renee on a few occasions and had seen her at the funeral and given her a hug. Why would she be calling me?

Cupping the phone, I lowered my voice. "Hi! How are you?"

Silence, then a deep sigh. I readied myself. I wasn't sure if I wanted to take this call.

Words began pouring from her. "Ah, yeah," she said nervously. "I hate to bother you with this, but Karen wrote and asked me if I would bag up all her things at her house and put them in a storage unit as soon as the police were done with their investigation and released her property. The landlord wants it out as soon as possible. The house is full of stuff. Clothes, toys, dishes, linens . . . it goes on and on. I'll pay for one month of storage. That's it. I don't want anything to do with Karen after this. I'm only doing it for her kids. I understand you are the only one communicating with her."

"Can you tell me where . . . ?" I tried to jump in.

"Make sure you tell her I will only pay for one month. I shouldn't even be doing that, but there are things the kids might need. It's up to someone else to get it out of storage." She was polite, but firm. I had always thought she seemed like a good person with a kind heart. I sensed she cared about the Bower children, and I had heard she was trying to get guardianship over at least some of them since the news of Hannah. Karen had spoken in the past about how Renee tried to help her at times. I was sure Renee was struggling with the loss of Hannah. I was all too familiar with that struggle.

My mind raced with questions. What could Karen have been thinking? Who did she think would take her belongings? What would happen to them at the end of a month? I wasn't sure what to say.

"Thank you for letting me know." I wanted to show grace. "I will, uh, figure out what to do."

Why did I say that? Why am I taking responsibility?

"Where is the storage unit?" I figured I had at least thirty days to work something out.

"It's on the west side of town. I know someone with a pickup truck who will move everything out if you have a place for it to go. I will give you his name and number. After this, I want *nothing* to do with it."

"Thank you for your call. That was kind of you."

She gave no response.

Hanging up the phone, I felt frustrated. Why did I feel responsible?

Karen's family can get it out of storage if they want it. If not, I'm sure it wouldn't be the first time someone left all their things and never came back for them. It's not my property. It's not my problem.

Grumbling made me more frustrated. I attempted a little self-counseling. Was I being *put upon* or was I *taking on*? I heard that voice again, prompting me to do this. The same one that said, *"Would I take her call?"* I wished that voice would choose someone else to speak to. I couldn't imagine what good could come from my involvement.

A week later, through various people, I learned where all the children were living, scattered among friends and family. DFS, strangely enough, was not answering any calls. There was not even a recording or voice mail box to leave information. When I called, the phone just rang and rang.

About that same time, Karen wrote asking for another visit. She wasn't allowed to call me from the Lusk women's prison, where they had moved her. She was only allowed to write letters. This letter informed me that they were soon bringing her back to the local jail to meet with her attorneys and that she would call me when she could.

Her call came one evening. The next day, I decided to go to the jail after getting my kids home from school. Not wanting to traumatize them further by telling them who I was going to visit, yet feeling as if I was sneaking off on a secret mission, I told them I had to run to town to do an errand and then drove to the jail.

I signed in as a clergy visit with Jean. As I walked to the visitation entrance, pressure filled my chest. I stared at the door handle for a moment. Reaching for it seemed to take all my energy as I pulled the door toward me. It was a reminder of what little strength I truly had without God. Like an electrical shock, doom shot through my veins as the security door slammed shut behind me.

I was surprised at my angst. Where was the peace of God I had at the first and second visits? My grief over Hannah and my struggle with forgiving Karen were fighting their way to the surface. Waiting between security doors, I prayed out loud, "Lord, be with me." Seconds later the door in front of me unlatched.

I entered the hall to the square cinder block special visitation rooms and passed a closed door to another room where low voices were coming from the other side. An attorney, religious leader, or lay chaplain was visiting with an inmate. Whenever there was more than one visit going on, the security doors to each individual room had to be closed and secured. I found myself not wanting to be so physically confined with Karen this time. I feared I would fall apart in tears or say terrible things.

My breathing became shallow as my heart raced. I didn't want this visit, but it was too late, as I'd be seeing her any minute. *Maybe my attitude will be better once I see her walking toward me.* I sat on the blue plastic chair facing the glass and waited, willing myself to surrender to the Lord's guidance during this visit.

Ten minutes passed. Fifteen. I looked at my watch. I didn't want to be late getting home to make dinner.

I began to hear radio chatter, and through the glass I finally saw Karen walking toward me. The officer reached for his radio and squeezed the transmit button.

"Control, open special visitation door, please." I rose to meet her as the lock released. When our eyes met, Karen gave me a quick smile. I returned one just as quick. Stepping forward, we embraced. Her hug was tight and, I sensed, genuine.

"How are you feeling? Is the baby moving much?" I wanted to have some control over the conversation, so I started with the obvious.

"I'm feeling okay. Every time they bring me back to Casper they put me in a cell in the infirmary. It's very boring. One of the nurses said it's not only because I'm pregnant but also for security reasons. It would be too dangerous for me in general population in the dorm or a housing unit."

I'd never thought of Karen being in danger in the jail, but suddenly that made sense. Child abusers and child murderers are often hated by other prisoners. I couldn't think of a response.

"Do you know anything about the kids?" Karen sat hunched over, her hair stringy; she began twisting her fingers.

"I don't know much. They're at different homes. Foster homes now, I believe. No one is talking, and I can't get DFS to answer their phone. Some say that they've shut down until an investigation is completed. That's crazy! There are foster parents who need to communicate with them. I know they are under tough scrutiny, and I guess it makes sense that there would be intense questioning. The community is outraged. You see it all through the newspaper. I hear it everywhere I go in town. People who know I am a foster parent stop me and ask if I know anything about the case."

Karen stared at me. For a moment, the focus was off of her and the bad guy was DFS. I found that my anger for the failure of the social system in Casper created an odd feeling of pity for Karen—as if this tragedy could have been averted if they had not returned the children to her prematurely. I found myself in an emotional tug-of-war that left me confused. DFS didn't take Hannah's life. I'd just hugged the person who had.

We sat silently again. There was so much to process. We both had questions. Where did we start? How comfortable were we to ask them? What could be the legal issues if we did ask—and answered?

I told her about Renee's call. Karen asked if I could pay another month's storage until she could figure out what to do.

I was frustrated that she'd ask that of me. "Karen, it's senseless to keep paying for storage. Isn't there someone who can get it out and store it? Your family? A friend?"

She shook her head as I continued to offer suggestions. There was no one.

"You are the only one who will help me." She wasn't begging. Just stating a fact.

"I'll see what I can do. I can't spend money on storage. Al would not be happy with that. I really have to go. Can I pray for you before I do?" I wanted to leave the jail. I felt pressured. Was it my conscience or God or because I had no answers? I pushed the button of the speaker on the wall, knowing we'd have time to pray before the officer came.

I wrapped my hands around hers, then prayed for the hearts of her children to be protected, for truth to be revealed, and for

God to work in Karen's spirit, that she would learn to trust him. She thanked me, and we sat in silence until the officer arrived to escort her back to the infirmary.

When I reached the parking lot, I poured out my frustration to God. "What do you want me to do? You give me Karen, who murdered her child, a child I loved. My family is hurting and angry and unhappy that I'm talking to Karen. I want to help her children, but they are all with other families. Who will care for them next? And then Karen has a baby on the way. Oh . . . and no one from DFS will answer my calls. I can't even talk to them about the two foster children I have in my home. And according to Karen, and now the newspapers, there is the possibility that Karen may be facing the death penalty. When do my heart and emotions get a break from all of this?" I whined and prayed as I whipped out of the parking lot, racing to get home.

Knowing I was running late, I rushed through the door when I reached home. My attempt to act nonchalant about where I had been was a struggle. *Slow down. Act calm. Walk, don't run. Behave as if this is just like any other day.* I hated all the pretense. It left me feeling so isolated.

I started pulling out pots and pans from the kitchen cupboard.

Al followed me, munching on crackers. "We were wondering when you would get home. Everyone is starving."

"Sorry. I was, uh, well, caught up in a conversation with someone." Al stared at me and stopped chomping.

Avoiding eye contact, I opened the refrigerator.

"A conversation with . . . *someone?*" He figured out where I had been. I was hyper and anxious under my phony smooth demeanor. "So what did you talk about?" He licked cracker crumbs off his fingers.

I answered in a whisper. "Karen wants to know if I can do something with all her stuff in storage."

"Like what?" A bit snappy with his reply, he took two big steps to the trash can, opened it, and forced the empty cracker box down into it.

"Well, what if I have it brought here and store it in the garage? I could go through it later and get things to her children. There might be things they need." I couldn't believe what I was saying. It was as if God put the words in my mouth right before they spilled out.

Al stared at me, his expression frozen, cold as stone. His silence spoke volumes. I didn't blame him. But I felt that same prodding from the Lord that I felt when I took Karen's first call from jail. It wasn't me offering to serve her in this way. It was Jesus in me prompting the offer. *He does seem to like volunteering me for his work.*

I stared back. It was a showdown, though not an angry one. Al shook his head. "Do what you think you need to do." Turning to walk out of the kitchen, he called back to me, "How long until dinner?"

I was reluctant to admit it, but it looked as though God had answered my prayers. I had asked him what I should do, and he had told me. I would receive the storage unit full of Karen's belongings and . . . then what? What would I do with it all? How much was there, anyway? I hadn't asked Renee how big the storage unit was or whether it was full. How much stuff could Karen have? And when was I supposed to find the time to sort through it all?

I was in the midst of preparing for the national Mrs. International pageant in Texas and would soon need to focus on the trip. I still had appearances to make as Mrs. Wyoming. I had my job, my family, and foster children to care for. Sure, I could receive the property and stick it in the back of my garage until I figured out what to do with it, but that left one other issue to deal with. How would I explain the stuff in our garage to my children who were still angry and suffering over Hannah's murder?

The next day, I called the number Renee gave me and made arrangements to have Karen's stuff delivered. Al was at work and the kids were at school when the man arrived in his pickup. The timing was perfect. I could tuck away the bags in the garage, on the other side of our boat, where hopefully the kids wouldn't notice them.

"Where do you want them?" he said gruffly, slipping on a worn pair of work gloves.

"Here on the driveway."

He clapped his hands together and said, "Let's get to it!"

The truck was full to the brim with black plastic garbage bags, fifteen to twenty of them. Climbing into the bed of the truck, the man threw them onto the driveway one by one.

Thud! Thud! Thud! As each bag hit the cement, I dragged it into the garage. This was far more than I'd feared. Why did God have me open my mouth to say I would accept them?

After the man had thrown the last bag from the truck, he got into the cab and drove off before I could thank him, the truck's wheels kicking up a cyclone of dust all the way down our road. I eyed the mound of bulging black plastic bags covering half the floor of my garage. I knew the bags would require hours of time. There would be no camouflaging them. No covering them up. No hiding them. It was too much. Too big.

Al and the kids will say I have lost my mind. Maybe I have.

It was only a matter of days before one of the children spotted the bags. I did my best to explain, but their anger at Karen surged once again, as did their frustration with me for visiting and helping her. I empathized with their frustration, but with Al's support I kept my course.

A few days later I was surprised to get a call from the police, asking if Al and I would come to the station to answer some questions. We agreed.

What would they ask us? What information could we offer

them? Karen had confessed to the police that she had taken Hannah's life. What could we say that would be of any help or shed any light on what Karen had already confessed to the police?

Still, we felt it was our responsibility to talk with the police since they requested it. We felt vulnerable. Would they ask me what Karen told me at our first visit? We wondered if we should hire an attorney but decided not to.

Detective Marsh met us in the police station lobby. He was dressed casually in an off-white golf shirt and dark grey khakis, with a shiny brass police badge clipped to his belt. His demeanor was as casual and welcoming as his appearance.

"Thank you for coming to the station. I'm sure this is difficult for your family. I understand you had the Bower children in your home for some time," he said, leading us to a room with several tables and chairs. Two other men and a woman were there, working at tables.

Pulling out a chair for me, the detective motioned to another for Al. "Have a seat. Would you like some water?" We shook our heads. We hoped we wouldn't have to stay long.

Detective Marsh scooted a chair up to the table and sat sideways on the seat, draping one arm over the back of his chair as if he were trying to take a relaxed pose to help us not feel intimidated. One of the other men walked over to our table and sat next to Al.

"How long have you been foster parents?" The first question came from Detective Marsh.

"Almost sixteen years, I think," I said, looking at Al for confirmation.

"Yes, I think it's going on sixteen years now," Al said.

"How long did you have the Bower children in your home?"

"Ten or eleven months, I think," I said, and Al nodded in agreement.

"Do you know anything about the fathers of the children?" When Detective Marsh asked the question, the man sitting next to Al cocked his head, listening intently.

"No, I have only met one briefly," I said. "Hannah's father."

From across the table, the other man finally introduced himself as a detective. He took over, asking if we would share what happened when the children were court ordered back to their mother and afterward. He asked if we saw Hannah during that time.

Suddenly, anger burned in my chest. *Now they ask! How many times did I call DFS about Hannah's safety? If anyone would have asked or listened then, we would not be having this meeting. Hannah would be alive and well.* I tried to calm myself. I knew it wasn't the fault of the police.

I explained that I had called DFS numerous times, expressing my concerns after the children went home. DFS had insisted that they were checking regularly on the children, including Hannah, and that all was well.

"I understand that you've met with Karen in jail. Will you tell me what the two of you discussed?" Detective Marsh asked.

"No, I don't believe I should divulge that," I said. "As her chaplain, our conversations were confidential." I felt I would need legal counsel to guide me before I could say anything about it.

Knowing Karen had confessed to the police the night they found Hannah's body, I didn't think they would need my testimony. I remembered a wise person told me once, "If you don't know what to do, do nothing until you do." I would do nothing and say nothing until I had clear understanding and direction from an attorney or from God.

I mentioned that I was storing Karen's property in our garage. Was it important to their investigation? Detective Marsh said no—the authorities had searched Karen's home and released the remaining contents.

Finally, the questions were over, the detectives thanked us, and Al and I were relieved to have that behind us. About a week passed and we got another call—this one from a private investigator asking if Al and I would meet with him at a restaurant or somewhere we felt comfortable.

Comfortable? We were anything but. We were not even sure who he was working for—DFS, Karen's attorneys, or her family. But we naively agreed to meet. His questions covered pretty much the same information as Detective Marsh's, so we repeated our answers.

Al and I returned home worn out and frustrated. What had I gotten us into when I answered that fateful call from Karen? I knew the Lord had prompted me to visit her, but now I was squirming. Not only did I have a garage filled with her belongings, but now I had the uncomfortable feeling that I was under legal scrutiny.

What was my involvement with Karen going to cost us?

Chapter 13

Sacred Conversations

KAREN HAD BEEN TRANSPORTED back to the prison in Lusk, a two-hour drive away. Though I felt compelled to visit her again, I allowed a few weeks to pass before I decided to make the trip.

Only Al knew where I was going that day. I couldn't tell my children or anyone else. I didn't want to hear any criticism or see any harsh looks from those who wouldn't understand my decision to visit Hannah's murderer. I left early in the morning to give myself plenty of time for the long drive.

As I approached Lusk, my heart raced. I drove along the quaint streets, then across the railroad tracks to the outskirts of town, and finally into the back row of the parking lot at the familiar prison facility. Twice a year for five years, as a speaker with a Christian women's jail and prison organization, I had spoken to female inmates at this facility. Now, in order to visit Karen as an individual inmate, I had to agree to no longer be a special guest speaker, which saddened me.

The huge gray cement building surrounded by a tall chain-link fence topped with razor wire looked menacing. This visit would be nothing like the ones at the local jail in Casper. This was an ominous prison. With the engine still running, I leaned back against the headrest and closed my eyes. I needed to take in a few deep breaths and seek God's grace and wisdom. Grace to make it through another visit with my own tumultuous feelings. Wisdom to know what to say and how to minister to Karen.

As I crossed the vast parking lot, I prayed, "Well, Lord. I'm here. Help me know what to say."

When I reached the small speaker box next to the gated entrance, I pushed the silver button on the box and waited. No response. As I pushed it again, a few people walked up behind me. This time a voice came over the speaker. "May I help you?"

A man standing next to me replied. "Yes. We are here for visitation."

"Who are you visiting?" the voice asked.

The man stated an inmate's name and number. A woman stepped up and gave a different name and number. I waited, knowing I would have to say Karen's name out loud. With the case still plastered all over the news, my secret visit was about to be exposed.

I moved closer to the box. "Karen Bower," I said quietly, hoping the others wouldn't hear. My face flushed with embarrassment as I moved behind them. I didn't look to see if any of them were looking at me. I stared at my driver's license, nervously flipping it between my fingers.

Finally, the gate opened and our little group passed through and into the prison lobby where we stored personal items in lockers. I stood away from the others while we waited another fifteen minutes for an officer to arrive. He asked that each visitor bring their license to the desk and sign in. I let everyone else go in front of me.

Once the others had signed in and walked through the scanner, the officer opened the door to let everyone into visitation— everyone but me. "Debra Moerke," he called out, in a voice that echoed throughout the waiting room. "Bower is at a high level of custody, so she cannot have a visit in the general visitation room. You will be having a closed visit in a separate room with a window and phone."

If the others didn't know who I was coming to see before, they knew now. The shame of her crime seemed to hang over me like a thick cloud. I gave the officer a weak smile.

"I'll be back for you in a minute," the officer said.

The security door slammed shut, and I was left alone in the silent, sterile lobby. Moments later, the officer appeared and told me to follow him. We walked down a short hall lined with doors of individual visitation rooms. Each door had a large window so visits could be visually monitored. The officer escorted me to one of the rooms. It had a plastic chair, a short counter, a phone, and a window that revealed the same kind of room on the opposite side. "They're getting Bower now," the officer said as he closed the door.

Moments later, two officers escorted Karen into the room across from me. She was dressed in orange scrubs and shackled in ankle chains that forced her to shuffle. A belly belt was wrapped around her waist, and her hands were cuffed to a large silver ring attached to the belt. My chest tightened at the sight of her chained and cuffed. I wasn't expecting to see her like that. In Casper, our visits had been one-on-one in the same room. There were no cuffs or ankle chains. Without warning, my eyes filled with tears. Once she saw me, tears filled her eyes as well, and she looked down as though she wanted to hide her face from me.

One of the officers took Karen's arm, helping her to the chair. She looked up at me as she sat. We stared at each other, watching tears stream down each other's faces.

I picked up the phone. Karen shifted to one side, trying to reach her phone on the other side. With her hands still cuffed to the belly belt, she could barely reach it. Holding it almost six inches from her face, she said, "We will have to talk loud so we can hear each other."

That's crazy. How do they expect an inmate to talk on the phone when she can't bring it to her ear? I had to remind myself that the prison wasn't there to accommodate an inmate but to restrict her. We would have to make the best of it.

"How are you doing?" I asked as I wiped tears from my face.

Karen's tears fell on her shirt. "It's not that bad. It's better than the jail. Well, other than having to be chained and cuffed like this." We both chuckled, pretending to make light of what was so serious.

"Have you heard anything from your attorney?" I asked.

"Just that they definitely plan to go for the death penalty. I don't know how all that will turn out. But that's what they are saying for now." Karen chewed the inside of her cheek as she stared at me through the glass.

The death penalty. Is this all really happening, Lord? My mind struggled to take in such horrendous information. "How do you feel about that?" I asked. *What a stupid question!*

"I don't know. It makes me sad for my children, but maybe it would be for the best. It's that or life in prison. I don't think I could spend the rest of my life here." Fresh tears sprang from her eyes. She shook her head as if she wasn't sure of what she was saying.

I didn't know what to say.

"Have you heard anything? Anything about the kids?" She wrestled with the phone as it began to slip from her fingers.

"No. I think they're all doing okay. Have you heard from your parents?"

"No. I don't hear from anyone except you." She gave me a warm smile. "I do have something very important to ask you though." Karen leaned closer to the window that separated us.

"What's that?" I drew closer too. We could almost hear each other better through the glass than through the phone.

"Would you consider taking legal guardianship of the baby when it's born? I don't want DFS to take it. I will never know what happens to it if they do." Her eyes narrowed as if pleading, hoping she would hear the answer she wanted.

I sat back in my chair in disbelief.

Lord, every time I think circumstances can't get more bizarre, another shock wave hits.

Trying to get a grip on my emotions, I peered through the window at the woman who hadn't wanted me to take Hannah, then murdered her, but now wanted me to take her unborn child when it arrived.

I don't know how long I sat there, just staring, trying to absorb this request. "Isn't there family or someone else you would rather have guardianship? Your parents or a friend?"

"No. You are the only one. I know the baby will be cared for and loved, and I will have peace knowing where it is." She sat motionless, waiting for my answer.

"I don't know." I stammered. "I can't tell you that now. I would have to talk to Al and my children. I'm not sure if that would be what's best for the baby. I will need to pray about it, and I ask you to pray about it as well." The whole idea threw me. I needed time to think and pray.

"I have prayed about it," Karen answered with confidence. "That's why I'm asking you." Our eyes locked, and a special connection we had never had before began to develop at that moment.

But why me? Wouldn't I be the last person she would want to take guardianship of her child? Isn't she the last person whose child I would want? Do I really want to have that kind of continued connection with her?

"I will talk to Al and let you know." I wanted the visit to end right then. Karen's request suddenly stirred feelings of deep anger. Anger that she took Hannah's life when she could have allowed her to stay with our family and prevented this nightmare. "When is the next time you will be in Casper? We could talk more about it then."

"I don't know. I never know until I'm in the van and on my

way. I can call you from the jail and we can talk about it again. Is that okay?" Her slight smile and raised brows held the expression of anticipation and hope. Clearly, she did not want no for an answer, nor did she want the visit to end.

"Yes, we can talk then." I returned the smile, though mine wasn't genuine.

Through the glass, I could see an officer nearby and waved to him that we were done. With one last look at each other, I waved good-bye as the officer helped Karen from her chair. She turned to shuffle away with him down the hall—such a disheartening sight.

As the final door to the prison unlocked, releasing me to the parking lot, tears streamed down my face. Before I reached my car, my tears had turned to sobs. I could hardly see to put the key in the lock of my car to open it. I hurriedly turned on the engine and threw the gearshift into reverse. I couldn't get out of Lusk fast enough, as far from the prison as I could get. I wanted to be alone with God.

As I drove the long stretch home, I asked God to fill me with peace. I needed it desperately. The anger in my chest seemed to be clawing its way up through my throat, and I wanted to scream. I had been devastated by Hannah's death, but I hadn't allowed myself to be angry. Really angry. I was afraid to let my anger surface. I didn't know what it would look like, and I was scared to let it out. What would happen if I did? Would it rip apart everything and everyone in my path? Family? Karen? I couldn't change anything. I couldn't bring Hannah back. I couldn't reverse what Karen had done. I had no control over the situation, and I didn't know how to process it all. It was as if I was releasing Hannah into Karen's care all over again.

Somehow, I managed to get myself together before I reached home. I didn't want Al or my children to see me in such an emotional mess.

A few days passed before I felt ready to talk to Al. I was waiting for a time when he and I could go for coffee and pie somewhere.

I didn't want to talk about it at home where kids, summer activities, and Al's job kept us from sneaking off for private, uninterrupted conversation. I wasn't sure I wanted to bring it up to Al in the first place. I was so confused. Finally, I told him I needed to talk to him about something Karen said.

As we sat down at Denny's Coffee Shop, I presented Al with the idea of guardianship. He rolled his eyes and shook his head.

"We can talk about it later, Deb. You need to concentrate on the pageant for now. Can we agree to pray about it and discuss it when we get home from Texas?" As usual, he made sense. We would wait until the national competition for the Mrs. International pageant was over.

I was obligated to compete in the pageant no matter what was going on in my private life. It was time to focus on the preparations. Two things I needed to find were a formal gown and a semiformal dress. Liz had recommended a lady in South Dakota who specialized in gowns for pageants. I called and we scheduled a time for me to come. I appreciated her availability but dreaded the long drive—it would take four to five hours. That would be an all-day, if not an overnight trip. I had no time for such a trivial trip, and I once again began to resent the pageant, wondering why God had prompted me to allow such a thing in my life when our family was so devastated by Hannah's death. What good was a sparkly crown and satin sash in light of such loss, murder, and possibly the death penalty? Couldn't I just excuse myself and tell the organizers that Mrs. Wyoming couldn't make it?

A friend suggested that one of the airlines might give me a discount for a quick round-trip flight to South Dakota in exchange for naming it as a sponsor. It was worth a try, so I went to the Natrona County airport. In the lobby, I ran into an acquaintance of Al's and mine, Dale Leatham. He worked as a part-time

US customs and border patrol officer and was a customer service agent for Delta Air Lines.

"Are you here to pick up someone?" he asked.

"No. I'm here to see if I can get a cheap flight, or even a sponsored flight, to South Dakota to buy a gown."

"Oh, that's right. I saw you won the Mrs. Wyoming pageant. Congratulations! I think that's great!" He put out his hand to shake mine. "As far as getting a sponsored flight, I don't think the airlines can do that. But I might be able to help." His words were encouraging, though I couldn't imagine what help he could be.

"I have a friend who flies cargo to different places. I know he goes to South Dakota. Maybe he would be willing to let you fly with him when he goes there. Would you like me to check with him? If I tell him why, he may go along with it."

I gave Dale a hug and wrote my number on a scrap paper, thinking how running into him was an unexpected answer to prayer.

Dale called the next day. "You're on! Can you leave Wednesday at six in the morning? The pilot will fly you there, then back to Casper a few hours later."

I scrambled to set up an early-morning appointment with the woman in South Dakota and make arrangements for my family's care. I would leave Casper at six and return before noon, dresses in hand.

I met the pilot at 5:30 a.m. Barely awake, I finished a cup of coffee I had bought on the way and climbed aboard the small cargo plane. It was much like the FedEx plane Tom Hanks flew on in the movie *Castaway*. I was actually in the compartment with all the cargo. Boxes and crates were strapped behind a netted safety barrier. I pulled down the jump seat behind the pilot and strapped myself in.

"It's going to get really loud and very bumpy, so make sure your belt is tight and secure," the pilot yelled over the roaring engine.

Barely believing this was actually happening, I gave a thumbs-up and the plane taxied away from the terminal. I hoped I wouldn't get airsick since I was facing the side of the plane and not forward. I took a deep breath as the engine whistled a high-pitched squeal and the plane forced its way into the sky. Wheels up. We were on our way.

For the next hour, there would be no conversation beyond a few shouted words from the pilot asking if I was all right.

No, I wasn't all right. There I was, high in the sky, the roar of an engine piercing my ears, the dips and shaking of the small plane upsetting my stomach, and memories of Hannah filling my mind. I hated that I was on my way to go gown shopping. *I should be doing something else. Something constructive. There is no purpose for this pageant.*

As I wrestled with sweet memories and bitter feelings, I knew that only God's Word would help me to focus and keep me from an emotional spill right there on the plane. I needed to hear from him. So I pulled out the small Bible I kept in my purse. Though the shaking and rattling of the plane made it difficult, I tried to focus on the small print. The brown silk ribbon marker rested in the book of James. I moved the ribbon aside and began to read.

> Consider it pure joy, my brothers and sisters, whenever
> you face trials of many kinds, because you know that
> the testing of your faith produces perseverance. Let
> perseverance finish its work so that you may be mature
> and complete, not lacking anything. If any of you lacks
> wisdom, you should ask God, who gives generously to
> all without finding fault, and it will be given to you.
> JAMES 1:2-5

The Lord was speaking directly to me. As I continued reading, another verse jumped out at me, gripping my heart.

Blessed is the one who perseveres under trial because,
having stood the test, that person will receive the crown
of life that the Lord has promised to those who love him.

JAMES 1:12

The crown. The crown of life.

I read verse twelve over and over again, my heart hammering with awe. I suddenly realized, beyond a doubt, what the Lord was telling me through my pageant participation. Yes, he was speaking about crowns . . . but he was teaching me that it's not the physical jeweled crown for worldly achievements that is important. What matters to God is the spiritual crown—the crown of life—we will receive for surrendering to God when we persevere through the trials of this life on earth.

I was thunderstruck, so it seemed only right that the plane dipped and vibrated in bone-rattling turbulence. I gripped the frame of my seat with confidence.

I can do this. I can face any turbulence that comes my way. This pageant isn't some frivolous side trip. My participation in these pageants is your grand object lesson for me. I am to be about my Father's business earning the crown of surrender and obedience, then lay that crown at the foot of the cross.

My part in these pageants, and in Hannah's story and its aftermath, was simply to surrender everything to my Father and do as he asked.

And there, literally flying through the heavens, I called out to my Lord, "I'm all in, dear Lord. Whatever you bring, I'm all in."

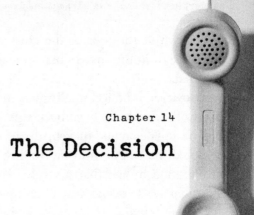

Chapter 14

The Decision

EVEN THOUGH THE KIDS WERE in the backseat, the long drive to Texas for the national pageant gave Al and me time to discuss the question of guardianship of Karen's unborn child, though it was too soon to come to any conclusions. We knew how to talk quietly in code.

Once we arrived in Tyler, my mind was totally focused on the pageant.

For four days, fifty women moved as one through the hotel, local restaurants, and community events. We all wore our sashes and were known by our states, not our names. I remember liking Mrs. Florida and Mrs. Missouri, but I can't remember their names.

I soon realized how seriously many of the other ladies were taking not only this pageant, but all the others in which they had participated. For some, it was one of the most significant events of their lives. There were those who found their identity in where they ranked in the final hours of the pageant. I thought frequently of my realization in the cargo plane that this experience was my opportunity to celebrate the crown of life, and that surrendering my crown at the foot of the cross was my ultimate goal. This freed me from the anxiety that so many of my fellow participants suffered.

However, I did feel small-town, unrefined, and clueless around most of the women. Even backstage, the clothes, undergarments, and personal hair and makeup artists that they brought with them tempted me to question my sophistication. I had to intentionally remind myself that my value lay in my identity in Christ. Fortunately, there was a small group of other Christians competing. I felt drawn to them and asked if they would like to share in prayer and a devotional between breakfast and lunch each morning. Five agreed, and we met in a small room off the banquet area. We prayed for one another during the daily process of the pageant. Hearing their prayers and sharing about what God had done in each of our lives put many of my insecurities to rest.

There were interviews, photo shoots, production rehearsals, banquets, and a husband-and-wife party night at a local country western restaurant. Four days and three nights flew by. I may have slept three hours a night the whole time there.

During my interview with the judges, one asked, "When this pageant is over, and you are on your way home, what would you like to be able to say that you accomplished during this time?"

"That's an easy question. I would like to know I accomplished the steps to the dance routine the night of the pageant and did it in three-inch heels." The judge laughed, not realizing I was serious.

During the final night of the pageant as I looked out at the audience and saw my children sitting next to Dale and Lauree, I felt so grateful for the love and support with which God had blessed me. I knew that my identity wasn't tied up in the outcome of this event. I was a beloved daughter of God, who had given me roles to play in the lives of these precious people. I thought of Karen and the child she was carrying. Was there a long-term role I was to play in their lives? I didn't know.

When the pageant ended, I was ready to go home. I can't even remember who won—except that it wasn't me. I just wanted to go back to Casper and the life God had given me there. I still wore the Wyoming crown, but more important, I knew I had obeyed God and done my best. I felt free knowing there would be no more events to compete in. I knew that my *crowning moment* had occurred not onstage, but in the air in the cargo plane. The experience left me thankful for my simple life with my family and more aware than ever before that wherever I went I wore the crown of life and was a representative of my heavenly Father.

On the drive home, I kept thinking of Karen and the life within her. When we returned to Casper, Al and I would be faced with a potentially life-changing decision.

I couldn't get past the thought that the temporary nature of guardianship didn't seem the best option for the baby. How would the child feel? Would Karen expect me to bring the child to the prison over the years? Would I have to explain the whole sad story to this child one day?

After a few days of traveling, our family arrived home. It was August, and shopping for school clothes and supplies was the first priority. Al and I put off the daunting discussion for another week.

Finally, it was time. On Saturday morning Al began the conversation in the kitchen. "I've thought about it, and I don't think guardianship would be the best thing for the baby," he said over a cup of coffee. "What security would that give the child growing up?" I was relieved that Al's thoughts resonated with my own.

"It would be different if we adopted the baby," I said. "The parents of an adopted child have total legal rights, whereas guardianship can change. I wouldn't want anyone else to be able to rip another child out of our care." My heart pounded as I reflected back to the desperate times when I had argued with the caseworker, pleading for protection for Hannah, but seemed to be ignored. I'd held no place of legal significance in Hannah's life other than that I was once a foster mother to her.

Al nodded. We sat silently for a moment. "So . . . what do you think about adoption?" I asked.

"I would say . . . that would be the only way we would agree to take the baby."

"So if Karen agrees to adoption, would we do it? I'm not sure that's what we want to do. But if we don't, then DFS would need to find a family to adopt it. Right?"

Al's expression didn't change. He was thinking.

Then he said, "Yes, but we know how that can go. The baby could end up in foster care for a long time before being adopted. I'm not sure what's best at this point." We both let out a sigh of frustration.

We sat there for a while drinking our coffee. Then Al looked me in the eyes and said, "What do you think?"

I suddenly became emotional. The weight of the decision hit me. Fighting tears that reminded me of how much healing I still needed, I said, "We tried everything to protect Hannah, but it was out of our hands. We couldn't do a thing. If we adopted this little one, we would have full legal control. We would not only have the responsibility, but also the ability to protect this one." Passion filled my heart and my words. "We couldn't save Hannah, but we could save this one. This is Hannah's brother or sister."

With his chin resting on his hand, Al looked at me and said, "Do you realize I will be almost seventy years old by the time this baby graduates from high school?" I looked at him, smiling. He continued, now grinning, "I'll probably be in a wheelchair by then."

I grinned back at him. "Well, look at it this way. You'll have somebody to push you around in the wheelchair." And we both laughed. We looked at each other and suddenly knew. Yes. If God opens this door. Yes. We had the confidence that if God chose us, then he would work it out. And if he did, then yes, our hearts were ready to receive this baby as our own.

We would agree to adoption, but not guardianship. If Karen

wanted us to adopt, we would. Our hearts were one on the matter. Now to ask the kids.

"We might adopt the baby? I'm in!" fourteen-year-old Helen said, wiggling with excitement. Helen, the baby-lover. We'd known what her answer would be before we even sat down with our kids to get their opinions on the adoption. Charles and Sadie? We were about to find out.

"It isn't fair. She wouldn't let us have Hannah, then she killed her," Charles said, resentment dripping from his words. "Now we're going to take care of her new baby?"

I understood my twelve-year-old's anger. Would he ever be able to see the baby as ours and not hers?

"Karen won't be allowed to keep this baby, no matter what," I explained. "Either she'll spend the rest of her life in prison or she'll get the death penalty. We didn't have the power to save Hannah. But if this baby becomes legally ours, we could protect it from Karen and the foster care system."

I watched his thinking shift. "Karen won't have anything to do with raising her?" he asked. "It would come home to us right from the hospital? It would be our baby and not hers?"

"That's right, Charles," Al assured him. "The baby would be a Moerke, not a Bower."

"Then yes," Charles announced.

Sadie, now sixteen, was clearly struggling with the pros and cons. As she mulled over the idea, she seemed hesitant. Finally, she spoke. "I give my approval, too," she said.

Our son Jason was still stationed in Germany with the air force, and our oldest, Elizabeth, was still away at college. They hadn't been living at home during our time with Hannah, though they'd been caring and supportive from a distance. They said they'd support us in whatever decision we made.

So now we knew how the Moerkes felt about adopting the baby. But what would Karen say? She hadn't offered us the option to adopt; she'd only asked us to take guardianship. Unless someone else stepped forward, which didn't seem likely, Karen would have to choose us as the adoptive parents or relinquish the child to DFS.

I sent Karen a letter telling her we could talk about the baby the next time she was in Casper. I would present the options and leave the outcome in God's hands.

As days passed, however, I realized with surprise that I still felt conflicted over the matter. Had Al and I made the right decision? Wouldn't this tie us forever to Hannah's murderer? Would we be able to celebrate this child without a cloud of grief always hovering? My ache for Hannah haunted me, and I realized that I still had a lot of grieving to do. I cried. I cried in the bathtub and when alone in the car. I cried when Al was at work and the kids were out of the house. I cried often, and I always cried alone. I knew I needed those tears to grieve Hannah, but I had to be selective of when and where I released that grief.

I decided not to discuss this with my local friends. They wanted to protect me from the agony I felt when I visited Karen—an agony that I couldn't deny even though I knew I was called to be involved with her. They would advise me to stop seeing Karen. Add to that the public sentiment that was so hostile toward her. Who would understand my decision to visit Hannah's murderer, pray with her, and consider the adoption of her child? I simply couldn't deal with the hatred of others toward her—it was all I could do to manage my own tumultuous feelings. It was all so complicated.

I did have Dale and Lauree in Texas to confide in. We called one another "covenant friends" because we'd made a covenant always to speak God's truth to one another, to hold one another accountable spiritually, and to encourage one another. I was up front about what I needed from them.

"Don't baby me," I told them. "And don't try to comfort me. Speak God's truth to me. That's what I need." They both expressed mixed feelings but said they'd support our decision to adopt and would pray that God's will be done.

Even so, I needed more time to wrestle through my emotions with God alone.

Within a few weeks of our family decision, I received a collect call from Karen at the Casper jail.

"Hello, Debra? I'm in Casper. Can you come see me?" Karen sounded better than she had at the prison. Her voice was strong with a note of excitement. She seemed happy just hearing my voice.

"Yes, I will come this evening."

"Good. I really want to see you. Did you talk to Al about the baby?"

"We did talk about it. I will let you know what we are thinking when I see you. I don't want to talk about it on the phone."

I watched a brilliant sunset through my kitchen window as I rinsed the dinner dishes and placed them in the drying rack on the counter. The children had finished their evening chores and gravitated to their bedrooms to finish their homework. Al relaxed in his recliner, watching the evening news.

I announced I was making a grocery store run and would be back soon. After a soft, "I'm leaving," to Al, along with a knowing look, I grabbed my keys.

When I arrived at the jail, a handful of people were in the lobby. At the security window Jean welcomed me with a sweet smile. "I think I know who you're here to see. I'll let you in and then I'll call for her."

I was grateful that Jean didn't announce my visit over the intercom with so many people within earshot. Even though two months had passed since the murder became public, the local media was still abuzz with news of the murder and pending trial, and public outrage remained high. I gave Jean a thumbs-up and a smile.

I made my way to a visitation cell and waited. Within minutes, an officer appeared at the door with Karen.

We exchanged hugs. Before Karen pulled out her chair, she asked, "What did you and Al decide about the baby?" Then she sat, resting her folded hands on the table. She was ready to talk business. I wasn't sure I was. I hadn't yet felt a final confirmation from the Lord, and I now felt unsure of the option I was about to offer her.

"We did talk." I sat back in my chair and rested my hands in my lap. I wanted the conversation to be relaxed, easy. I didn't want it to appear that this was all business.

"So, this is how Al and I feel about your request."

Karen tilted her head, ready to listen.

"We do not believe guardianship would be in the best interest of the baby."

Karen's look of anticipation fell into disappointment.

"Wait. I'm not done yet," I said. "You know you will never be able to raise this baby. With you in prison and no family to call its own, guardianship would leave this little one in limbo all its life. If DFS takes guardianship of the child, they will go to court to have your rights relinquished. Then they will adopt or foster the baby out to strangers because no family member is stepping forward. It's your decision. Al and I are willing to adopt the baby, but we will not take guardianship. You can let DFS make the decision, or you can make it. You need to give careful thought and prayer as to what will be best for the baby."

Karen and I locked eyes as we had so many times before. It seemed that we found understanding deep in each other's eyes. A truth that words could not convey. Something within me began to stir. A new depth of positive feelings for her began to take root—feelings that only God could bring. A slowly emerging love was taking us out of the harsh reality we were living and moving us to a place of pure grace.

"I don't know," Karen said. "I don't want DFS to take the baby, but I'm not sure if I'm ready to relinquish my rights and give the baby up for adoption."

I sat silently, letting Karen process her choices.

"The baby is not due until the end of October," I said. "You have some time to think, but not that much time. If you decide that you want us to adopt, we need to find an attorney to start the process. We'll talk again. It's your decision. I trust God will help you make it."

I needed to take my own advice. I needed to trust God for the outcome as well. I couldn't allow myself to get emotionally attached to one outcome or the other. Not while my emotions were still so raw. I couldn't trust myself to know what would be best for the innocent, unsuspecting infant who continued to grow in Karen's womb. I, along with Karen, would have to wait to hear from God.

The visit was short, maybe fifteen minutes. When I got home I walked into the living room where Al looked up at me with questions in his eyes. With a smile and a wink, I let him know I had delivered the message. We would wait on God to speak to Karen. However long that would be.

Two days later, I called the jail and learned that Karen had been returned to Lusk. I would have to wait until I received a letter to know when to set up another visit.

A few days passed, and then a letter came from Karen with the name and number of an attorney. She wanted me to call the woman and discuss adoption with her. Karen wasn't saying she was ready to relinquish her rights; she was just taking the first step. I contacted the lawyer, and she informed me about the process. I told her I would get back to her.

I wrote to Karen, telling her I could come to Lusk for another visit. We would talk about what she had decided to do.

I prayed during the drive to the prison in Lusk. Was I the best mother for this baby? Was it wise to raise this baby in a home that would always have the memory of Hannah's brutal death? Would some young couple, not able to have children, living somewhere far from this tragedy, be a better choice? I had struggled, wrestled, and lost sleep over such thoughts. Only God knew what was best for this little one. We had sought his will, and I needed to rest in that.

At the prison, I sat in the small room and watched as an officer brought Karen inside. She was still in ankle chains and cuffed to a belly belt, but this time he uncuffed one of her hands so she could hold the phone more easily.

She didn't waste any time telling me her decision. "I have decided to relinquish the baby to you and Al. The attorney I wrote to you about wants to help. She will do the paperwork for me at a low cost, but I don't have any money. Can you pay her? You would have to pay for your own attorney as well, I guess. Can you do that?" Her drawn face and bloodshot eyes showed the stress and wrestling she had been going through.

My throat tightened. I found it hard to speak. "If we do this, we'll use your attorney. I want to make sure that we both agree about everything, without any regrets. Are you okay with that?"

I kept my eyes locked on her, trying to read her eyes, her face. I was looking for sincerity. For conviction. I wasn't going to play around with such an important decision. I needed to know she was sure of what she was saying.

"Yes," she said, her eyes never leaving mine.

Our joint decision had now been made. God's decision had yet to be revealed.

Chapter 15

Unexpected Standoff

THE SILENCE WAS DEAFENING.

For sixteen years, as an extremely active foster mom, I was used to frequent communication with DFS. Whether discussing new children arriving, current children leaving, upcoming or recent home visits, health updates, or progress reports, I'd always appreciated the excellent communication we had. My yellow phone had been like an umbilical cord passing critical information back and forth and connecting each of our 140 foster children to the agency that bore responsibility for their well-being—until the Bower children were abruptly placed back with Karen. Then it had become my useless conduit for concerns about Hannah that went into what seemed to me like a black hole of apparent DFS incompetence. Even then I'd placed hope in every call I'd made. During those frustrating months that Hannah was missing, I'd continued to accept calls from DFS, taking in the foster children who needed a home.

Now, as the community's anger boiled over a child lying dead in a garage for nine months while DFS didn't even know she was missing, DFS went silent—not for a matter of days but for weeks. And not just with me, but with everyone—the press and other foster families included. It was as if they had shut their doors and pulled the shades until attorneys instructed them how to handle the community that had united in outrage. Letters to the editor, newspaper articles, and general conversations throughout Casper appeared to focus even more outrage toward the Department of Family Services than toward Karen.

"I bet heads are rolling there."

"They are sure to have a major lawsuit against them."

"They dropped the ball on this one. How could a child fall through the cracks like that?"

According to the Casper *Star Tribune*, Hannah's father had filed a lawsuit against DFS.

I resonated with the anger and criticism in the community. We all wanted answers.

Then, the first week of September, two months after the heart-wrenching call that Hannah's body had been discovered, I received a call from a DFS caseworker. It was someone I was unfamiliar with. Though surprised at the call, I felt hopeful that communication with the government agency was about to resume. The woman on the phone told me, rather firmly, that our conversation would be limited to only the needs of the two children I was fostering—a premature infant and an eight-year-old boy. No other questions would be answered. Her statement sounded rehearsed, a directive I guessed came from attorneys and her supervisors.

Our conversation was brief. I said nothing of my visits with Karen. I felt I needed to keep that information to myself until I knew the intent of DFS in this case. Though glad to have finally received a call from someone at the agency, I continued to wonder what was going on behind the closed doors and why the phones went unanswered.

Meanwhile, the adoption attorney gave us papers to fill out and asked for copies of certificates and documents. We had maybe five weeks before the baby was due to have everything in order so she could present our case to the court.

Then we hit a snag. Karen wanted us to keep Bower as the last name for the child. Al and I strongly disagreed with her. If we were to adopt, the last name would have to be our family name. We talked about keeping Karen's last name as, perhaps, a middle name. I agreed we would think about that, but Moerke needed to be the legal last name. The child would otherwise always feel he or she was not a full member of our family in the same way our other children were.

Working out an agreeable adoption plan took time—time we didn't have. A date for Karen's C-section was planned for late October, but the baby could come early. If we didn't have everything signed and in place prior to its birth, DFS could step in and take the infant. We had to compromise. We agreed to pray about it once again and do what we all felt was best for the child.

As I prayed, giving the decision up to God, I felt drawn to the story in the Bible from 1 Kings 3:16-28 in which two prostitutes living in the same house each had a baby son, born three days apart. During the night, one woman inadvertently rolled over onto her son, killing him. So she sneaked to the bedside of the other woman who was sound asleep and switched babies.

The next morning when the woman awoke, she saw that the baby by her side was not only dead but was not her child. The two appeared before King Solomon, each arguing that the living child was her own. Neither would relent in their argument, so finally the king said, "Bring me a sword." Then he issued an order: "Cut the living child in two and give half to one and half to the other."

The real mother, moved out of love for her son, said to the king, "Please, my lord, give her the living baby! Don't kill him!"

But the other woman said, "Neither I nor you shall have him. Cut him in two!"

The king then instructed that the baby be given to the first woman, declaring her as the baby's mother. Scripture then says,

"When all Israel heard the verdict the king had given, they held the king in awe, because they saw that he had wisdom from God to administer justice" (1 Kings 3:28).

Peace filled my heart as I contemplated the story. I was reminded that the Lord, the ultimate judge, saw Karen's and my heart and knew we wanted what was best for the infant. As the perfect judge, the Lord already knew the best option for this child, even if that meant placing the infant with DFS. I had to be open to whatever the Lord decided. I needed to be willing to surrender this child into his hands, giving up my rights and desires. I wanted to trust his will, because I knew his ways are so far beyond what we can understand.

After a few weeks of working through the adoption plan, Karen decided to give up her legal rights and her desire to have the baby bear her last name in order that her unborn child would have the chance at a good life, with loving people she knew. In return, the reward for her would be knowing who parented her baby and being able to know how the child was doing as it grew up.

The attorney drew up the documents, we both signed, and then we waited. As the papers were being filed with the court, I received a call from our attorney. She said, "I want to warn you. DFS knows you are working with Karen to adopt the baby. They plan to show up on the hearing date and fight you for guardianship. They plan to get custody of the infant as soon as it is born."

Her words pierced my heart, and I felt a bolt of panic surge through me. I couldn't speak. A sudden ringing filled my ears, and my eyes couldn't focus clearly. DFS was going to "fight us" for the baby? The words alone felt like an attack. I was overwhelmed with hurt that they would wage a campaign against my husband and me after we'd worked so closely with them for sixteen years. Why? I'd seen us as a team, wanting to protect and help children. Now, they were out to fight us for custody? It couldn't be because the agency thought we were unfit. We still had two foster children in our home.

I decided to call the caseworker I had come to care about and value over the past year—Jill, the one who trusted me enough to call and ask me if I had any information that might help with locating Hannah when they couldn't find her. The one who had enough concern for me to call and let me know Hannah's body was found before I saw it on the evening news. I wanted to hear from her why they were going to fight to keep us from adopting Karen's baby.

I paced the floor of my kitchen, listening to the endless ringing of the DFS line. I yelled into the receiver, "Someone pick up!"

A feeling of betrayal raged through my heart. These were the very people I had come to trust through the years, some of whom I respected and would even say I loved. I knew in my heart they didn't think we were unfit to parent the child. But what had I done that they wanted to fight me? There had to be more to this decision.

I gasped with relief as a live person came on the phone.

"Department of Family Services, how may I help you?"

"I would like to speak with Jill, please." I drew in a breath to try to calm my quivering voice.

"May I ask who's calling?" I recognized the voice of the receptionist.

"Debra Moerke," I said, my heart pounding.

She told me Jill was in a meeting and she would be happy to connect me to her voice mail if I would like.

Having no choice, I agreed.

"Hi, Jill. This is Deb Moerke. Would you please give me a call back? Today? Thank you." My message was short and almost curt.

She'll know. She'll know that I heard about the agency's plan to fight the adoption. But that doesn't matter. She has to talk to me. I need her to explain what is going on.

The day ended with no call from Jill. My frustration grew deeper, and I decided that I'd go downtown to the DFS office in the morning and wait in the lobby until someone would meet with me.

The next day, after Al went to work and all the kids were at school, I drove to the DFS office and stood in line to talk to the receptionist. Through a glass window I could see office workers at their desks. One woman glanced up at me with a surprised look. Watching me, she picked up the phone on her desk, pushed a few buttons, and spoke into the receiver. Suddenly, a side door to the lobby opened and Jill was standing there.

"Deb! Hi. You want to follow me?" She sounded friendly, but her cheeks appeared flushed as I walked across the lobby to meet her.

"It's good to see you," Jill said with a professional tone as she began walking down a long hallway. As I passed open office doors, caseworkers at their desks looked up and took a double take. From the stunned expressions on their faces, I felt they all knew why I was there.

Jill entered a large office and motioned toward a chair. "Have a seat." Then she took a seat behind her desk. "What can I do for you?" Her smile appeared forced.

Where was the warm young Christian caseworker I had grown so fond of? Jill's behavior made me uneasy. I looked around the office, wondering if there was a two-way mirror or a tape recorder hidden somewhere. As my eyes searched the room I could sense Jill watching me. I believed she knew I didn't trust the environment.

I flashed her a quick smile as I settled in the chair. "I heard that DFS is going to fight us on adopting Karen Bower's baby. I don't understand why, and thought you might be able to fill me in."

I knew the visit had to be difficult for Jill. She represented DFS, and we both knew that since Hannah's body was found, our relationship had to change. Hannah's murder had placed us on opposing sides. I wasn't looking out for DFS, but I knew she needed to. I respected Jill and tried to make it easier on her, wondering if ears might be listening or eyes might be watching.

Sitting up straight, Jill took a deep breath and quietly said, "We know you have been visiting Karen at the jail and prison. Our job is to protect children"—my stomach lurched at those words—"and we feel that your relationship with Karen would put the baby in harm's way if you were to have guardianship. You may take the child to the prison, and that could be dangerous. So, DFS feels that in the best interest of the child, we need to take guardianship and custody."

My eyes narrowed and locked in on Jill's. I paused for a moment and thought, *Your agency has been on lockdown for weeks because of the murder of a child that was under the supervision of DFS, and you are worried about us?* Fury rose from my heart, and through my clenched jaw I said, "Really?"

Jill's eyes widened as if she were preparing for me to blow up.

Leaning toward her, I drew in a deep breath, readying myself to speak my heart. "You know this baby would not only be safe with us, but loved as well. I believe DFS wants to save face and have control over all of Karen's other children since they failed to protect Hannah. I know there is a lawsuit being brought against DFS, and I suspect DFS is trying to present itself as the best option for this baby. But it wasn't me who had authority over Hannah and her sisters and brothers for fourteen months. It wasn't me who failed to keep an eye on what was going on in their mother's home after they left mine. And it wasn't me who failed to find out, for nine months, that Hannah had been beaten to death by her mother and her body stuffed in a garbage bag stashed in the garage of her home."

In a deep, unwavering tone, I went on. "We have been foster parents for sixteen years with this agency. My husband and I have been asked, on a number of occasions, to share at trainings for new foster families because DFS felt we were such great examples of a successful foster family. When the news team in Casper wanted to do a special Mother's Day highlight on their show and wanted to use a foster mother in the community, DFS gave them my name.

We have two foster children right now. You haven't pulled them out, saying we are an unfit or questionable foster home. Now caseworkers feel I would put Karen's unborn baby in harm's way if we were to go for adoption?"

Jill said nothing.

Though my tone was low, my words were firm. "I know you are in a tough position. I don't know if I am being recorded or watched right now, but I will tell you this. I will do what God calls me to do before I do what man wants me to do. You are a Christian. I know you understand what I am saying. God has called Al and me to move forward in adopting this baby, and that is what we will do. I have gone to court in support of DFS in the past. It looks like this time we will be on opposite sides. That makes me very sad, but even so, I will fight for this baby. I had no authority to protect Hannah, but I do have the opportunity to protect this little one, and I believe God is calling me to do so."

Jill didn't speak. I could see a little sparkle in her eye and the slightest hint of a smile. Was she trying to say something? The stiffness in her body appeared to dissipate. Her shoulders relaxed.

We sat for a moment studying each other. Neither of us spoke.

Then I stood, thanked Jill for her time, and walked out of her office.

The Arrival

THE PHONE RECORDING FROM the Casper jail played the familiar message. Karen was in town. I knew her time would be limited and that within a day or two she would be returned to the women's prison in Lusk. It would be important that my short time with her be used to finalize our plan.

It had been a week since I had spoken with Jill at DFS. My frustration simmered, and my concern for the future of Karen's baby haunted me as the birth date grew closer. I wanted my trust in God to be unwavering, but waver it did. I had to keep reminding myself to fully surrender this to God's will—that however it unfolded would be perfect.

Evening came, and the dinner dishes were put away. Al and I gathered our children in the living room to discuss where we were with the adoption process. Our kids admitted to mixed feelings. What would be best for the baby? Would it be difficult to have Hannah's sibling in our home as a constant reminder of Hannah and what had happened? Would there be people in the community who would think we should not adopt Karen's infant, believing that DFS should have the baby adopted out of state or, at least, out of Casper? All were great questions. Then came the big one. If God had called us to adopt this little one, would we be able to protect it from going into the foster care system knowing we hadn't been able to protect Hannah?

The decision was unanimous. We would move forward and see what God had in store for the baby as well as for our family.

As our conversation ended, I told my children I was going to town. "Karen is in Casper at the jail. I want to tell her how we all feel." I watched as everyone's demeanor changed when I mentioned Karen. Folded arms, stares out the window, shaking heads—disgust written all over their faces. But no one commented. No one said not to go.

I kissed Al and each of our children on the top of their heads, then picked up my keys and left. The drive to the jail was lonely. A heaviness of responsibility and uncertainty, of what the future held, weighed on my soul. The questions my family had were the very questions I had mulled over for weeks. As I pulled into the parking lot of the detention center, my silent prayer was one of complete confusion. *What am I to do, God? This is so hard. I believe I am to keep moving forward.* Was I doubting God, or myself? I bowed my head and closed my eyes. *I need confirmation from you, Lord.*

Alone in the visiting area, I paced the short hall remembering every conversation with Karen. We had come far in our relationship over the past three months. What would the sentence be—the death penalty or life in prison? After sentencing, would our talks continue? If DFS ended up with the baby, what would we talk about? What, other than God, would connect us?

When Karen finally arrived, she appeared so much more pregnant than when I had seen her just weeks prior. She rubbed her stomach as she walked toward me. Her cheeks were flushed with a pink glow and her hair was neatly combed. We both chuckled as we attempted to give each other a hug around her big belly.

"You look great! How are you feeling?" I asked as we both sat down.

"I'm feeling good. I can finally sleep. I was brought to Casper for a doctor's appointment tomorrow. I think we are still looking at the end of October or first of November, but I'll see what the doctor says. At my last appointment she said everything was looking good." Karen spoke with a lift in her voice. She appeared at peace and not stressed. I had to wonder if part of the reason was because she wasn't wearing a belly belt or ankle chains for this visit.

"I talked with my family. We are all on board for the adoption but not without reservations. There are some mixed feelings. I didn't tell my children yet, but I found out last week that DFS is planning to fight us for the baby." I watched Karen's face closely for how she would respond.

Karen puckered her lips and shook her head as she often did when she disagreed with something. "I know. The attorney told me. I can't believe it! But she says there isn't any legitimate reason why DFS should get custody. We have a good chance for the adoption to go through."

I shrugged. "I don't know. They seem to think they have grounds to prevent the adoption."

Karen leaned back abruptly. The shirt of her navy-blue scrubs began to dance across her stomach. We both laughed as the baby kicked and moved within her. At the sight, my heart opened up to the reality of the life within her. I could feel myself becoming drawn to the unborn child. For a sweet moment I focused on the baby and off the tragedy of Hannah. I sensed God turning our hearts to life and away from death.

"May I rest my hands on your belly and pray a blessing and protection over the baby?"

Karen nodded and smiled. I pulled my chair closer to hers, facing her, knee to knee. Resting both my hands on her belly, feeling the firmness of the baby inside her, I began to pray. Karen placed her hands on top of mine.

At first her hands felt warm and comforting. But then I remembered that these were the hands that had stuffed Hannah's little body into a trash bag and carried her to the garage where she was tucked away for almost a year. I slipped my hands out from under hers and placed them on top. That simple act freed me emotionally to pray for both the baby and Karen and for God's will and perfect plan. By letting go of my will, my desires, and my hurt and confusion, I gave both mother and child to God. He was in control, not I. His plan for both of them was already set in motion. How I would be used in their lives was still left to be seen. I felt a step closer to the full surrender I wanted to have.

After Karen's doctor appointment the next day, she was transported back to the prison. I would not see her for at least two weeks. The waiting for the birth began.

My friend Pammy had offered to join me at the hospital if Al was not in town, so I called her with the new date for the C-section: November 5. With only weeks before the birth, I wondered what the people at DFS were planning. Surely, they would also have the new date. Would they swoop in and take the child immediately? For now, all any of us could do was wait. Would the baby come before the scheduled C-section? If not, November 5 was circled on my calendar, and I would be prayed up, ready for the birth and the court battle. Our attorney had explained to us that adoption would require a two-stage process. First, we would have to win guardianship at a hearing. Then we'd await court approval of the adoption. When would that guardianship hearing take place? We could only hope to have all of that resolved before the birth.

On October 28 I received a call from the lieutenant at the jail, telling me Karen would be brought to Casper that evening. The baby was ready, so the doctor scheduled the C-section the next morning at 5:00 a.m. The lieutenant said I had permission to be present at the hospital, but for security reasons, I could tell no one except my family. I explained that Al was out of town and I was planning to bring Pammy, so he gave permission for her to know.

The next morning, I drove to the hospital around 4:30, leaving Sadie in charge and sleeping children in their beds. A light morning snow fell as I drove to town. It seemed as if I were the only person in the world awake.

When I arrived, the worn oak bench in the hospital corridor was a welcome sight, offering a place for me to rest from my sleepless night. I wrapped my coat around me and sat down at the end. Snow dripped from my boots and formed a small puddle.

I fixed my eyes on the door to the delivery room at the end of the hall and wondered, *Have they started yet?*

The dim, vacant waiting area had an eerie feel to it. Patients were still asleep, and the nursing staff was reviewing medical charts, preparing for a shift change. The memory of being on the same floor only two years before to pick up Hannah's baby sister as our foster child, flashed across my mind. That event had launched me on this journey. Would I be bringing this baby home just as I had baby Ally?

Suddenly, the elevator dinged. The metal doors slid open, and like floating spirits, four silhouettes exited and walked toward me. I could see Pammy behind three others. She was a comforting sight. But I dreaded seeing the three who preceded her—a policeman accompanying two social service caseworkers, one of whom was Jill.

Seriously? A police escort? Why? Are they afraid I'm going to make some kind of trouble?

Pammy maneuvered her way around the trio and tucked herself in close to me on the bench, giving me a supportive hug, then wrapped her arm through mine.

An angel unaware. I tried to ignore the unwelcomed opposition now sitting across from us.

Do they have to sit so close?

The presence of the three intruders left little privacy for Pammy and me to talk. There was only so much five people in a small hospital waiting area could do to avoid eye contact. Minutes passed. Pammy and I sat silently. There was no place to go. We had to wait for word of the baby's birth, but I decided I couldn't submit to another moment of silent intimidation. Taking a deep breath, I looked directly at the three who were staring right at us. Their eyes widened as I offered an introductory smile.

"Good morning," I said.

Each of the three gave a quick, uncomfortable nod. One of the caseworkers whispered, "Good morning." It was as if none of them knew whether they should be speaking to me.

When on opposing sides of a battle, should one speak with the enemy? I mentally chastised myself. *They are not the enemy. They are all just doing their jobs. I am not their enemy either. Months ago, we would all have been sitting on the same bench.*

But for now, there was conflict, division, and mistrust. It was appropriate that we sit across from one another this morning. It was also sad to know that the relationship my family and I had had with DFS for sixteen years seemed to have evaporated overnight. Now, all of us had become victims.

At 5:35 a.m. the delivery room doors swung open. Dr. Myers, draped in drab green scrubs, paper bonnet, and surgical mask, made his grand entrance into the hallway. He carried a bundle in a white hospital blanket. The cowboy doc was in true character, wearing western boots under his sterile paper booties. With a Clydesdale stride down the long hallway, I could see his eyes shift from the DFS entourage to Pammy and me.

Like three birds perched on a wire, the caseworkers and officer came to attention.

Shifting his glance sharply, he focused on me and his eyes brightened. I could see a smile under the rim of his mask as it rose up his cheeks.

Dr. Myers was our beloved family pediatrician who had cared for our five children as well as the nearly 140 foster children we had had in our home. At my request, and with Karen's approval, he had agreed to take care of this baby after its birth.

I remained expressionless, not moving from the bench. Though my heart was racing, I didn't want to appear to be challenging the three officials across from me. Pammy followed my lead.

Marching up to me, Dr. Myers leaned forward and gently unwrapped the bundle, enough for a peek. He winked, then announced quietly, "It's a girl." Ignoring the other visitors, he covered the infant and continued with a clomp, clomp, clomp down the hall to the nursery with the bundle safe in his arms.

Resting the palm of my hand on my chest to quiet my pounding heart, I bowed my head and whispered a prayer. "Thank you, Jesus, for this precious new life."

As morning darkness gave way to daylight, Pammy needed to get home to her own children. She gave me another hug before leaving. "Call me later," she whispered.

I sat alone, left with three bewildered faces staring at me. I felt an unwarranted responsibility to be the birth announcer. I crossed the invisible boundary in the middle of the hall and uncomfortably entered their territory.

"It's a girl," I whispered, as if I was supposed to keep it a secret.

We all smiled at each other, and for a moment it appeared as if we were all family members sharing in the joy of the new birth. Within seconds, the reality of who we *really* were darkened the moment, and we found ourselves soberly straight-faced once again.

"Thank you," Jill said, as the three got up and headed toward the elevator. *That's it? They're leaving?*

I waited until they were out of sight, then quickly made my way to the nursery just as the hospital lights came on for the day.

Through the nursery window, I could see a nurse bathing the new arrival. The unhappy infant bellowed and waved tiny closed fists, letting everyone know she was not happy. I smiled as tears rolled down my cheeks. *Heavenly Father, you are amazing.*

Karen was still in recovery. I would come back later in the day. For now, five children at home were waking up for school. They would be hungry and needing Mom to give the morning instructions. Breakfast, bed making, teeth brushing, and school dressing would fill the next hour. I headed home. No sweet baby girl to tuck into an infant seat this time. I would have to go before a judge and wait to hear recommendations for the future of this little one.

It was unnerving to still have guardianship unresolved. We expected that DFS would be at that hearing fighting us for guardianship. I found some comfort knowing that Karen's and my attorney would guide us through that ordeal. More important, I knew God would be there at the courthouse. I would entrust the judge into God's hands.

As I headed down the highway to Goose Egg Road, Proverbs 3:5 came to mind. *"Trust in the LORD with all your heart and lean not on your own understanding."* I recited the Scripture over in my head as I drove home to care for the children who awaited me.

Chapter 17

The Painted Stone

Around noon that day, I received a call from our adoption attorney telling me the hearing was scheduled for ten o'clock the next morning in the judge's chambers. DFS would definitely be there trying to win guardianship. While I wasn't looking forward to a court battle with my former allies, I was grateful to know that our wait was almost over.

After a busy day of transporting children and working at the rescue mission, I brought pizza home for the kids for dinner so I could go see Karen. Helen and Charles were excited about the baby. Sadie was quiet and reserved. I called Al with the news. He said he wished he could be with me but would be praying about the hearing. With the kids settled in for the evening, I gave them a kiss, then left for the hospital.

Hoping to get more than just a peek at the little girl I'd glimpsed in the early hours, I peered through the nursery window at the row of sleeping infants. Soft brown hair and a round pudgy little face were all I could see of the only girl newborn. The tag on her bassinet was labeled Bower. Her body was wrapped snugly, like a burrito, in a pale green nursery blanket. Her long eyelashes feathered under her closed eyelids, and her tiny lips pressed together as if she were nursing. I chuckled. Even in her sleep, she was dreaming of food.

"Excuse me," I said as I approached the nurses' station. "Can you tell me what room Karen Bower is in?"

The woman looked up from her desk at me, sliding her reading glasses to the end of her nose. "She is in a special room off the nursery. You will need to talk with the nurse on duty. Are you the chaplain from the jail? She said you might be coming by to see her."

Relieved that I was expected, I confirmed that I was.

"We understand that you can visit her. She is under security watch, as I'm sure you know." The woman smiled, then went back to tapping away on her keyboard.

I stepped into the nursery. The on-duty nurse was charting information on a clipboard. "May I help you?" she said.

"I was told you could show me where Karen Bower is. I'm here for a visit."

"Are you the chaplain?"

I nodded.

With her hands full, she nodded toward the door next to me. "Push it open. She's in there."

The room was not much bigger than the hospital bed Karen lay in. A small counter with a sink and emergency medical equipment attached to the wall made the room seem crowded and sterile. I closed the door quietly behind me and tiptoed to the right side of the bed. Karen lay asleep, with her left wrist handcuffed to the side rail.

Really? Do they think she'll run away after just having a C-section? I had to remind myself that she'd confessed to murder and the security was necessary. I watched her sleep for a few minutes. Before waking her, I remembered something I had read on a plaque at my children's Christian school. "Sin will always take you further than you want to go . . . cost you more than you want to pay . . . and keep you longer than you want to stay." Karen was living that out and would do so for the rest of her life. I could give her a few minutes of sleep and rest from her consequences.

Suddenly, I realized I had no business wrestling with Karen's sin. I had my own to deal with. Like Paul the apostle, I do what I don't want to do and don't do what I should. And yet, like me, Karen had the promise from God to forgive her and cleanse her from all unrighteousness. I had to remember that.

Karen took in a deep breath and let out a waking sigh. Her eyelids fluttered slightly before she opened them and smiled weakly at me. She attempted to shift her body using her right hand, but she could barely brace herself with the little strength of her left handcuffed wrist.

"Ouch!" She rolled to one side. "I forgot about the stitches." She laughed faintly.

"How are you doing?" I whispered.

"I'm okay, I guess." She leaned on her left elbow, trying to get more comfortable. "I've been sleeping most the day. Whatever they gave me pretty well knocked me out. What time is it?"

I looked around the room for a clock. There was none. Thinking about what time I had left the house, I took a guess. "It's almost 7:30 in the evening."

"Did you get to see her? I haven't seen her. They won't bring her to me because of my security status. They strapped both my hands down for the C-section and knocked me out. I wasn't awake to see her. I just want to hold her for a minute. I don't know when I will be transported back to the prison, but I don't think they will keep me here long. I wish I could see her before I leave."

As a mother, my heart filled with sorrow for her. I couldn't imagine not being able to see my baby and hold her. But there was protocol to be followed. Due to the circumstances, there was little pity for a mother who gave birth after taking the life of one of her other children.

"Have you thought of a name?" I asked, focusing on something positive.

"I like the name Courtney a lot. What do you think?" Karen's face seemed to light up just saying the name.

"It's a cute name. What about a middle name?"

"I thought I would leave that up to you. You should be able to have a say in the name. At least part of it."

"I like Grace or Faith or Hope," I said. "Any of them would say what God has brought into our lives with her birth."

"I like Faith. Courtney Faith. It's all about our faith in what God can and will do in our lives, don't you think?"

Was Karen already shifting her heart toward the Lord? It was the first time I had ever heard her speak about God or faith other than during our forgiveness discussion. I dared to believe at that moment that she was truly at the beginning of listening to God and responding to his voice.

"Faith, it is!"

Karen and I grinned. However big or small our faith was, it felt huge that evening. Courtney Faith had entered the world, and with her entrance, she brought life and joy.

Though I didn't want to interrupt the sweet moment, I needed to talk to Karen about the next day. "The court hearing is at ten o'clock. Can we pray together now—for God's will and for the judge to decide what will be best for Courtney?" I reached out my hands, palms up, to take Karen's. She reached across her still swollen stomach with her right hand and opened her left, cuffed hand to welcome mine.

"Dear heavenly Father, we come before you with humble hearts. We ask that you forgive us for our sins and that you would hear our joint prayer for the future of Courtney Faith. We pray for the judge, that you prepare his heart and mind to hear truth. Give him wisdom to make the best decision for Courtney. Help us to accept that decision and to trust that you know what the future holds for this new life and only you know what will be best for her.

Continue to work in Karen's life and heart and help her to know you as her Lord and Savior and to trust you with her life, as well. Thank you, Father. Amen."

As we ended our prayer, the nurse entered the room to take Karen's vital signs. It seemed like a good time for me to leave.

"If I can, I will let you know how everything goes tomorrow. If I can't, I'm sure our attorney will come to tell you." I squeezed Karen's hand. She nodded and gave a squeeze in return. I marveled at the tenderness I was feeling toward this woman—evidence that God was at work in my heart.

The sky darkened as I drove home. Clouds full of forecasted snow hovered over Casper Mountain. A light rain had dampened the road while I visited Karen. The day had warmed up and the cool air that had moved down from the mountain brought a mist that floated across the highway. Fall, like spring in Wyoming, was unpredictable. Tomorrow there could be sunshine or snow showers. Either way, my black suit-dress and pumps would be the most appropriate to wear to court.

I spent much of the evening formulating a plan for the following day. Sadie would drive the van to take our kids to school and pick them up. I'd drive the Skunk Truck. Though it was an eyesore and a challenge to shift at times, the old truck was reliable and available. It was the one vehicle that pulled all the others out of the snow and mud. The Skunk Truck always started, even in subzero temperatures.

The next morning, I dressed in my court clothes and met Sadie at the front door with keys to the van. "I don't know what will happen this morning," I said, hugging her before she, Helen, and Charles loaded up in the van. "Get the kids to school and pick them up on time. I should know by late this morning if I will be bringing home the baby later today or not. I will call you from work and let you know if anything changes."

My midcalf black suit-dress with brass buttons up the front and black pumps gave me the confidence I needed to appear before the judge. Before climbing into the Skunk Truck, I strapped seat belts across our two foster children. One was only months old herself. Climbing into the front seat and strapping myself in, I followed the family van into town. By 8:30 a.m., all the children were at their intended destinations for the day.

As silly as I felt for it, I didn't want to be seen driving the Skunk Truck in town any more than my daughter would have wanted to drive it to her high school, so I wore my sunglasses and took the tree-lined side streets to the old stucco Wyoming Rescue Mission downtown.

The truck bounced over the curb and rolled to a stop in the parking lot. As ladylike as I could in a fitted dress and pantyhose, I opened the door to the truck, turned my body, slid to the left, and swung my legs out of the truck. Looking to see if anyone was watching, I jumped down onto the blacktop. My dress rose a little and twisted. The center buttons were now on the side of my thigh instead of the front of my body, so I tugged and straightened my dress to look presentable. I felt awkward, as though I were climbing out of a Sherman tank all dressed up. How fitting for such an awkward day with a court battle before me.

Entering the Little House (the nickname for the old building that had once been a small home), I made my way around the rectangular table where six men, gruff and worn from street life, leaned over paperback Bibles. One of the residents, just as scruffy as the others, led the study. A few of the men scooted their metal chairs so I could make my way to my office door.

"Morning, gentlemen," I said.

"Morning, Miss Deb," the men mumbled.

"You sure look nice today," one announced. They had not seen me so dressed up before. The usual dress for staff at the mission was much more casual, usually blue jeans.

None of the men looked quite awake. Coffee was not offered at the mission. The director felt it was a stimulant the guests did not need. I sure needed it. I had to drink two cups before heading to work in the morning and usually could use a third, though I dared not bring a to-go cup of the wretched caffeine into the building.

My office was toasty. I was sure it was Joe who had gone in early and turned the antique heater on for me. Files were stacked on the old, distressed wooden desk. Sad files. Files with stories of broken women who stayed at the mission needing help, love, and hope. Some of the women came fresh out of prison. Many had lost everything. Their home, husband, job, and sometimes, even children. Most had lost their dignity. I thought of Karen. She'd never need our services. She was never getting out. My job as chaplain was to give these women hope. I could use some hope myself this morning.

The knock at my office door was a familiar sound for that time of the morning. Only Maureen came to my office first thing. Maureen's home was the mission. She had been there so long she was almost considered an employee. Maureen would gather stones on her daily walks around town. She was quite selective. Bringing the stones back to the mission, she would wash them and then, using acrylic paints, paint little landscapes on one side and Scripture on the other—Maureen's personalized gifts. Often she would come to my office in the mornings and share her most recent creations with me.

She took a seat in the antique wood rocker next to my desk and began to rock without saying a word.

Staring at me for a moment, she blurted out, "Are you going to a funeral today?"

"No. I'm going to court."

"Court?" Maureen would always probe, even though she bragged about never wanting to intrude. "So, you dress in black to go to court? Are you in trouble?"

"No. It's just something I need to take care of. It will be fine, really."

Maureen handed me a small white box tied with coral-colored ribbon. I held the little lightly stained box with both hands, handling it as if it were breakable glass.

"Well . . . before you go, you might want to open your gift. Since I'm always showing you the stones I paint for other people, I asked God what I should paint for you. This is what he told me." Maureen sat up taller, displaying pride and a little sass.

Lifting the lid, I found Kleenex cradling the treasure inside. I carefully lifted out a stone and placed it in my open palm so I could read the painted words.

BE NOT AFRAID . . . ONLY BELIEVE. MARK 5:36

The shiny white paint sparkled against the smooth, smoky gray stone. Tears sprang to my eyes as I wrapped my fingers around the smooth stone, hugging it to my chest.

"Are you okay?" Maureen asked. "I didn't mean to upset you."

"This is exactly what I needed this morning." My throat tightened. I could hardly speak. I stood and took her face in my hands. Looking directly into her eyes I said, "You could never have known, but God did. He used you to remind me that he is with me. Thank you for listening to him." I kissed her forehead and gave her a hug.

"You are welcome," Maureen announced with conviction. "Isn't he great!"

"Yes. He is, Maureen. I know he will be with me today in court."

"What time is court?" Maureen asked.

Looking at my watch, I saw it was already after nine o'clock.

"Oh! I need to go. Court is at ten. I can't be late." I gathered my keys, hugged Maureen again, and with the stone in hand, ran out the door.

"Don't you have a coat or sweater?" Maureen yelled out to me. "It's supposed to snow today."

I had asked friends and family to intercede for me during the hearing. As I drove toward the downtown business area, I asked God to stir their spirits to start praying.

I arrived at the courthouse forty minutes early. I hoped my attorney would be there on time to meet me before I had to enter the judge's chambers.

Holding tightly to my dress this time, I jumped down from the Skunk Truck. I nearly stumbled out of a shoe as I quickly climbed the steps to the old municipal courthouse. As always, I admired the brass door handles, cement statues, and marble floors of the historic structure built in the early 1900s. My black pumps echoed down the cathedral-like hall as I walked briskly to the courtrooms next to the judge's chambers, passing men and women in suits waiting outside courtroom doors and a couple quietly arguing next to a water fountain. The smell of cedar wood and leather briefcases filled the air as I quickly made my way to the judge's chambers. I did not open the door but looked for a quiet, secluded place to sit and wait for my attorney.

The hallway's walls were lined with framed portraits of judges, past and present. Some looked very distinguished. Some a little creepy. Honorable this, and Honorable that. I didn't recognize any of them. Why would I? I hadn't been to court for anything before. One retired judge's name stood out, though. He was *the* judge who had ordered the five Bower children home. Home without a plan. No warning. No reason. No preparation. Then, leaving many questions unanswered, he retired.

Seeing the judge's picture, my heart began to pound. I nervously twisted my ring. Would *today's* judge listen to all sides? What would he decide?

I glanced at my watch: 9:50. Where was my attorney? Time was running out to be briefed.

I hope she's not late, I thought, as I twisted my ring a few more times.

Hearing voices and footsteps, I saw two DFS caseworkers I recognized heading toward me. Accompanying them was a man I hadn't seen before. He was tall, had a receding hairline, and was wearing thick, dark-framed glasses. His starched white dress shirt and argyle knitted vest didn't seem to be an attorney's attire. At least not in my experience. *Is he an attorney? Or is he someone with DFS?*

The three didn't seem to notice me, before disappearing behind the door of room 305.

As I was about to panic, my attorney appeared out of the stairwell a few yards away. Approaching quickly and out of breath, she asked, "Have you spoken to anyone?"

"No. I've been waiting for you." My hands were wet with sweat, and my mouth felt dry and pasty. I desperately wanted a drink of water, but there was no time.

"Follow me," she said. We entered room 305 and a legal assistant led us to the judge's chambers.

Inside, diplomas, group pictures of judges, and a huge watercolor mural of the city of Casper from the early 1900s hung on the paneled walls. A rich, dark wood conference table with a dozen high-back swivel chairs filled the room. At the end of the long table, an oversized black leather chair, with a cushioned headrest and armrests signified that someone of great responsibility and power would be sitting there.

I followed my attorney's lead as we entered the room and chose chairs directly across from the DFS caseworkers and the mysterious man.

I squeezed the stone I still held in my sweaty hand. I would do what was written on it. BE NOT AFRAID . . . ONLY BELIEVE!
I will believe!

I was reminded of the armor God gives those who love and choose to put their trust in him. To the others sitting across from me, my black suit-dress and black pumps were not intimidating. But if they knew, really knew, the God I served, they would be nervous. Armored up, I knew prayer for this very hour had me well covered.

Cupping my fingers around the stone, I looked across the massive table toward the judge's empty chair. A peaceful strength came over me.

My attorney leaned toward me and whispered, "What is in your hand?"

Still looking forward, I unfurled my fingers, revealing the stone and the Scripture, then slowly closed them back around it.

"What is that for?" she whispered.

"I am holding on to it, asking God to show grace and favor through the judge this morning," I whispered.

"And what if the judge doesn't show this grace you talk about?"

"Then I will stone him," I said with a wink and a slight grin.

Chapter 18

The Ruling

THE DOOR OF THE JUDGE's chambers opened abruptly, and the court assistant entered. Walking briskly around the huge conference table, she firmly instructed, "All rise!"

The judge, clad in a black flowing robe, glided past the assistant. He was distinguished looking, maybe in his early fifties, with black hair and a little graying at the temples.

A lingering hush hovered over the room as he drew his chair to the table. Opening a thick brown file folder, he handed a single document to his assistant seated at his right. A moment or two passed, and then, looking up, with a friendly but sober welcome, he announced, "Good morning!"

Soft murmurs of collective good mornings floated around the table.

"We are here this morning to consider temporary guardianship of an infant whose name is . . ." he paused and shuffled through his papers, "Courtney Faith Bower." The judge glanced at those at the table, confirming everyone was there for the right hearing.

"Would legal counsel in the room please identify yourself and provide an opening statement of who you are and who you represent? Let's start with those of you on my right." The judge's eyes fixed on the man wearing the argyle vest. He appeared to recognize him.

"Your Honor, my name is Dan Sims. I am an attorney representing the Department of Family Services. I have with me Mr. Mark Schmitt, a supervisor for the Department, and Ms. Jill Clark, a caseworker, who also works for the Department."

"Thank you, Mr. Sims."

I smiled awkwardly at the two DFS staff members whom I knew well. They avoided acknowledging me, staring at the table, then looking round the room. A rush of emotion slipped from my control, and my bottom lip began to quiver. I would fight tears at all cost. I could not let this wave of sorrow and disappointment overtake me. The devastating loss of Hannah, and now, feelings of betrayal, especially by these caseworkers, engulfed me. Hurt and rage threatened their way into my heart. I wouldn't allow it. I needed to focus. I needed to speak God's will today. I could not let my emotions preempt my words.

Looking up from his paperwork, the judge addressed my attorney and me. "Ladies?"

"Your Honor, my name is Cheryl Pryor. I am an attorney representing Mr. and Mrs. Moerke, who are seeking temporary guardianship of the infant."

"Thank you, Ms. Pryor." The judge flipped through the papers in his file. Stopping to study one, he looked up quickly and addressed Mr. Sims. "Let's begin with the Department of Family Services. Counselor, would you like to start?"

"Thank you, your Honor. As I am sure you can see in your file, the infant we are here to discuss this morning is under the Department of Family Service's legal custody. She was born yesterday morning. The infant's mother, Ms. Karen Bower, has been in prison awaiting trial for the fatal beating of one of her children. She was pregnant when picked up and arrested by the police four months ago. Five of her children have been placed in foster care since then. One is being raised by family members. The Department believes the infant should be placed in DFS custody, in an unknown protective foster home, to ensure the child's safety and care. The Department is aware that this is a high-profile case, and the protection of the Bower children is our first concern. We believe this infant could be in jeopardy if the wrong people could get access to her."

"Isn't Mrs. Moerke a foster parent with the Department of Family Services?" The judge's hands, now folded, rested on top of the file. "In fact, doesn't she have a few foster children in her home right now?"

"Yes . . . yes, your Honor," the attorney stammered.

The judge wrinkled his brow, appearing puzzled. "Why wouldn't Mrs. Moerke be considered as a foster parent for the infant since she is also seeking temporary guardianship?"

"The Department is aware that Mrs. Moerke has built a relationship with Karen Bower, the infant's birth mother. She visits her in prison and at our local detention center when she is transported here for hearings. We are concerned that, in this case, Mrs. Moerke's decision-making may be compromised."

"Thank you, Mr. Sims. Do you have any documentation for your concerns?"

A short sigh. "No, your Honor."

"Mr. Schmitt and Ms. Clark, do you have documented concerns for this infant if placed in the care of Mrs. Moerke and her family?"

The two looked at each other, then to their attorney. Mr. Sims shifted in his seat. "Well, your Honor, sir, ah, we do have our concerns since Mrs. Moerke does visit Ms. Bower at the prison. That is what we have documented."

I sat expressionless and studied the two caseworkers I had known for years. These were people I had worked side by side with for the benefit of children who had been neglected or abused.

I had suffered alongside them over sad cases of innocent children harmed emotionally, psychologically, and physically. I had rejoiced with them when children were returned to parents who loved them and simply needed parental training. Al and I had consistently made the special needs of our foster children a priority in our lives. When new foster parents asked what made us so successful with the children placed in our home, I would tell them our secret. "We offer lots of love, structure, and prayer." Some would smile, thinking there had to be much more to our techniques. I knew the truth. Strategies with love go a long way with a child. I knew prayer went even further.

I understood that the two caseworkers were under pressure and in a difficult position. I shouldn't blame them for what they had to do and say in order to protect the Department as well as their own reputations. I believed they didn't want to speak against my family or me. They were under authority to do what they were doing. I was a big believer in the principle of authority. I knew we all have the capacity to rebel against it, even though it is intended for our protection. DFS wanted to protect themselves. We wanted to protect Courtney.

The judge looked down at his file as he reclined in his tall leather chair, then took a moment to study the three professionals he had questioned. Smiling at each one, he thanked them. The caseworkers and their attorney all relaxed.

Have they won? Is that all the judge is going to ask them? Can it be that simple? Has the judge taken their side even before the hearing has begun? I sat paralyzed, squeezing the stone in the palm of my hand. *Surrender, Deb, surrender*, I reminded myself.

I had prayed that God would show me the right decision for Courtney's future through the judge's decision. Al and I had felt led by the Lord to move forward in guardianship proceedings with the plan to adopt. But I knew that God gives us direction, yet he doesn't necessarily tell us what the outcome will be. I hoped that the outcome would be for me to bring the baby home. And yet,

I believed God might want me to go through this process for some other reason. Maybe he had a different plan for the child. Was I willing to surrender to his will and embrace the outcome, no matter what?

I'd chosen to surrender to God's prompting by extending his love to Karen even though she had committed a brutal crime against an innocent child. A child I loved. As painful and difficult as it had been, in my heart I knew I'd followed God's leading. Was I correctly discerning his leading concerning guardianship and adoption? I believed I was. But now I readied myself for the judge's ruling to reveal God's will in the matter. Would I now allow the Holy Spirit to dictate my actions—to trust God no matter what— or would I choose to fear or even resent the outcome?

Surrender. It all came down to my willingness to surrender to God's will.

I again thought of King Solomon judging the case of the two women who argued over one child, still alive, and the child who had died. How would *this* judge rule? Wasn't it God who gave Solomon his wisdom? If so, he could give this judge wisdom to make the best decision.

DFS had not visited Karen in prison, placed their hands on her belly, and prayed over her infant. They hadn't prayed for Karen's health and protection as she carried the child in her womb.

The warmth of the smooth, round stone in my fist distracted me from my rising anxiety. *Be not afraid . . . Only believe.* Even if it meant the baby would remain in DFS custody, I would choose to trust God.

The judge looked at me but directed his next question to my attorney. "Ms. Pryor, did you have a statement you wanted to make on behalf of your client?"

"Yes, your Honor. My client has been a foster parent for sixteen years with the Department of Family Services. She and her husband have fostered well over a hundred children in addition to having five children of their own. Mr. and Mrs. Moerke are not only interested in temporary guardianship at this time, but wish to take steps to move forward seeking full adoption. They are serious about their commitment to the infant and would do nothing to put her in harm's way. We are asking that the court rule in favor of Mr. and Mrs. Moerke, for temporary guardianship, your Honor."

The judge rocked a little in his chair as if each movement helped him process the information. Then, with a sudden halt, he simply said, "Thank you, Counselor." He folded his hands, leaned back, and stared for a moment at the three sitting across from me. Then, he directed a pensive gaze at me. I had no idea what he could be thinking. I braced myself for the questions about to come. *If only Al were here.* I could hear the pounding of my own heart throbbing in my ears.

"Mrs. Moerke." The judge leaned forward. "I would like to hear from *you.* Why are you interested in adopting this child? You have five children of your own."

I squeezed the stone now sandwiched between both palms. This is where I needed to *believe.* This is where I needed to *be not afraid.*

"Your Honor, my husband and I have cared for many children over many years. We have loved them and brought structure and hope to their lives by welcoming them into our family as people to be cherished, respected, and loved. We are foster parents because we want to help children who are in need. We have been considered a successful foster family because the children in our home, over time, move toward becoming healthy, physically and emotionally. They begin to thrive and do well in school and learn how to function in a family with respect and love for one another. We would do nothing to allow harm to come to any of them while they are under our care. But we can only protect them as far as the laws allow.

"We could not protect Hannah, the child who died. The courts sent her home, and we had no legal say in her care or welfare. We realize that the only way we can protect this new baby, whom the mother has requested we adopt, is by doing it the right way. We will submit to the laws of our state and make sure that we are given legal rights to protect her. That is why I am here today. My husband and I are appealing to the courts to give us legal guardianship so that we can move forward in making this child our own. We want to adopt her. We ask nothing of the state. We will raise her as our child, taking care of all her needs."

I was confident in my statement, even if I was not confident in what way the judge might rule.

As the judge reflected on my words, I noticed a slight grin before he gently sighed.

"I have not met you before, Mrs. Moerke," the judge stated. "But my wife has spoken of you. She has heard you speak on behalf of the crisis pregnancy center. She has heard of you through others who have attended women's retreats where you have been the keynote speaker. Even my pastor knows you and speaks highly of you. Your family's reputation as foster parents in our community is well known and respected. I want you to know I hear your heart. I know, unfortunately, our community questions DFS's ability to protect the children in their care since this tragic death of the five-year-old sibling of this infant. I believe it is in the best interest of this child . . ." He paused for a moment, and I realized I was holding my breath, "to be placed in your home, giving you temporary guardianship as you move forward with your adoption plans. My assistant will have papers for you to sign. I wish you and your family the best. You can arrange with the Department of Family Services as to how and when you can receive the child today. Thank you all for attending the hearing."

The DFS attorney looked down at his papers, shaking his head from side to side. My attorney tugged at my arm, indicating that we needed to stand as the judge rose and left the room.

I stood, in shock. *Is it over? Really? Did God decide and choose our family to be the ones to love and protect this precious new life?*

Tears pooled in my eyes as my attorney and I waited for the

other three to leave the room. Then I hugged her. "I so appreciate you being here."

She hugged me and said, "I didn't actually do anything, but you did make me nervous with that stone in your hand. Congratulations. Remember, though, the battle is not over. DFS is not going to back down easily. They are under great pressure from the community and have serious legal issues they have to deal with concerning Hannah's death. I can be there when you pick up the baby, if you would like. I don't want you to be alone."

Tears ran down my cheeks. I was tingling with excitement over the decision. "I will be fine. God will be with me. I am not worried." God had demonstrated his love and grace with a few words painted on a small stone. *Be not afraid . . . Only believe.*

Hannah would be happy. I am sure she is in heaven clapping her little hands. An image of her sweet, dimpled cheeks and big dark brown eyes flashed in my mind. I could see the shiny black ponytail with a ringlet at the end. Joy filled my heart, reminding me that God will replace ashes with beauty if we will trust in him to do so.

I met with the judge's assistant and signed the document giving us the desire of our heart, knowing now with confidence that it was God's desire as well.

It was 10:45 a.m. I had arranged to be off work for the rest of the day. I hadn't realized that in less than an hour's time, my life would change so drastically. I would contact my children to tell them the great news and get to the mall for all the newborn's needs. *Clothes, blankets, diapers, bottles . . .* the list started to add up in my mind. I planned to lavish the newborn with everything new, just for her. I couldn't wait to call Al and the friends who had been praying. I was especially excited for Karen to hear and found myself wishing that I were the one who could tell her in person, mother to mother.

Chapter 19

Obstacle Course

I STEPPED OUT OF THE COURTHOUSE and took a long, deep breath of the crisp October air, inhaling anticipation and exhaling all the worry and tension I'd been carrying with me. Courtney was ours! I wasn't holding her in my arms yet, but the Lord had ruled, and we could take her home.

Flakes of snow drifted through the air as if they didn't know where to land. *It's just flurries*, I thought as bits of white fell onto my lashes. As I raised my hand to brush them from my face, I realized I still carried the stone of hope. I recited the verse, "Be not afraid . . . Only believe." *I do believe, Lord. You have demonstrated your love and shown me your presence in this sad but hopeful story.*

I climbed into the truck in as ladylike a manner as I could. My plan was to go to the mission and call family and friends with the good news. I'd pick up our foster children at three o'clock, drive them home, and then race to the mall for newborn necessities. I didn't know what time DFS would release Courtney, or if it even would be today. Who knew what hoops DFS might still want me to jump through before I could take her home? No matter. I was up for any challenge now. We'd won!

The mission was quiet, with only a few cars in the parking lot when I arrived. Opening the door to my office, I saw the small red light flashing on my desk phone. *This may be the news I'm waiting for.*

"Hello, Deb. This is Tom at the Department of Family Services. I was asked to give you a call to let you know you can pick up the Bower baby after the office closes at five o'clock today. Wait in the lobby. Once everyone is out of the waiting area, a caseworker will bring the infant to you. If you have any questions, please call the office and ask for me."

I had known Tom for years. We had joked and laughed with each other on most occasions. His usual friendly lightheartedness sounded cool and stale this morning, but the instructions were clear. I had no questions, and even if I did, I wouldn't call to ask them. I just wanted to get Courtney home.

By the time I picked up the children and dropped them off at home and raced back to town, the temperature had dropped significantly. I hadn't changed clothes or grabbed a coat. My mind was focused on what I needed at the mall and then getting to DFS.

When I finished my shopping, the view of Casper Mountain was disappearing behind a curtain of snowflakes. My black pumps left a path of shoeprints across the parking lot as I hurried to the truck with arms full of baby goods. The clock was ticking. I was starting to feel anxious about who would meet me at the DFS office and whether they'd be kind or cold. I couldn't wait for this to be over and finally be home with Courtney. I pictured myself in my living room next to a cozy fire, rocking Courtney and surrounded by all the children. Suddenly, I longed to have Al home from his business trip.

It was minutes before five when I parked the truck in the lot beside the two-story brick DFS building. Powdery white snow swirled around the few parked cars left in the parking lot. As I jumped down from the seat of the truck and made my way to the front doors of the building, I didn't feel the cold, only a mixture of joy and anticipation.

Flakes of snow fell from my hair and dress as I pushed the button for the second-floor office. When I stepped from the elevator, I quickly scanned the lobby. Two people were waiting to be helped. One woman stood at the tall counter, speaking to the receptionist. The other was sitting, reading a storybook to a child on her lap.

I spotted a chair in the corner of the room and slumped there, trying to look inconspicuous. It was too late. The receptionist noticed me, and in the middle of talking to the woman in front of her, immediately picked up her desk phone to make a call. The "alert" that I had arrived was now in motion.

The minutes ticked by slowly. At 5:15, the last visitor left, with the receptionist following behind to lock the door. "Someone will be with you shortly," she announced.

"Thank you," I said, offering a quick smile. Sitting alone in the lobby, I could see lights being turned off or dimmed on the other side of the reception counter. The office was shutting down. It was time to go home for the day. I wanted nothing more than to get Courtney and go home as well.

Minutes went by, and then two caseworkers entered the lobby, one holding the bundled infant in her arms. I knew the two caseworkers but was not sure how they would treat me. As I walked across the room, they both smiled tenderly.

"She is so sweet," one commented, as she kissed the infant on her forehead.

"You are going to a very loving home, little one," the other worker said, as she smoothed the baby's hair. Their kind words calmed my heart as I held out my arms to receive Courtney.

I tucked the corner of the blanket around her tiny face, kissed her on the cheek, and hugged her close. Looking up at the women to say thank you, I saw tears in their eyes. I began to weep as well, and to my surprise, one of the women embraced Courtney . . .

and me. "We want you to know that we are so happy she is going to be with you."

I was taken aback, considering all that had happened over the past four months.

"Do you have a car seat to take her home?"

"Yes. I have everything I need for her. Thank you." My heart was full of gratitude. I knew these two women were not responsible for Hannah's death. They were not the ones wanting to fight me in court. They were women who, much like myself, were heartbroken over what had transpired. They worked for an agency that was set up to support and protect children. That agency was now under scrutiny and publicly criticized. I was not to judge. *There but for the grace of God go I.* I had made mistakes in life. Some were big ones. God had shown me grace and forgiveness. I needed to show the people at DFS the same.

Riding the elevator to the main floor, I embraced the warm little baby I held in my arms. I couldn't believe I was really taking Courtney home. We would be able to love, protect, and raise her. I could not wait to introduce her to the children and to Al and share all that God had done.

As I exited the building and heard the door lock behind me, I saw that night had already crept in, and the Skunk Truck was alone in the lot. The caseworkers had gone through a back door, and I saw them drive away. In the short time I was inside, the snow flurries had turned into a blizzard. The snow fell fast and hard and the wind whipped sharply, making it difficult to see. I wrapped Courtney as best I could, thankful she had on a knitted hat, and held her close.

Brushing the snow off the passenger door handle with my bare hand, I pulled the door open and securely buckled Courtney into the car seat. The temperature was continuing to drop, and my legs were feeling the bite of the frigid air whipping around me. As I made my way around to the driver's side, I couldn't see my shoes anymore. All I could see were legs, ankles, and then snow. My feet were numb, wet snow dripped down my face, and my hands were icy cold and red. With fingers stinging, I cleaned off the handle of the driver's door. Stomping snow off my shoes, I hiked up my dress with no attempt to appear ladylike and climbed into the cab. Shivering, I dug into my purse for my keys. My stiff fingers could hardly grasp the right key to put it into the ignition. I needed to get the truck started and the engine warm for Courtney.

When I turned the key, there was no roar under the hood. No knocking and clanking. Just a click.

"No! Lord! The truck worked fine all day. What could be the problem? Don't tell me the battery is dead." I tried a few more times, but with each try, the clicking became fainter until there was no clicking at all.

I remembered turning on the lights as I left the mall. I didn't remember turning them off once I reached DFS and parked the truck. The short time I was in the building, combined with the cold temperatures, must have been enough to drain the battery.

"Really?" I mumbled to myself. I'd had so much on my mind all day that a little thing like turning off the headlights hadn't crossed my mind. Now I was stuck in a deserted parking lot in the dark with a dead battery, a winter storm underway, and a newborn sleeping next to me. I needed to think fast.

I'm not one to quickly assume that the devil is behind every inconvenience, but I couldn't help but feel that he, thwarted at every turn in trying to disrupt God's plan for placing Courtney in our care, was taking one last stand against me, determined that if he couldn't keep her out of our lives then he'd work to steal my joy at taking her home. But my God was victorious! Courtney belonged to the Lord and to us, and nothing would steal my joy. I'd face this latest challenge head-on.

There was a hotel down the hill. If I could get the truck to the street and roll it down the hill, maybe it could build up enough momentum so I could pop the clutch, get the engine going, and make it to the hotel parking lot. Someone inside the hotel could help me, and I could call my children to let them know I was okay.

I grabbed a package of flannel blankets out of a shopping bag and fashioned a tent out of two blankets, which I draped over Courtney in the car seat.

"God, please give me strength to push the truck across the parking lot," I whispered. I knew that once I got to the street, I could jump in and coast down the hill to the hotel.

My sense of spiritual warfare grew more intense. "Satan is still trying to get to us, but he will *not* win," I declared boldly to Courtney as she slept. "Jesus is our cover. This battle is already won! Sweet baby, you are in my care and under the protection of my Savior. No man and no power of Satan can harm us now. Thank you, God, for loving us!" I sounded like I was preaching to the universe. Maybe I was. I knew God would provide the strength I needed.

Releasing the emergency brake, I put the truck into neutral, jumped out, and ground my black pumps into the white powder until I could feel the blacktop under my feet. With the driver's door open, I grabbed the doorframe with one hand and the steering wheel with the other. I gave a deep grunt and then a ninja yell as I put all my weight into pushing the truck forward. Snowy wind whipped at my body, slapping my head, hands, and face. I had to squint to see.

The truck did not budge.

I realized I would need to rock the truck back and forth. My first efforts did nothing, but then the truck began to rock, very slightly. I kept up the momentum, yelling out, "We can do this! God, Courtney, and I can do this!" *What a sight I must be. If only there were someone to see me!*

Once or twice I slipped, and I had to grab tighter to the steering wheel to keep from falling. I dug in again and continued pushing and rocking. Back and forth. Back and forth. The truck began to move forward. I turned the steering wheel sharply, trying to get the vehicle to turn. It was facing the opposite way I needed it to go, and getting it turned around to head down the hill would be a challenge. Since the parking lot was flat, it offered no help. Finally, with me pushing as hard as I could, the truck turned and headed in the right direction. I pushed it all the way to the parking lot exit. As the truck rolled onto the street, I jumped in the driver's seat and turned the steering wheel as hard as I could, directing the truck down the hill.

My hands were so numb that I could hardly feel them to grasp the wheel and pull the door closed. The speed of the truck picked up; I would need to go fast enough to try and pop the clutch. If that didn't work, I would have to roll all the way to the hotel. With no power steering, I would have to pull hard to turn the truck into the parking lot and not hit a pole or miss the driveway entrance. With no working headlights, it was difficult to discern where the road was and where the driveway to the hotel parking lot began.

Courtney slept, unaware of the battle I was going through to get her home. The hotel driveway entrance came up faster than I had anticipated. I grabbed the wheel as tightly as I could and eased up on the brake, pulling with all my strength to turn to the right. The truck bounced hard as the back wheel jumped the curb. Then the truck glided across the hotel parking lot and rolled to a stop halfway between the street and the hotel entrance. *I'll take it!* I was happy to be within walking distance of the entrance.

Getting out of the truck, I hugged the hood to keep from slipping and carefully made my way around to the passenger side to get Courtney.

Sound asleep. What a picture of trust she was. *Lord, that's the kind of trust I want to have in you—so filled with faith that I can sleep soundly while you wage battle on my behalf!*

I unbuckled the covered car seat and lifted it out of the truck, trying not to wake Courtney. Shuffling through the snow, now more than three inches deep, I couldn't feel my feet. When I entered the hotel lobby, the two young women at the front desk looked at me in shock. I'm sure I looked like the abominable snowman, carrying a large basket.

"Hello," I said, trying to sound normal. "My truck's battery is dead, and I am carrying a newborn. I need help."

One woman hurried round the desk and guided me to a couch. Brushing the snow off the blanket covering Courtney, she peeked under the flannel tent.

The other woman made her way to me. "You poor thing. Let me brush you off. Would you like some coffee or water or . . . something?"

"Thank you. I need to call my children to tell them why I'm not home yet. I also need someone to jump my truck. Is there someone who could do that for me?"

One of them hurried to the desk and called hotel maintenance. Within minutes, two men arrived. I gave them my keys with one hand and welcomed a cup of coffee from one of the desk clerks with the other. I felt almost foolish as the women commented on how little clothing I had on considering the storm. I didn't bother to explain how many hours ago I'd first left home dressed for the crisp October morning.

Within thirty minutes, the Skunk Truck was charged, running, warm, and waiting at the hotel entrance. I thanked the wonderful people who had helped me as I strapped in the car seat. My hair was straggly and wet. My feet were still cold, but I could feel the cold now. The heater had been running for at least fifteen minutes, and the cab of the truck was toasty. I sighed with contentment as I climbed behind the steering wheel.

The storm had worsened, but I had headlights and four-wheel drive to get us home. Once again, God had won. We were in his care and under his watch. I didn't doubt we would make it home.

I thought about the children waiting for us there. The woodburning stove would need to be lit and dinner prepared, but Courtney would finally be with her new family.

Part Four

Going
the Distance

Chapter 20

A Tender Hello

AND THEY ALL LIVED happily ever after.

Somehow when I awoke the next morning—Courtney's first morning in her new home—I felt as if we all deserved a fairy-tale existence for a while. After all, we had endured more than a year of the anxiety of a missing child whom we loved, the horror and shock of her murder, the unsettling news of Karen's new pregnancy, the indecision over our willingness to take guardianship or adopt, the stress of being pulled into an investigation, the unexpected standoff with DFS that broke our long-held trust of them, and finally the court battle for Courtney. In addition, during the past four months, our family had been torn over my decision to visit with the murderer of the child we'd loved. The previous night's misadventures with the Skunk Truck topped off the entire ordeal in a battle with nature and mechanics. In short, we'd been through the wringer and I felt ready for a respite.

But life isn't a fairy tale, and we are not owed blissful happy endings. We are called to run the race marked out for us until we are called heavenward, and that, I was assuming, was a long-distance run. Now I had a grieving family to shepherd through an adjustment and healing period, and two foster children with needs of their own.

Happily, the delight of having a newborn to cuddle and care for proved to be a great source of healing for all of us. We realized that Courtney was not a substitute for Hannah. Each one of us still struggled with various degrees of anger and resentment not only toward Karen but toward DFS as well. Only time and the Holy Spirit could bring about any changes of heart in those two areas, but at least everyone was able to voice their thoughts and feelings and be respected for their opinions. Our adjustment went as smoothly as Al and I could possibly have hoped.

Meanwhile, Karen had asked me if I would bring Courtney to visit her. After much prayer, I decided to let her see the baby just once. When Courtney was older, if she requested to meet her birth mother, I would bring her back. Al and I agreed that the children didn't need to know about the one visit as it would likely upset them all, so I told only a few close friends who would pray for me. Even they were resistant to the idea, as showing any grace to a mother who takes the life of her child is painful. Besides, they knew it would be an emotionally difficult visit for me, and they felt protective. But I knew I had to depend on God to direct me.

The first week of December 1998, when Courtney was about five weeks old, I felt the time was right. The air was frigid and gray clouds hovered overhead, threatening a weather change. As I drove in silence, the wind grew stronger. Glancing in my rearview mirror, I could see Courtney sound asleep in her car seat. Her soft, dark hair peeked out from the front of her pink knitted cap. I'd draped a fluffy lime-green blanket over her, with only her face visible, wanting her to be warm and cozy. I smiled. She was a gift.

As the wind picked up, I fought against the steering wheel just as I fought against my doubts about this visit. Was I doing the right thing? I thought back to the day Courtney was born. Karen never saw her. In spite of my second thoughts, I felt I was doing the best thing. I felt led to show mercy and grace to Karen as evidence of God's love for her. Although there had been no trial or sentencing yet, Karen's confession meant that she'd never be free again.

I drove through Lusk, passed the old brick houses with wide front porches scattered along one side of Main Street, and crossed over the railroad tracks. As I turned onto the long driveway of the prison, I found myself letting up on the accelerator. I was in no rush to go through with this visit. Though my car was slowing, my heart was racing. I was in utter turmoil second-guessing what I was doing and why.

I thought of Hannah. If she could see me, what would she think? Would she cry out in shock? Would she tell me, *No, don't go in there. My mother doesn't deserve to see Courtney. She doesn't deserve anything. She was mean and heartless and brutal. She killed me. How could you bring Courtney here, after all that she's done?* Or would she say she has forgiven her mother and I needed to show grace and bring Courtney to see her? Hannah had a sweet and tender heart. I believed she would have told me to do what I knew God was prompting me to do.

The words of Ephesians 2:4-5 rolled across my mind and heart:

But because of his great love for us, God, who is rich in mercy, made us alive with Christ even when we were dead in transgressions—it is by grace you have been saved.

I couldn't begin to guess why God was sending me to the prison with a precious newborn for a visit that would prove to be heart-wrenching for me and for the mother. I simply knew grace had something to do with it, and I knew God wanted me to show grace. How many times had he shown his grace to me?

Tears streamed down my cheeks as I parked the truck. I looked up to the sky as if God were waiting for my decision.

"Lord, I don't think I can do this," I prayed. "I couldn't protect

Hannah. Am I failing to do what's best for Courtney by bringing her here?"

Leaning over the steering wheel, I sobbed. In sharp contrast, Courtney slept peacefully. Time was running out. Visitation would start soon, and if I wasn't on time, I would not be able to go in. I knew I needed to obey what God was clearly leading me to do.

I dried my tears, and a deep peace filled the spaces of my heart where fear had tried to take over. I would obey. As I opened the door to the back seat, I had to fight against the wind. *Even the wind is wrestling with me, Lord.* I unbuckled Courtney and wrapped the blanket around her so she looked like a little burrito. The sweet smell of baby lotion from her morning bath reminded me of how innocent and vulnerable she was. Holding her tightly against my chest, I walked to the metal box to announce our arrival.

Once inside the visitor area, I unwrapped my precious bundle. A few visitors smiled as I slipped the little winter cap off Courtney's head, letting her dark hair escape. The visitation officer behind the counter smiled as well. "Are you here to see Karen Bower?" she asked.

I didn't want her to say Karen's name so loudly. Her name was now notorious throughout Wyoming and had even made national news. Would one of these visitors tell people I had brought the baby for Karen to see? Would the guards give me those looks that said I was crazy for even visiting Karen? I knew my pride was breaking through, the enemy looking to win a small battle in the face of God's grace winning out in my visit.

"Make sure everything is out of your pockets and in a locker," the officer called out to the handful of visitors. "Oh, miss, you'll need to put the baby blanket in a locker." There went my cover. Courtney and I were both exposed as we walked through the scan and stood in line to go into the visitation room.

The smell of unlaundered clothes hung in the air, reminding me that many people had sat in here before me—people I would not have necessarily wanted around Courtney or any of my children. I eyed the bookshelves of children's books and games and thought of other children visiting their mothers. Through the windows, I could see the outside courtyard enclosed by cinder block walls and razor wire. I scanned the room for privacy, but found none. This would be the first time I visited Karen here without glass between us. We could finally sit together in an open room.

I watched as each inmate passed through the door until, finally, Karen appeared. She smiled at me, then, seeing the baby, began to cry. I started to cry as well. We embraced with Courtney tucked between us. It felt strange and yet right sitting next to each other watching Courtney sleep. After a few silent moments, Karen spoke.

"May I hold her?"

I didn't want her to, and yet I did. We both knew she would never hold Courtney again—not as a baby or small child and maybe never. Karen cried as she rocked her daughter. I cried watching her. It would break my heart if I could only hold my babies one time in my life. My heart broke for Karen. My heart broke for Hannah. My heart broke for Courtney. How did we all find ourselves here?

Karen stroked her baby's arms and head. She kissed her softly and gave her tender hugs. I knew Courtney would want a bottle soon. I wasn't permitted to bring one in to visitation, but I knew this would be my way out of the visit if it was not going well. I hugged Karen as she held her baby and prayed over both of them. We sat in silence for the longest time, Karen watching Courtney sleep, smoothing her soft baby hair to one side. Then Courtney woke and started to fuss. I knew she was getting hungry.

"We have to go. She needs a bottle," I whispered.

"I know. I don't want you to leave. I know I won't see her again." Karen began to cry, though she appeared to be trying to hold back in order not to cause a scene. She kissed Courtney's forehead. I wanted to respect Karen as a mother, yet my own motherly love for Hannah took over. Where were the kisses from her mother when she was alive? Resentment began to creep inside me.

I asked God to push the anger back down and let this moment be one of grace. While doing God's will in visiting this mother with her baby in my arms, I could not have resentment in my heart. I must have love. I must have compassion. I must trust God to help me to raise this little one with the spirit of forgiveness. One day, Courtney and I would both need to walk in such grace if we were to be free of bitterness. I knew that was what God was calling me to do.

Together we walked to the officer on duty, whose eyes were full of compassion. I was surprised as much by her compassion as I was by how calm I was lifting Courtney from Karen's arms. I hated for an innocent baby to be in prison surroundings. I wanted her out of there as soon as I could make it through the security doors.

The officer radioed to open the visitation door for me to leave. Standing at the door, Karen gave me a hug. "Thank you for bringing her."

Hugging Karen one last time, I turned, then walked down the hall. As I left the facility, I pictured her being escorted back to her cell. She must have such mixed feelings, as I did. Sorrow. Regret. Loneliness. Heartache for her newborn child and for all of her children.

I sat with Courtney in the back seat of my car feeding her a well-deserved bottle. It was time for her to go home and live her life. I prayed that God would protect her tender heart in the future when she would have to come to terms with the actions and fate of her birthmother.

A sudden pang of anxiety surged through me. How and when would I possibly mother this precious child through the realization that her birth mother had murdered her sister?

"That is in my hands," I sensed God telling me. For now, my calling was simply to walk in the light that I had.

Chapter 21

The Garage

IN SPRING OF 1999 two significant events took place in the Moerke household. The first was long awaited and brought relief and closure. In May, Courtney's adoption was finalized, and she joined our family as an official Moerke. We were delighted and sighed with relief, knowing there would be no more fear of her being taken from us.

The second event took us by complete surprise and initially seemed unwelcome news. Within a month of the adoption, Al received notice that a new company would be managing the food service at the Casper Events Center. We would need to transfer to Arizona. No one in our family wanted to move. We loved the Rocky Mountains, our church family, and our friends. Phoenix would mean big-city living and high temperatures, and we didn't know anyone there. Our oldest two, Elizabeth and Jason, were now twenty-four and twenty-three years old and independent, so our move wouldn't affect them much. But our four youngest had all been born in Casper. Sadie was seventeen and in her senior year of high school—an especially difficult year to move. Helen was fifteen, and Charles twelve. Courtney, only seven months, would be the only child for whom the move would not be difficult. In fact, we saw definite advantages for her to leave Casper where her mother's crime continued to fascinate the community.

Al went on ahead to Phoenix to start work and look for our new home. The rest of us stayed in Casper, and I put our house on the market. We still had one nine-year-old foster son who had been with us for some time. We couldn't bring him with us, but he had a family in Casper who could take him. I hoped to make his summer fun before we had to leave.

Moving meant packing. And beyond all our own belongings in the house, I still had to contend with Karen's property stored in our garage.

It was time. The pile of black bags was beginning to look like a dusty sleeping buffalo in the corner. I hadn't put it off for so long because of laziness or lack of time. It was just that when I would go out to our garage and see the pile of black trash bags stacked high, I would picture Hannah's little body curled up inside them. I would stare at the suffocating plastic and feel my own breathing tighten within my chest.

Though nearly a year had passed since her body had been discovered, I still found it painful that no one had known. No one went looking for her. For months and months, no one guessed she had been murdered and hidden in the house where her mother, sisters, and brothers continued on with their lives. I was facing nearly twenty trash bags, each one reminding me of precious Hannah.

Now that we were moving, I was forced either to put all of the bags in a dumpster unopened, or go through them, as I told Karen I would. I decided to honor my promise. I waited until the kids were either at school or doing homework to start the process, two bags at a time. I had no idea what I'd find, so I wanted to allow myself time to digest anything that might be upsetting.

I pulled at the tightly secured knot on the first bag, and after much frustration, closed my eyes, dug my fingers into the side of the bag, and stretched it until a huge hole popped open, exposing the contents. Bath towels and sheets. *That isn't so bad.* Setting them aside for Goodwill, I breathed in a breath of courage and grabbed a second smaller bag. I found bras, underwear, and other lingerie, obviously Karen's.

I turned the bag upside down and shook out the contents; Polaroid photos fell out as well. There were five or six pictures of Karen with a man. They were pictures not meant for my eyes or anyone else's. I was sure Karen would have been embarrassed that I found them. I certainly was. I sorted through the lingerie to make sure I collected all of the photos. I wasn't comfortable putting them in my trash can, so I decided to burn them. After throwing the lingerie away I looked for a container in which to safely burn the pictures.

What about the kids? I thought, as I dug through aluminum cans and tools on a narrow wooden shelf against a wall. *What if they smell the smoke and come out to the garage?* I found a rusty coffee can full of nails and screws and emptied it. As the contents spilled out of the can, chills ran up my spine as if something had scurried up my wrist. I looked down at the two faces in the photo, and though both Karen and the man were smiling, I sensed *evil* darting at me from the man's eyes.

I quickly dropped the pictures into the can, set it down on the garage floor, and went looking for matches in the house. I hoped the kids were distracted enough to not notice me sneaking into the kitchen to rummage through the junk drawer.

Finding the long-handled BBQ lighter, I tiptoed back to the garage.

Carrying the coffee can outside, I set it down on the driveway, clicked the lighter, and watched the flames devour the photos. Once the photos were nothing but ashes, I tossed a handful of dirt into the can.

I glanced over at the sheets and towels and decided I didn't want to have anything in my home that didn't belong to the Bower children. I grabbed the linens and threw them away. *This was only two bags. Can I do the rest?*

I went into the house to wash up. Though my hands were scrubbed clean, I still felt dirty and tainted. It wasn't the lewdness in the pictures that upset me as much as the evil I felt from the eyes of the man. His eyes and smile sent a haunting chill through me. And in my mind, I could see Karen wrapped in his arms, like an unsuspecting fly caught on a sticky bug strip.

Over the next several days I found energy to keep unpacking the bags. I would open them, pull out the children's clothes and toys, and separate their personal items from everything else. Then I would wash the clothes and clean the toys for the children. Out of all the heartache, confusion, and turmoil, this was something I could do to bring some joy to Karen's children and partial closure to my own broken heart.

One morning, after dropping the kids off at school, I went into the garage to finish the job. Within a week's time, I had gone through all but two bags. I pulled one across the cement floor and ripped into the plastic. Inside I found Karen's clothes, her wallet, and shoes. A pair of sandals with wooden soles fell out of the bag with a clunk, and I scooted away quickly. The sight of the shoes sent my mind into an instant flashback of my first visit with Karen in jail when she described to me what had happened the night Hannah died. Tears filled my eyes as I replayed the horrific details of Karen kicking Hannah all over her entire body, including the powerful blows to her head that had crushed her skull.

I sat frozen for several minutes, staring at the shoes in front of me. Were these the murder weapons? Reluctantly, I picked up one in each hand and held them against my chest and squeezed my eyes shut. *If only I could have kept these from you,* I cried out to Hannah. *If only I could have protected you from the blows.* Silently, tears streamed down my face as I embraced the shoes. I found myself gently rocking back and forth as if I were holding Hannah. A verse came to my mind.

I have told you all this so that you will have peace of heart and mind. Here on earth you will have many trials and sorrow; but cheer up, for I have overcome the world.

JOHN 16:33, TLB

I could sense Jesus saying, "*You could not have protected Hannah her whole life. You cannot protect your own children from the sin in this world. But out of what Satan uses for evil and what sinful man can do, I can bring life and restoration. Trust me. There is life, love, and hope beyond what you see. Beyond what you are experiencing now.*"

A silent wailing scream stuck in my throat. My hands trembled as I carefully set the shoes down. My mind kept telling me to breathe, but I couldn't. I started getting dizzy, and I knew I would pass out if I didn't force myself to inhale. Taking small breaths in between, I sobbed as if there would be no end to it.

Twenty minutes passed. I was numb, but numb was a good place to be at that point. I prayed and thanked God for being with me in the garage as I grieved. I was being given a breath of his strength. Gathering the contents of the bag, including the shoes, I threw them into the trash can. Leaving the last bag unopened, I just threw it away. I was done.

I swept the corner clean with a broom. It was over. Now it was time to wash the last of the children's clothes, clean up their toys, and take a step toward hope.

"Lord," I prayed, "please cleanse our garage and our home. Bring peace to us and guide me to what you would have me to do."

Next, I called Jill. She was now the caseworker in charge of the Bower children. She didn't answer, so I left a voice mail, asking her to call me. Within minutes, she called back.

"Hi, Deb . . . this is Jill. I got your call. What can I do for you?" Ever since we'd been awarded custody of Courtney, she'd always sounded a little guarded when we spoke. I understood and tried not to react to it.

"I wonder if you could help me with something. I have . . . uh . . . collected the Bower children's clothes and toys that had been left at their home. I was thinking that I could have lunch or a cookie and milk reunion for them at my home and give them their things. What do you think?"

Silence.

I chewed my thumbnail and paced the kitchen floor. "Jill, are you there?"

"I'm here. Just thinking. I will have to ask my supervisor. If he says I can call the families who are caring for the children now, and they agree, then maybe we can work it out. The children haven't seen one another in months. One is undergoing serious counseling, and I am not sure if that child would be able to come. I don't know if it would be too emotional for them all or if it would be a good thing. I'll get back to you," she said, with compassion in her voice.

"Thank you. It may be something that brings some happiness to the kids. I will wait to hear." I was hopeful when I hung up.

Days later, Jill called back. The children could come, and their guardians would bring them to our home for the get-together. Even Karen's parents agreed DeAnn could attend. I couldn't have been happier. I planned it for a Saturday afternoon. My daughters helped plan the menu and were excited to be part of the event.

The big day came. I put the last plate of cookies on the kitchen table just as I saw a few cars making their way up the dirt road. Excited but nervous, I called out to my children, "They're here!"

The first car pulled through the gate and parked in front of our home. Two children climbed out. Their faces were serious, somber. I wondered what they could be thinking. The doorbell rang. I opened the door and gave them a big smile. "Kyle! Kyra! It's so good to see you." They smiled short, quick smiles. Apparently nervous, they walked a bit stiffly, so the woman accompanying them nudged them into the living room.

They must be confused and not know how to act. I allowed for their confusion and determined to show love and warmth no matter how they reacted. My children greeted them with reserved smiles and kept their distance. They were uncomfortable as well. It was an awkward few minutes.

The doorbell rang again, and two more women with Andrew, Ally, and Steven stood on the threshold. As I welcomed them in, the last car drove up with DeAnn, the oldest. All six children had arrived.

The siblings grinned when they saw one another, and joy danced in their eyes. They kept hugging each other. The sound of the Bower children's giggling filled our home once again.

The night before, I had put sheets and blankets over all the clothes and toys in our sunroom so no one could see what they were until they were unveiled. After a few minutes I said, "I have a surprise for all of you! Follow me into the sunroom."

My two girls went ahead of us and lifted the sheet and blankets. The faces of the children beamed. They talked excitedly as they looked through their familiar belongings. Dolls, a noisy fire truck, Hot Wheels cars . . . they each remembered which ones were theirs. Laughter filled the sunroom. It was all I could do to contain myself. My girls and I exchanged smiles. My heart was full.

With their special toys in hand, the children went into the living room to play.

It was time to introduce Courtney to her brothers and sisters. They gathered round her, gently touching the baby and softly talking to her. It was a tender moment.

Then we all gathered in the kitchen for finger foods, cookies, and punch. The next two hours flew by, and it was time for them all to leave. I asked if I could take a picture of them with their new baby sister. They climbed onto one of the couches and as older siblings held younger ones, they smiled and said, "Cheese!"

Two hours of love and happiness. Two hours of forgetting the horror of why they were separated. Two hours of giggles and chatter and wrestling; snacks and punch and cookies; crumbs and messes and joy; reconnecting. Then the time came to leave and go back to separate homes with people who were not their parents, to continue their now separate lives. But for two hours, there was joy. Pure joy!

Chapter 22

The Witness Stand

THE SUMMER OF 1999 proved to be quiet and calm—a welcome relief—until one afternoon in July when I heard a knock on my door. To my surprise, an officer was standing there with an envelope.

"Are you Debra Moerke?"

"Yes."

With that, he handed me a subpoena to appear in court in August for a hearing concerning Karen's case. I couldn't imagine why *I* was being called to court. Karen had confessed to the police. They had it all on a recording. What more could I possibly contribute?

Since Al was still settling into his new job in Arizona, I had to face a judge alone—again. I asked my faithful friend Charlene to go with me. When we arrived, we joined hands in a corner of the lobby and prayed. I didn't doubt God would be with me, but I was nervous and missed Al. I was grateful for his prayers and those of friends who'd offered their support. I drew in a deep breath for courage as I heard my name called. Charlene and I entered the sparsely filled courtroom and took seats near the back.

Minutes later, as a court officer entered with Karen at his side, an eerie silence washed over the room. Her ankle chains dragged across the floor and echoed throughout the room as she shuffled to the defendant's table. One of her attorneys assisted her in taking a seat. She rested her cuffed hands in her lap and looked quickly across the room at me before looking down. She and her legal counsel then huddled together, whispering.

"All rise," the court officer bellowed as the judge entered the courtroom. He took his seat, cracked the gavel on the sound block, and ordered the hearing to begin.

"I'm ready to hear your opening statements," the judge announced as he looked at the prosecuting and defending attorneys. Still baffled as to why I'd been subpoenaed, I was eager to hear what they would say.

What took place over the next hour was complicated and tedious, but slowly through their opening statements and their many questions to me I realized why both Karen's lawyer and the prosecutor wanted my testimony at this hearing and just how much was at stake. The issue boiled down to this: They knew that Karen had made a confession to me. They also knew that I'd been questioned by Detective Marsh and had opted not to disclose what Karen had told me out of my concern over breaking confidentiality. What they did not know was *what* Karen had actually told me, and whether, since I was a lay chaplain, her conversations with me were legally confidential or not. Nor did they know how much help or damage I might do to the cases they were each building if I were to be called as a witness during her trial.

I also learned that there was no legal statute in Wyoming that covered the question of confidentiality of information given to a lay chaplain, and therefore it was entirely possible they might use my case to establish one. That alone would have been overwhelming to me, but it paled in comparison to the realization that both sides saw me as a potential threat to their cases and therefore were trying to discredit me in some way.

At one point during his opening comments, the defense attorney's words made my blood run ice-cold in my veins.

". . . during this whole period of time, Ms. Moerke was attempting to adopt Ms. Bower's youngest child. That adoption went through in May of this year. On May fourteenth, the order was signed.

"After that adoption went through, Ms. Moerke apparently felt she no longer had to invoke any kind of privilege and was free to talk to law enforcement officers or the district attorney's office or anyone else that she wanted.

"We think that [confidentiality] privilege existed because Ms. Bower was under the impression that Ms. Moerke was a clergyman. She entered the cell as a clergyman. She signed into the jail as a clergyman. There was no discussion that we're aware of as to whether or not she was an ordained minister at that time.

"We think that under *In Re Grand Jury Investigation* [a reference to a confidential Grand Jury investigation], that qualifies her as a clergyman and the fact that she invoked the privilege, qualifies her as a clergyman. We also believe evidence will show she acted in a role as a clergyman through this whole proceeding until after the adoption went through. At that point she felt she could say anything she wanted to anyone. That evidence we plan to present to the Court today."

I sat stunned, my heart pounding. If it were true, I supposed he would have a good case. But I knew the truth. Karen knew the truth as well. I looked at her, but Karen looked anywhere but at me. It was understandable why her attorney didn't want me to testify at Karen's trial. But manipulating the truth would be the only way their argument could hold up.

The prosecutor, I assumed, would want to be able to put me on the stand and reveal what Karen told me about how Hannah died. I wondered if my supposition was correct.

As the prosecutor spoke at length, my head spun in an effort to grasp all that was being presented to the judge.

"It's our position, your Honor," he eventually said, "that after hearing testimony in this case, you will conclude that Debra Moerke is nothing more than a lay minister, providing spiritual counseling and guidance and prayer to an inmate at the jail, as are dozens of other lay people who are called jail chaplains, who are not ordained ministers or clergy.

"She has no formal theological training, which makes her a simple lay member of her church who participates in jail ministry, for which she is passionate.

"Ms. Moerke answers to an ordained pastor who is one of the sponsors for her to enter the jail chaplain program. She is in a church that does not have a belief system in a confession-type right [sic] or sacrament of confession, and furthermore, does not believe that either Ms. Moerke or her pastor would have authority to absolve sins. So it's not the traditional priest-penitent-clergyman relationship. She did not have that authority."

I couldn't help but nod. I may be teased by friends and family of having many superpowers, but absolution of sin was certainly not one of them. But what did my belief system concerning the absolution of sin have to do with the trial?

"Ms. Moerke's in the capacity a counselor would be in. She'd like to invoke the privilege of a psychiatrist or psychologist, but cannot do so because of her status. She doesn't meet that threshold question.

"Secondly, your Honor, the testimony is going to establish that when you look at the total picture—contrary to the defense counsel's representations—the testimony will be that Ms. Moerke, in fact, advised Karen Bower, and what Ms. Bower said to her was not confidential and was not privileged.

"There was no professional capacity as far as confidentiality. Ms. Moerke was not acting as an agent of the State, nor was she acting as an agent for the police trying to gain information. She was simply there, at the request of Karen Bower, immediately upon her arrest back in July of last year.

"Ms. Moerke's first visit to Ms. Bower really was because Ms. Bower knew her and because Debra Moerke—as the evidence will clarify—was a foster parent of many of Ms. Bower's children. They had a relationship existing prior to their communication at the jail.

"Now, since then the State acknowledges that Ms. Moerke went to the jail, prayed, gave guidance, and read [S]cripture, there was no expectation ascribed of confidentiality. There was no reasonable expectation on Ms. Bower's part that Debra Moerke was anything other than a lay person coming to visit with her at the jail.

"We believe, the testimony of Ms. Moerke, and Lieutenant Shift, will explain the chaplain program to the Court. The Court will conclude the privilege did not apply, and Ms. Moerke would be allow[ed] to testify as to anything Ms. Bower said to her concerning the death of Hannah Bower."

"Thank you, gentlemen." The judge signaled with a nod to call me to the stand.

After hearing their opening arguments, I understood why I had been subpoenaed. The judge could rule whether I would be called to testify at Karen's trial or not. The prosecution, as well as the defense attorneys, knew Karen had talked to me about Hannah's death. Would I be an asset or a liability?

It depended on which side got their way.

I felt like a bone between two dogs facing off.

However, I continued to wonder why it would be so important either for me to be a witness against Karen or why I would be a threat for the defense if called upon. Wasn't Karen's recorded confession to the police enough? The thought of being called as a witness in Karen's trial sickened me. Might my testimony lead to her receiving the death penalty?

"I would call Debra Moerke," the defense attorney announced.

I walked down the side of the courtroom to the dais where the judge sat.

As I approached, my heart pounded and I felt shaky. I thought about the advice the witness advocate had given me earlier: answer the questions the best I can, offer no additional information, remember that attorneys will try to trip me up, and finally, relax. Relaxing seemed quite beyond me at the moment.

While being sworn in, I looked at Charlene. She smiled and gave a little nod, reminding me God had me covered. I tried to smile back just as the judge began to speak. For a split second, Karen and I looked at each other. We both knew the truth. But we were under the jurisdiction of the courts now and had to let the hearing play out however it would.

The distinguished judge wasn't as scary as I had imagined. His features were soft and his eyes kind. He instructed me to answer the questions but to stop if there was something I didn't understand, then asked if his directions were clear. I assured him they were.

The defense attorney proceeded with establishing who I was and asking me to explain my relationship to Karen.

"Today my relationship with her is sort of a combination. It has become a friendship, but I have been a mentor, spiritual mother, counselor, and foster parent to her children."

The attorney nodded. "Did you have any special type of interview or anything of another nature that allowed you to become a chaplain at the jail here in Casper?"

I told him about the chaplain training I had received.

"You were foster mother to Karen Bower's children, right?" The attorney examined some documents in his hand, then peered at me.

"Yes, I was."

"How long did you have her children?"

"Approximately ten . . . ten and a half months."

"Did Karen see her children while you had them in your custody?"

"Yes, she did."

"And where did those meetings take place?"

The questioning seemed relentless, covering all kinds of details about my relationship with Karen, but always coming back to the confidentiality issue.

Then the prosecutor stood to begin his questioning.

"Ms. Moerke, in your conversations with Ms. Bower, during the time she was arrested, to the present day, did you and she ever discuss the confidentiality of her conversation with you?"

"Not that I recall." I wondered what direction his questioning would take.

"Did you ever indicate to Ms. Bower that you would not lie for her as to what she told you?"

Karen looked over at me, her eyes a bit squinted and her jaw locked, waiting for my answers. *What had she told them?*

I didn't want my words or my intent to be misunderstood. I knew I was counseled to only answer the questions and not add to my answers, but I had to make sure that neither I nor Karen was being misrepresented at the hearing.

"I want to answer that, but I also want to clarify that Ms. Bower has never asked me to lie. But I did make it clear to her I never would lie for her. I thought that was important to express."

"Did it ever come up about whether what she told you was going to be confidential or not in your conversation together?"

"Yes, it did."

"And what was that conversation, and when did that occur? Do you remember?"

Did they want an exact date? I hoped not. The best I could give was an estimate. "It was sometime between . . . before counsel was appointed to her."

The attorney turned to the court reporter, directing his statement more to her than to me, though his question was for me. "I want to clarify for the record one final question in this regard. At no time, did you tell Karen Bower that you would keep in strict confidence everything she told you about the death of Hannah Bower, did you?"

"No." How many ways can one ask the same question? I had to be patient. There was obviously something the attorney was trying to get out of me. I could only tell him the truth. That was all I knew.

"That's all at this time, your Honor. Thank you." The prosecutor offered the floor back to the defense for further questioning. The tall attorney stood and walked up to me. He narrowed his eyes as he approached the witness stand. I wasn't sure what that meant. What information could I have that needed a confrontation, other than Karen's confession? I realized this attorney was hoping I would *not* be able to testify due to a confidentiality position that, evidently, was in question.

"In July of 1998, Karen Bower had been arrested for the death of Hannah Bower. Do you recall that?" he began.

"Yes."

"Okay. And she called you?"

"Yes."

"And she had not been appointed an attorney when you first talked to her, is that correct?"

His tone had grown deeper and louder. His faced flushed a little as he waited almost impatiently for my answer.

"That's correct."

"She asked you to come see her?"

"Yes."

"And did you go see her?"

"Yes, I did." I was getting a little frustrated with the questioning. *Haven't we established all of this?*

"Where did you meet with her?" the attorney continued.

"I met with her at the detention center here in Casper." *Where else would we meet? She had been arrested.*

"And did you meet with her in person?"

"Yes, I did."

"How did you get in to see her in person?"

"Because I have chaplaincy clearance, I was able to see her in person."

"Did anybody at the jail question you about your standing in your church?"

"No." I was beginning to see where he was going. I knew I needed to listen carefully to each question.

"Did anyone ask you if you were an ordained minister?"

"No."

The tedious questioning went on and on concerning the clergy privilege status. Realizing I could be a part of a case that could establish a new legal principle, I wasn't feeling comfortable being put in that position, but I had no choice.

I answered his questions to the best of my ability, even though the attorney put the pressure on. When he asked about my church and my belief system, I shared the details about my Christian belief. When he asked me about the forgiveness of sins, I spoke freely about what I had told Karen.

The attorney moved a step closer to where I sat. "What are the types of things your church believes as far as basic fundamental religious beliefs?"

Did I hear him right? This was a question I would gladly answer with confidence.

"We believe in the [T]rinity, the Father, the Son, and the Holy Spirit. And we believe that Christ came to die on the cross for our sins. We believe that there is forgiveness for sins through Christ's death. We believe that when we receive Christ as our Lord and Savior, we receive the gift of the Holy Spirit that can lead us into all truth, and that he communicates before the Father for us. We believe in the Bible as the final Word of God. And those are our basic beliefs." I never imagined I would be in a place to share the gospel in a court of law. Whatever else was going on in this strange hearing, God was working in a mysterious way.

The defense attorney wasn't finished with me yet. "Do you believe you must confess your sins?"

"Yes, I do."

"Did you tell Karen Bower about these beliefs that your religion holds?"

"Yes."

"And did you discuss those with her?"

"Yes."

"And you prayed with her?"

"Yes."

"And you advised her to ask for forgiveness?"

"Yes."

I got the distinct impression that the attorney was trying to compare forgiveness of sins with pardoning of a crime. Surely he didn't think I would tell Karen she could be pardoned if she confessed everything to me? The forgiveness of sins doesn't mean we escape consequences. I wasn't sure what he was getting at. The judge stopped the questioning with his own question. I found it curious that the judge would want me to clarify what I had just said. Was it for the court or for himself?

"Let me interrupt you, if I might—and I hate to interrupt— but let me be specific. Is it the belief of your church that the ordained pastor may *not* grant forgiveness?" He leaned over the dais and looked into my eyes with sincerity.

"That's true," I answered, smiling back at him. I was finally feeling a sense of relief and excitement over sharing my faith. But what came next blindsided me.

The defense attorney then said, "Do you have interest in seeing Karen go to prison for a long time?"

"Do I have any interest?" *What is he getting at?* Afraid of what his intentions were, I felt manipulated by his question and shot up a quick prayer.

The lawyer raised his voice a little. "Now, if my client's in prison, she doesn't have any chance of getting Courtney back, is that correct?"

My heart started to hammer. *Does he really think I was manipulating the adoption, using Karen's confession as a bargaining tool to adopt Courtney?* Fire burned in my chest. He had no under-standing of what really went on inside of me, and court was not the place for me to share my heart—especially with an attorney who was trying to discredit me. I had to remember his position. He was just doing his job, but in doing so, the truth was being distorted.

"In May of this year, the adoption of Courtney went through?"

"Yes," I said, working my jaw a bit to make sure I didn't speak through clenched teeth.

"And at that time, you wrote Karen and said that the adoption was final, and that she didn't have to worry about anything anymore, correct?"

Confused as to what information he thought he had that could be detrimental, I felt my body stiffen at what he might twist or turn into wrong actions on my part. "I could have. I don't recall that particular time, but I could have said that."

"I can tell you your exact words. Let me get the letter." Reaching for two papers that lay on the corner of the table where Karen and her other attorney sat, he handed them to me and asked me to read specific paragraphs. I looked up at the attorney and nodded when I finished. It took every ounce of strength to suppress a grin. This was almost humorous. There wasn't anything questionable in the letter. I gave simple information about how the adoption was going and told Karen that I had contacted the attorney who agreed to help with that process. I handed the letter back to him.

His voice was stern. "Did you write those letters?'

"I believe so."

"You do know that one of Karen Bower's goals and her focus in life is getting her children back. Is that correct?"

What is the point of this? "Yes."

"Now, if she's in prison, she doesn't have any chance of getting Courtney back, is that correct?"

"I would assume that is correct."

I was confused. The questioning ping-ponged from forgiveness to the adoption. All I could glean from it was that the defense wanted to discredit me as a potential witness—making me look manipulative—using my status as a jail chaplain to adopt Karen's baby. With five of my own children, I was not someone desperate to adopt another baby. The call to do so came from God. But I wasn't given an opportunity to correct the misconception of me that he had just insinuated.

The attorney, apparently frustrated, returned to his chair. "Thank you. That's all my questions."

Once again, I was handed over to the prosecutor for a brief recross examination.

Then suddenly, the questioning was over.

And with that, the hearing was apparently over.

Or at least my part in it. I was stunned with the abrupt end.

The court officer escorted Karen out the same door they had entered over an hour ago. The prosecutor asked the judge to allow me to be dismissed from the courtroom and released from the subpoena. I stepped down from the stand, walked across the courtroom, and rejoined Charlene.

The judge would decide later regarding whether or not I'd be called to testify at the trial. I couldn't help but feel cheated somehow—as if I were owed some kind of explanation or conclusion. But clearly, that was not to be.

"I hope I did what God wanted me to do," I whispered to Charlene.

"You spoke the truth. Now it's up to the judge to make his decision."

As I drove home after the proceedings, I wrestled with conflicting emotions. On the one hand, I felt battered, bruised, and misused. All I'd done from the beginning was try to follow God's call to minister to Karen in spite of the fact that she'd murdered precious Hannah. For that, I'd just been dragged through a hearing where my character was smeared with innuendo. On the other hand, I'd stood steadfast in spite of my jangled nerves and had even shared the gospel in a court of law. God had proven himself trustworthy once again.

Several days after the hearing, I went to the jail to visit Karen. She had been held over in Casper for more meetings with her attorneys. When I told her I didn't understand why I might be called to testify at the trial, she told me that the quality of the tape with her confession to the police was poor. It wasn't clear enough to be admissible in court.

In that moment I knew why I was either the prosecutor's best hope . . . or the defense attorney's biggest fear. But I still had no idea if I'd be called to testify at Karen's trial. All I could do was hope that I would not. The thought of Karen's life or death hinging on my words was unthinkable.

Chapter 23

New Territories

MOVING FROM OUR GOOSE EGG ROAD home to Arizona left our family torn. On the one hand, it was good to be far away from court hearings and news coverage of Hannah's death and Karen's pending trial. On the other hand, Casper was our home, and saying good-bye to the hometown and house that held so many good memories of our own family and the many children we'd fostered tugged at our hearts.

In October of 1999, we arrived in Arizona and the six of us moved into a two-bedroom apartment near Phoenix until the house we were buying was finished being built. Charles slept on the couch. Sadie and Helen shared one bedroom, and Al, Courtney, and I shared the second. It was cozy but not ideal. The only perk was the pool that the kids enjoyed. It seemed odd to enjoy swimming in October. I missed the crisp fall air and brilliant colors back home.

Arizona plunged us into a different lifestyle. We knew to expect seasonal rainy monsoons instead of freezing snowy blizzards, and we began adapting to scorching heat instead of extreme cold.

Navigating traffic across town could take an hour rather than ten minutes. Instead of cruising quiet Highway 220 along the flowing North Platte River to Casper, we listened each morning for car accident reports so we would know which detours to take into Phoenix.

Our house, completed just before Christmas, was located in a town named Surprise. What an appropriate place to live given all that was to come.

The house was beautiful, and everyone settled into his or her own room. Sadie left for Casper to live with some friends and complete her senior year with her class.

During the holiday season, I missed the grand fir we usually brought home to decorate. However, we learned that one *could* string lights on a saguaro cactus, if you do it very carefully. The holiday without snow, our church family, and our friends dampened our spirits, but the services at The Church at Arrowhead, the church we found when we first arrived, fed our family with God's Word and new friendships.

Then one day in December we received a tremendous Christmas surprise. A letter arrived from Karen. In it she told us that the judge had ruled that there was no premeditation in Hannah's death; therefore, Karen would not be given the death penalty! Karen agreed to a plea bargain to avoid putting her family through a long trial that would only cause more hurt and pain for all of them. So finally, it was decided. Karen would serve a life sentence.

I was relieved she wouldn't be put to death. By this time, I was seeing evidence of her slow yet steady spiritual growth. With the prison's permission, I had given her a leather Bible with her name engraved on it a few months before. She'd been reading it and was asking me more and more questions about God through our letters.

I also appreciated that one day our precious Courtney would not have to be told her birth mother had been executed. I had no idea, of course, at what age Courtney would learn the events behind her adoption, nor how she would respond to the horrific truth of her sister's murder, but somehow it seemed to me that with Karen still alive there might be more hope for a positive outcome of the story—a story God was still writing. When he is the author, there is always hope.

Finally, I was relieved to know that I would not be called to testify in a trial. Ever since learning that the taped confession was not presentable as evidence, I'd worried that Karen's detailed confession to me might be the evidence that would send her to her death. With that weight now lifted, I celebrated in prayer and thanksgiving.

As the new year began, I decided to register for college classes at Wayland Baptist University, a few miles from our home. I was excited to go back to school to get a degree so I could enter the prison system as a fully employed chaplain. My connection with Karen further spurred me on in my desire for this line of work as it made me realize more than ever how God could use prison time to work in a prisoner's heart. I wanted to be a part of what God was doing behind the razor wire. I would attend evening classes when the family was home so Courtney, a year old, could be cared for by Al and the kids.

By this time in my life I felt I'd earned a master's degree in the practice of surrender. Foster parenting had been a lifestyle of surrender—surrendering self to meet the needs of children. Over the years I'd found a sense of beautiful spiritual growth in investing myself in the needs of young impressionable hearts and participating in their discoveries of obedience, trust, discipline, and love. My own obedience and trust in God had grown, an appreciation of the Lord's discipline and grace had developed, and my love for him had deepened.

The day I'd had to peel Hannah's terrified grasp away and leave her at her mother's home had nearly undone me. Driving away from her that day had been an unparalleled milestone on my surrender journey, for I'd been obedient and clung to the Lord— surrender lesson learned. What I had discovered in the months that followed was that my powerlessness over seeing and confirming Hannah's well-being took me to deeper degrees of surrender— a continual painful surrender over the long haul. Surely, I'd learned all that the Lord had to teach me about surrender.

But not so. God had then called me to endure Hannah's death and submit to his will by visiting her mother and murderer, sharing the gospel with her, and demonstrating God's unconditional love, while fighting bitterness and suffering heartrending grief. This was an ongoing surrender I was still working out through my growing relationship with Karen. Grief, I was discovering, when entrusted to God, was another form of surrender. I could choose to rail against God for the atrocity of Hannah's murder or entrust my broken heart to the God who gave his own Son to suffer and die for me. I'd chosen the latter and was discovering a tenderness from the Lord unlike any I'd known.

I've got this surrender principle conquered, I thought with confidence. *I can handle an unwanted move.*

But then began a series of events that demanded an even deeper surrender.

First, only weeks after Sadie returned to Casper, Helen was diagnosed with osteosarcoma. The cancerous tumor in her leg needed chemotherapy and eventually surgery. Helen had survived leukemia when she was a little girl, and we always knew she was susceptible to another cancer. Still, we'd hoped and prayed we would never hear the word *cancer* linked to her name again. The evening the doctor called with the report, we all wept.

On her first day in the hospital, I smiled at Helen and said, "Well, it looks like we're back in the hospital ministry!" She remembered well her leukemia days, and we knew another tough road lay ahead. Together, however, we filled our days with sharing our faith with other struggling children and their parents.

Al was working at the Peoria Sports Complex, the spring training home of the San Diego Padres and Seattle Mariners baseball teams. His days were long, and he found it a different world going to work in Bermuda shorts and a golf shirt instead of a shirt and tie each morning. I stayed home with Courtney during the day and went to my night classes after our family finished dinner.

Life was full in our new surroundings during our first few months of 2000. Adjusting to a new home, Al's new job, chemotherapy for Helen, two teenagers at home, a year-old baby, and me in college made for a significant challenge. Then, just days after I returned to school, a medical procedure for Helen that was supposed to be a four-hour outpatient procedure ended up requiring an emergency airlift to Phoenix Children's Hospital, where she was admitted to the ICU for ten days.

I had to face the question: Would my faith survive if Helen were taken from me? Fortunately, faith is a gift, given by God, and he gave it to me generously. Yes, I could and would trust God through this ordeal, no matter the outcome.

Once out of the ICU, it would be weeks before she would be able to go home. I wrestled with continuing my classes at the university, but Helen argued that I should stay in school. She would be fine with me not being at the hospital all the time.

God, in his glorious grace, then gave us an unexpected gift in a woman named Sandy Meyerson. We met her at the high school. She was the counselor for Helen and Charles, and as soon as she realized the challenges we were facing she stepped in at every turn. She called us, checking on our needs. She took care of all the homeschooling for Helen during the long bouts in and out of the hospital. She took Courtney for afternoons of fun and entertainment and met me for lunch monthly so she could be a support and a friend. Every hospital stay, chemo treatment, and surgery, Sandy was nearby. She was Jewish and I would lovingly call her my Jewish mother. She was a constant reminder to me that God was with us, meeting our needs.

Al and I soon realized that juggling life with a sick child in the hospital meant more than a drain on our time and energy. It hit our finances hard. I needed to go back to work because our health insurance would not cover all of Helen's medical expenses. Thankfully, I found a wonderful woman at our church who cared for Courtney while I waitressed at a local restaurant. But as Helen insisted, I kept up with my classes.

Helen's surgery had to be delayed until she was strong enough. We were troubled that the tumor in her leg continued to grow, compromising her chances of a successful surgery. We didn't want her leg to be amputated. Our family, friends, and church members prayed that the surgeon would be able to save her leg. Our close friends, John and Chris, drove from Wyoming and joined us the day of Helen's operation—evidence that the body of Christ was alive and well and ministering God's grace. We were tremendously relieved and grateful when Helen came out of surgery with both legs, minus a tumor.

Since Helen would be homebound for months, her best friend in Wyoming, Tricia, asked if she could come live with us and be with Helen until the end of the school year. What a blessing she brought to our family. She attended our local high school during the day, and she and Helen would giggle every night, sometimes all night. Tricia, only fifteen years old, saved Helen from a season of depression and isolation and was a daily reminder of God's provision.

May arrived, and our family, along with Tricia, traveled home to celebrate Sadie's high school graduation in Casper. Springtime weather in the Rockies was a welcome relief from 115-degree temperatures. We would stay only a few days, but we were all aware that we didn't want to return to Arizona. Though grateful that living in the desert removed us from the reminders of Hannah's death as well as providing the best medical care for Helen, we were fish out of water. We wanted to move back "home" to Casper. Al and I constantly looked for opportunities to transfer back to Wyoming, but none opened up. We had to surrender to the fact that God knew best.

While in Casper, I visited Karen at the prison. I was genuinely looking forward to seeing her. She and I had continued to exchange letters, and I had been sending her pictures of Courtney, along with Christian books to keep her growing in her newfound faith.

During the visit, Karen and I talked about the judge's decision regarding her sentence. I found her depressed at the thought of living in prison for the rest of her life, and there was little I could do to give her hope. I prayed silently as we chatted during the visit that day, and the Lord had me remind her of how important the prayers of a mother are for her children.

"Your prayers asking God to intervene in your children's lives will be heard. Your journey will require that you trust God for their future as well as for your own. Your life still has value. God isn't finished with you yet. As long as you have breath, there is hope."

The visit was emotional for both of us. We cried together, though perhaps for different reasons. As always, we didn't talk about Hannah, though my memories of her were heavy on my heart. I still grieved, but I was learning to allow the Holy Spirit to use it to draw me closer to the Father.

In the fall of 2000, Sadie packed up for college, and after hugs all around, she and Al drove to Wyoming where she'd attend Wyoming University. Helen returned to Cactus High School with Charles, and I resumed my evening classes. Courtney, two years old, and I took Helen to clinic visits and checkups, and she and Charles loved to wrestle each evening when the family was at home. A two-year-old and a six-foot-tall teenage boy wrestling kept us well entertained.

In October 2001 we celebrated Courtney's third birthday. Life felt as though it was moving further away from the heartache of Hannah's death. Then one day a registered letter arrived in the mail.

Some of Hannah's family had brought a lawsuit against the Department of Family Services in Casper, and a settlement had been reached. A sum of money had been put in a trust for all of the surviving Bower children. The attorney who sent the letter asked if we wanted a portion to be set aside for Courtney. We needed to answer yes or no and send the letter back by registered mail to his office.

As soon as I read the letter, my eyes welled up. A flood of sorrow washed over me as I saw this money as blood money. I didn't want any part of it. I didn't want to connect our innocent child to the horrible history of her sibling's death. The drama surrounding the murder wouldn't go away, and it seemed we couldn't move away from it either.

When Al returned home from work that evening, we both agreed to mark no and send the letter back. We could take care of Courtney. She didn't need to be tied to the money from Hannah's death.

I had recently begun introducing Courtney to the concept of adoption by reading her children's stories of bunny rabbits taking in baby squirrels as their own. We had a long way to go before ever telling her the circumstances surrounding her adoption, but Al and I had decided that Courtney would always know that she was adopted, and when she was old enough to understand, we'd tell her more of her story if she asked. I knew from experience that some children hunger to know of their past, while others are content to live in the present. Who knew where Courtney would land?

At Wayland Baptist University, prayer requests were commonly shared in class. One evening, my professor asked if anyone had a need for prayer. I raised my hand. "My teenage daughter is being treated for osteosarcoma. I'm asking for prayer for her health and for wisdom for the doctors and nurses who are caring for her."

The professor asked the class to stop and join him in prayer. As they did, I silently asked God to help me discern how I could better help pay for Helen's medical expenses.

I had no inkling that God would use that prayer to lead me into what would be perhaps the most unlikely role I have ever played in my life.

Shortly after the touching prayer, we had a break before class resumed. A funny and intelligent gentleman in my class approached me, asking if I would be interested in experiencing the jail system in a position other than as a chaplain.

I laughed as I held my cup under the coffee dispenser. "Do you mean as an inmate?"

Chuckling, he said, "No. As an officer for the sheriff's department."

I was so jolted by his response that when I turned to give him a dumbfounded look, my coffee cup overflowed. "An officer? Are you joking?"

"Believe me," he said, "if you really have a heart for prisoners, there's no more up-close-and-personal way to have an impact on them than to feed and clothe and care for them where they live and breathe. There you can make a real difference in their daily lives."

It turned out that he was a captain of one of the jails in Maricopa County. He knew the department was hiring and told me he thought I would be an asset. He offered to write me a letter of recommendation.

"Deb, you can gain a far richer perspective on inmates and the jail system wearing a uniform with a star rather than wearing street clothes and carrying a Bible."

At first I dismissed the idea as absurd. Me? An officer? In a jail? The Bible-study-rescue-mission-Sunday-school-teacher-pregnancy-center-director-foster-mom? With two teenagers and a toddler at home? I wanted to be a chaplain, not an officer. It was laughable. Except for two facts. It would mean a paycheck right away—something we needed to help with medical costs. And my heart stirred with that familiar inexplicable sense of calling. A calling to surrender once again.

I said nothing to my family until the next evening at dinner. When I recounted the conversation I had with my classmate, the clicking of forks and knives against ceramic plates ceased, and all eyes fell on me.

"Are you crazy?" my protective Charles asked.

"Maybe a little. I would like to look into it at least. I've never thought of working as an officer before, but I could gain better insight from a whole different position."

"That position is what makes us nervous." Al didn't sound convinced that it was such a good idea. But my baffled husband, after first laughing it off as crazy, joined me in praying about it and eventually gave his blessing.

The next day I called to set up an appointment and an interview. The first went well, leading to weeks of additional interviews, psychological testing, and a lie detector test. Finally I was hired. Boot camp would begin a few weeks later, but before starting the six-week program, I began running each day, working out, and dieting. It reminded me of preparing for the pageant.

As I entered the meeting room on the first day of boot camp, I saw a variety of diverse ethnicities of young people between the ages of twenty and thirty. Only one other person was close to my age of forty-eight.

What have I gotten myself into?

But in no time at all I was learning, of all things, how to use a Taser and flip people onto thick mats.

This is even more bizarre than my pageant experience!

I didn't know whether to laugh or cringe the first time I put on my official uniform and looked at myself in the mirror. So I did both. Let's just say that the boxy, khaki short-sleeved button-up shirt and high-waisted dark brown pants with cargo pockets were far less flattering than my Mrs. Wyoming gowns. And as for accessories, the duty belt that held a radio, handcuffs, glove pouch, Taser, and pepper spray added a good four inches to my hips. I will say, however, that it was far easier to walk (and run) in the heavy regulation black army-style boots than to dance in three-inch heels. And the boots didn't make my toes hurt.

Stepping through the gates of Estrella Jail on my first day was sobering. It was one thing to enter a prison as a visitor for one hour, but the thought of being locked inside the facility for many hours, day after day, made the razor wire curled atop the fences and walls look far more threatening. Security doors slammed shut with an eerie clank. A stale locker room smell hung in the air. And faces with sad, hopeless, often empty eyes looked back at me from every direction. I could see right away that the captain was right. Within those walls, life was raw and hard. Everything is stripped away except the bare essentials. If I wanted to make a difference in any of these women's lives, spending time in their reality was the place to do it.

I thought I was going there to have an impact on the prisoners. Little did I know the impact they would have on me.

Chapter 24

Boots and a Badge

I HAD TOUCHED DEATH ONLY twice before. One of the bodies I had wrapped in an old washrag and buried in a shoebox in my backyard when I was six years old. The other I had scooped up in a dustpan and carried to the trash. This time, I was holding up the limp body of a woman hanging by her neck.

It didn't seem that long since I'd worn my jeweled crown and three-inch heels as Mrs. Wyoming. Now I had traded them in for boots and a badge as Officer Moerke at Estrella Jail in Phoenix, Arizona. An officer only weeks out of field training, I was assigned this fateful morning to A-Tower. Estrella (es-tray-ya) was divided into dorms and tower housing, with each identified by a letter. There were only four towers. A and B towers were for females only. They stood next to each other, connected by a long hallway. The towers housing males, C and D, were some distance away in another part of the 1,700-plus-inmate prison.

Each square tower was a huge two-story cement and cinder block detention area separated into quarters, called pods. In the center of each tower stood a cylindrical guard tower. An officer could stand in the middle of the windowed tower and, by slowly turning around, see everything in the four two-story pods, identified as 100, 200, 300, and 400. All security doors in a tower were controlled electronically at a panel within the guard tower.

A and B towers each housed four classifications of female inmates: medium, maximum, closed custody (CC—referring to high-security inmates), and special administration segregate inmates, called ad segs. (Their separation was due to the type of charges against them—high profile, violence, child abuse, sexual abuse, etc.—that rendered them at greater risk if they were not segregated from the general population.)

I radioed my partner as I finished my security walk in the 400 pod. "Officer Moerke to A-Tower."

"Go ahead, Moerke."

"Security walk is complete. Open 400 pod slider, please."

The steel-framed, windowed door slid open. Once I'd entered the corridor that circles the guard tower, it closed sharply behind me with a grinding squeal. It was early in my shift, around 0840. I was approaching the security door to the guard tower when an officer's scream blasted over the radio, shattering the quiet of the morning.

"B-Tower . . . a . . . in . . . ahh!"

The main security control center for the entire jail responded: "Security control to B-Tower officer. 10-9?" That was a request to repeat the radio call.

"B-Tower to security control. Inmate hanging! Assistance needed!" screamed the female voice. Clear and deliberate this time. "Hurry!" Her voice broke into crying.

I froze with one foot still on the cement entry to the tower, my fingers gripping the door handle. I looked up the metal steps and saw my partner jump to her feet from the stool at the control panel.

"I'll go!" I yelled to her. To this day I'm not sure why I volunteered so quickly. I was still so new, so green. But the distress in the officer's voice on the radio call stirred me to respond. A tower must be manned by at least one officer at all times, 24/7. Only a second officer can leave to assist elsewhere in the jail, so I left my partner to man the post, slammed the tower door, and ran across the concrete hall toward B-Tower.

My boots felt heavy. My mind replayed the panicked voice of the officer. Running in response to a radio call for officer assistance due to an inmate fight was not uncommon. But in my first month on the job, I'd never before heard the words "inmate hanging." As I ran, I reached to the back of my duty belt for my glove pouch, ripped open the Velcro flap, and pulled out a pair of blue latex gloves. Gloves were required when handling inmates or their property.

I saw another officer sprinting into B-Tower ahead of me, and the sound of pounding boots coming from different halls assured me more help was on the way. I turned into B-Tower, and through the security windows the officer waved me on to 300 pod. The slider into the pod was already open and all inmates locked down in their cells. Only one cell door remained open. Dodging tables as I ran through the general eating area of the pod, I heard inmates calling out, screaming, crying, and beating on their cell doors.

"What's happening down there?"

"What's going on?"

"Is someone hurt?"

The din grew louder as more inmates joined in. Yelling. Pounding. I ran into the corner cell where an officer stood with arms around the torso of a woman hanging from her bunk, a knotted bra her makeshift noose. He was panting, his face red and damp with sweat, his voice desperate. "Grab her legs. Help me hold her up!" The hanging woman's arms were limp at her sides. The female officer who had made the call was also there, crying, too hysterical to be much help.

I tucked myself between the metal bunk frame and the hanging woman. Leaning against the other officer, I folded my arms tightly around the woman's legs and lifted, my cheek against her thigh. I smelled urine and other bodily fluids that were draining from her, saturating her striped uniform, and I soon felt the dampness on my cheek and shirt. She was lifeless. Heavy. Together the other officer and I tried to lift her high enough to release the pressure from the ligature around her neck.

Adrenaline rushed through me. I'm sure it was only seconds, though it seemed much longer, until half the jail officers appeared in the pod.

"Fire department is on the way. You both need to hold her up till they get here," the sergeant ordered, stating the policy we already knew.

Sarge told the crying officer to go to the office. Though a seasoned officer, she was a mess and needed to let others take over.

"Is she dead?" she asked. "Is she? I just finished a security walk. She was fine. She can't be dead." She wept as she walked out of the pod. I prayed. My heart hurt for the officers of B-Tower as much as for the woman in my arms. It hadn't taken long for me to discover the unique bond that forms between some officers and the inmates they oversee. The weeping officer's emotional state underscored that reality.

Soon, firemen, EMTs, jail officials, and officers filled 300 pod. Medical personnel brought a gurney into the cell. The other officer and I relinquished the hanging woman to the EMTs. Checking her neck, they loosened the bra, untied it from the bunk rails, and laid her gently on the gurney. I knew there was no life in her, though that would need to be legally determined by a doctor.

The sergeant told me to take over the vacated position in B-Tower and help the assigned officer quiet the other pods. I made my way through the crowd of officials and waved to the guard tower to open the security door for me. As I walked the short hall to the door, I could see (and hear) that pods 100, 200, and 400 were out of control, unlike 300 pod that had now grown deathly still. I gulped.

How would I quiet them? All inmates were locked down in their cells, but the volume was so loud I couldn't hear my radio.

Like caged animals sensing a tiger lurking, they were anxious, beating and slamming against the doors of their individual cells. They were safe—they just didn't know what was happening, only that officers and medical personnel had rushed through the facility. Although there was an intercom system to communicate instructions, the women were so loud they could barely hear the tower officer's commands to quiet down. Praying silently, I radioed the tower officer to let me into 100 pod. It would take personal attention, not a loudspeaker, to calm them.

I entered 100 pod and stood silently in the middle of the dayroom until I could get the women to quiet down enough to listen. "There is an emergency in 300 pod. A woman is hurt." I spoke softly, calmly, calling on the Holy Spirit for wisdom. "You all need to quiet down and let the EMTs do their job. If it were one of you or a friend of yours, you would want everyone to be quiet and let the medical people do what they needed to do to help you. Right?" I hoped that by speaking personally to them, with respect, they would calm down. It worked.

I delivered the same talk in each pod until B-Tower as a whole was quieted. Then, I went back to the control tower and climbed the stairs to find the tower officer, a young woman, staring out the windows at the medical personnel at work. She was sobbing.

"You okay?" I hugged the officer. She sobbed harder.

"No. I'm not okay. This is horrible. Is she dead?"

I nodded. Together we watched through the windows as the EMTs strapped the woman to the gurney and rolled it out of 300 pod. The sergeant closed the hanged woman's cell door, and all the officers returned to their posts.

Sarge radioed me as she passed the tower security windows. "Moerke. Turn your radio to channel two." Using that channel allowed us to talk without interfering with communications on the standard jail channel.

"How's the officer in the tower doing?"

"She needs to leave B-Tower, Sarge. She's not doing well," I radioed back.

"Send her out. I'll take her with me. You have the tower now. I'll send an officer to do your security walks, and he'll take care of lunch chow as well. You're in charge for the rest of first shift. Log everything that happened and record all officer names and 'A' numbers [officer ID numbers] of those who responded. Can you handle that?"

"10-4, Sarge." I opened the security door to the tower so that the weeping officer could leave.

After I watched the sergeant and the officer disappear down the hallway, I sat tentatively on the tall stool facing the pods.

Silence.

A silence so still I could hear my heart beat.

My body was stinging from the drama of the whole insane event. *What horrible hopelessness she must have felt.* My uniform stank from my own sweat and from the bodily fluids of the woman who had rested in my arms, dead.

She'd rested in *my* arms. Dead. I was too stunned to cry and realized with surprise that I was still trying to catch my breath. *I'm just a fish.* (The nickname inmates gave rookie officers.) *What do I know? How did I end up in charge?* My mind was stuck on rewind. Over and over I relived the sights and smells of the hanging. Feeling caught in a fog, I knew I had to begin my work in the logbook.

Fortunately, other than meal service, all the inmates stayed locked down in their cells the rest of my shift. The tower remained quiet.

Every twenty-five minutes an officer did my usual security walk through all the pods. He checked each cell carefully. No one wanted a copycat hanging or anyone else trying to hurt themselves. I logged each walk during the seemingly endless wait until 1455, when second-shift officers would relieve me. They, along with all officers that day and night, would be briefed on the hanging.

As I waited, I thought of Karen back in the prison in Lusk. What hopelessness was she fighting? What must she witness on a regular basis? Had any inmates around her attempted or committed suicide? I lifted her in prayer, asking that God would fill her with purpose and hope and prayed that the Lord would continue to grow her faith deeper and develop her reliance on him. Then I prayed for Courtney. One day, she'd be a young woman coming to terms with having her birth mother serving a life sentence for murder. My mother's heart wanted to spare her that pain, but I knew there was no avoiding it. All I could do was model a life of dependence on God—a dependence I felt as I sat at my post recovering from the day's trauma.

I somehow sensed that this role would play a vital part in what was to me a great mystery—that which the apostle Paul describes in Colossians 1:27: "This mystery, which is Christ in you, the hope of glory." I prayed that Christ in me—a holy mystery still unfolding in my life—would grow deeper roots and that God would use my "jail time" to further change me.

At 1455, I stood at the control panel watching for my relief. I was grateful when two second-shift officers appeared at the tower door. I popped the security door open from the control panel and spent a few minutes going over the logbook. Before I could head home for the day, I still needed to get names and A numbers from some of the officers who had come to assist. Exhausted, I grabbed my backpack and thermos and headed down the metal stairs. A few inmates watched me leave. Their eyes seemed sad and hollow, and I realized from their faces that they had heard. News had spread as to who had died and how. I gave them a soft smile, hoping to show some compassion.

Walking the hall to the sergeant's office, a few first-shift officers joined me. "Hey, Moerke, did you hear what happened in B-Tower today?"

I nodded sadly, relieved that soon I'd be resting in the comforts of home and my family's loving arms. But I'd be leaving behind well over a thousand women for whom this tragic place *was* home. Women like Karen. I was determined to return the next day looking for ways to let each inmate whose path I crossed know that she mattered—that she had value and worth. Hopelessness was one of the enemies I'd been called to fight here.

The longer I served at Estrella, the more God revealed himself to me, showing me who he was and what he was doing in such a dark place. Unlike my pageant experience, I didn't have to wonder what God was accomplishing in me through this experience. I was learning to love in new and concrete ways, with a kind tone of voice, eye contact, and carefully chosen words that communicated respect and value. I was doing what I could to bring a touch of Jesus' love into the lives of these women. Though I wanted to have the heart of Jesus, I was a person in a serious position of authority and responsible to keep order and discipline in a tough jail environment. I was about to discover that balancing compassion and authority could be far more difficult than I expected.

B-Tower 400 pod housed closed custody (CC) inmates. These women with nothin'-to-lose lives could be dangerous and violent. Some were in for murder or attempted murder. Sadly, many had mental problems, which multiplied the tragedy of their stories. Most CC cells were on the upper tier of the two-tiered pod. No officer was permitted to let any of these special-class inmates out of their cells without a second officer present. Some inmates had stabbed people or attacked them violently with their bare hands. CC inmates could unexpectedly demonstrate out-of-control behavior.

Before a CC inmate was allowed to be escorted from her pod, guards attached to the prisoner a four-inch-wide leather belly belt with an attached metal ring and a set of handcuffs looped through the ring. In some cases, ankle chains were also required—another reminder of Karen. It didn't matter if an inmate was being transported to court in a vehicle or walking down the hall to the infirmary. The procedure, policy, and requirements were the same.

To belly-belt and cuff an inmate, officers used a small drop-door on the individual's cell door, about waist high, through which food trays were also passed. It opened from the outside. When an officer was ready to take the inmate out of the cell, the inmate would put both hands through the drop-door opening, just past their wrists. Through the drop-door, I had been spit on and had food, drinks, and urine thrown at me. Not the most pleasant conditions.

I had no problem working with the CC inmates. I was respectful of the dangers. Strangely enough, I never minded guarding them or caring for them. I may not have had issues with B-Tower CC inmates, but A-Tower 400 pod inmates were a different story.

No, they weren't dangerous or violent CC inmates—at least not dangerous to the guards. Their crimes had been against children, mostly their own. Physical abuse. Sexual abuse. Some women had pimped their small children, boys and girls, for drugs. Some had locked their children up for days in dark closets or basements with no food or water. Their children were often told they were being punished or "in the way" of the mother's lifestyle, which often involved drugs, alcohol, and prostitution. In some instances, male family members or live-in boyfriends burned the children with cigarettes if they didn't listen. Children were whipped with household objects, and babies were thrown against walls like footballs by enraged adults. One woman gave birth to a baby girl who died days later, poisoned by toxic fumes her mother created while making meth in a hotel room.

It was my job to feed, clothe, inspect, and take care of the needs of these women just like anyone else in the jail. I took my responsibility seriously, and I genuinely wanted to have a Christian attitude toward them. But when assigned to these women, I discovered it was hard—terribly hard—to love them. It was downright painful even to serve them.

I didn't want to talk to them or even acknowledge them. I felt they were a species I couldn't comprehend. Reading some of their intake information cards listing the crimes they had committed, I recoiled over the acts they had done, or allowed to be done, to their children. How could these mothers' hearts be so disconnected from their children? Did they have no love, compassion, or tenderness? I'd spent eighteen years caring for the children of women like these—nursing their pain, trying to win their trust, yearning to reach their guarded hearts with love—my own, Al's, our family's, and Jesus' love. But their little hearts were all too often deeply, irreparably scarred because of what their mothers had done to them. Mothers like the women in A-400 pod.

Women I believed were nothing like me at all.

I didn't want to love them. I wanted to avoid A-400 pod completely. It brought out the worst in me—a side of myself that I didn't want to see.

I wanted to shake them, scream at them, and even worse, hurt them with the same objects they had used on their children. Never in my life had I even considered being violent with anyone, but there was no question that desire in me was strong toward them. I didn't want to touch them or their belongings. A creepy crawling chill shivered through my body whenever I had to look at them face-to-face. When I'd come home and look in the mirror, I was incredibly disappointed in the woman looking back at me.

I wasn't alone in my feelings. I watched other officers assigned to A-Tower do their security walks in A-400 pod. In other pods, officers often took their time—visiting with inmates while doing cell checks, telling women to clean up their cells, or pulling contraband such as leftover food or too many books. But when officers came to A-400, their eyes looked everywhere except at the women. They walked more quickly and placed only one foot in each cell, gave it a quick glance, then hurried to the next cell. A few female officers talked to the inmates as they did their walk, but they were the exception to the rule. Most officers ignored the women and spoke only when they had to. These officers were parents and grandparents who, like me, could not imagine intentionally hurting their children, selling them for drugs, or watching boyfriends sexually abuse them.

The inmates as well as the officers were silent during the security walks. The women quietly shuffled cards, wrote letters, rested their heads on the metal tables, or flipped through tattered paperbacks. Conversation and eye contact were avoided. With folded arms and locked jaws, a few of the inmates would lean against open cell doors watching the officers. They all knew that officers, as well as other inmates in the jail, saw them as the lowest of the low, less than human—scum.

I watched the women in A-400 pod through the tower windows and couldn't escape the obvious comparison—Karen, back at Lusk, would be watched the same way. I remembered the reaction of the guard at Casper that first night I went to see her—that look that said, *Are you sure you want to see that inmate?* But I had greeted her with an embrace and begun a relationship with her. And she had murdered precious Hannah. Why, then, my issue with A-400 pod?

I had decided long ago I would choose to love and forgive whenever given the opportunity. It was a commitment I made to God. Now, when faced with a pod full of "Karens," torrid emotions enveloped my chest. I pictured what these women had done to their children—the images nagged at my spirit and twisted my heart and called me to hate. They told me that I'd never do the crimes these women had done.

Al and I had cared for children who had been abused or neglected by adults. For us to intentionally hurt our own children was unthinkable. No. Not me. I love children. I want to protect them from such people. But my controlled rage now showed me that without God, without the Holy Spirit working in me, I am no better, no different. I wanted to violently hurt these women. My sins didn't stink any less than what these women had done.

I hated A-400 pod. It showed me who I really am without Christ.

I needed to find a flicker of love and hope in my heart for these inmates. Some people might argue that even God didn't love them. How could he if he is a good God and loves children? Others might justify my disgust and my avoidance. But I didn't answer to others. I knew I couldn't love these women on my own. I was an ordinary person, with a fallen, sinful heart. It would take God moving in me to have a heart for them.

One morning as I walked A-400 pod, an old saying came to mind: "We like someone *because*. We love someone *although*."

I meditated all day on that thought. *If true love is unconditional, then we must love although. Isn't although how God loves us? When I can't seem to find love in my own heart, I need to ask God to give me his heart for the unlovable.* That day God reminded me of times when I was unlovable and when my slate was not so clean. When my sin was disgusting. When I wanted to lash out and hurt these women.

God, I know you could not look on me if not for your Son taking my sin and cleaning me up. They need someone to care about them as you do. They need someone to show them who you are.

I felt led that the next time I was working in A-400 pod, I should say, "Good morning" to the women. I said it to all the other inmates. I would start to say it to these women as well. That was all. Just "Good morning." And yet . . . I found it uncomfortable. I balked and squirmed at the very thought of it. But I would be obedient and do it. Or, at least, give it a shot. Almost immediately, I was surprised and disappointed when I had to admit to myself that I believed if I let God change my heart toward these inmates, other officers would ridicule me. I knew the ugly truth that I'd rather shun the women than face that ridicule.

I didn't have to wait very long for my new resolve to be tested. The very next morning I was assigned meal service duty for all pods in A-Tower. My partner in the tower announced over the speaker that chow was going to be served, and all inmates were to be dressed and lined up at the sliders. (Here in A pod, unlike the CC cells, food was served through the open slider doors with the assistance of inmate trustees.) I left the tower to meet the trustees who would help serve.

"I will start at 100 pod first," I told them. As the slider to 100 pod opened, I hollered across the dayroom, "Line up, ladies, and have your IDs ready for chow." I pulled my pen from my uniform pocket, ready to mark the roster. Lunch bags were handed out. As I finished up pods 100, 200, and 300, my stomach started to get queasy. I knew the last pod would be where my test awaited me.

I reached the slider to 400 pod, but it didn't open. Why? *I want to get this over with.* I looked up at the tower window and could see that the tower officer was sidetracked by an inmate in 200 pod. I stood at the slider impatiently and waited for the officer's attention.

Minutes passed. I had hoped to get my test over with quickly, and these minutes of standing face-to-face with these particular inmates were making me squirm all the more. "Moerke to A-Tower," I said into my radio. "Chow in 400 pod. Open slider, please."

"10-12, Moerke. Dealing with inmate in 200."

The tower officer was telling me to "hold on a second" in radio terms, and I knew there was no rushing her. She didn't want to open another pod until she could have her full attention on me, nor should she. It was a protective policy all officers must adhere to.

As I waited, I shifted from foot to foot, avoiding looking at the women visible through the window by pretending to look over the roster. The delay seemed to be taking forever, and I could feel the inmates almost breathing down my neck. I knew they were staring at me. I could feel it. I could see it in the eyes of my trustees as they looked at me.

"Moerke to A-Tower. Do you need me to check on something

in 200 pod?" Maybe there was an issue going on that needed an officer to physically go in and take care of. That would be a relief.

"Negative, Moerke. All is 10-4."

Finally, the officer up in the tower turned toward me, and the 400 pod slider opened. Seventeen women faced the security slider, lined up, waiting for their meal. This was it. I made myself look each of them in the eye as they stepped up to me with their ID. As the trustee handed each woman her lunch bag, I marked the inmate's name on the roster and gave her a friendly, "Good morning."

Most of them immediately looked down at the ground after flashing their ID, taking the food and walking off. Others, however, looked up at me in surprise, but said nothing. Two said "Good morning" back.

To my amazement, I could feel my natural smile begin to come through, and a strange connection engaged us. I even saw one woman return the slightest smile when we made eye contact.

"Officer Moerke to A-Tower," I radioed, keeping my professional composure in spite of the tears I wanted to shed.

"Go ahead, Moerke."

"Chow is completed. Starting security walk in 400 pod."

"10-4."

I stepped fully into the pod and the slider closed behind me. I quickly scanned the pod as I moved to each cell on the bottom floor. Inmates filled the seats at the metal tables, digging into their lunch bags, putting lunchmeats and cheese on their bread slices, and opening pint-size milk cartons. I could hear whispers as I crossed the dayroom. I made myself cover the distance more slowly than usual. Scanning the dayroom, I caught sight of a few of the women looking up and then quickly dropping their heads. Two women leaned against their cell doors and tracked me as they chewed their food. Only the clomping from my regulation boots broke the near-silence.

As I climbed the stairs to the upper tier, I felt eyes watching me from below. Glancing down, I saw that most of the women were observing me as I walked. I stopped and smiled—yes smiled— down at them. I surprised myself more than them. Then, unlocking the dividing security door to the next pod, I stepped across the threshold into 100 pod and locked the door behind me. Resting my ear to the door, I could hear the women start up their chatter.

As I walked to my next duties, my mind wrestled with my spirit over 400 pod. *Lord, why was that so hard? And what are they thinking and saying?*

It's not for you to be concerned with. Just obey. I could hear God speaking to my spirit. I wasn't showing the love of Christ just for them. God was changing *my* heart—softening it toward these women just as he'd been softening my heart toward Karen.

Chapter 25

Ticking Time Bomb

Stepping in and out of Estrella jail on a near-daily basis was like stepping in and out of a time warp. Even how I thought about time had to change as the prison used military time. Inside, time seemed to stand still. There was an oppressive sameness to the days. At 0700 the lights went from the dim sleeping setting to full day-time brightness. ID head count was taken, then inmates showered, cleaned their living areas, and those with court dates, visitation, or medical visits were escorted to and from their appointments. Lunch was served around 1000 and dinner at 1730. The only things that would change from day to day might be who won a card game, or the swapping of paperbacks, or an occasional inmate fight. Monotony is a curse of the imprisoned.

Unlike the inmates, I'd step out of the jail and back into my fast-paced but rich life as a wife, manager of my household, and mother of Courtney and two teens. I worked a five-day week—weekends and three school days, usually from 7:00 a.m. to 3:00 p.m., so I only needed childcare for Courtney three school days per week. Al worked very long hours as a general manager of food and beverages at the Peoria Sports Complex, but fortunately was home in the mornings to take Courtney to childcare. Somehow, Charles and Helen gave Courtney ample care amidst the whirlwind of their comings and goings. Even though they were teens, they often showed more maturity than some of the officers with whom I worked.

At Estrella there were officers who just did their job, some who genuinely cared about the inmates, and sadly, a few who treated inmates terribly. One of those officers was . . . well . . . I'll call her Miller. She enjoyed throwing her weight around, insulting the inmates, and reminding them of their powerlessness. Thankfully, officers like Miller were not plentiful in my experience. I was grateful for that because one bad seed like her could sow enough dissension to spark some potentially explosive situations—like one I remember all too well. It took place after I'd been working at the prison for just over a year.

I can't quite describe the sound of approximately 150 women all screaming at once, but even above the deafening din I could hear the hammering of my heart in my ears. I'd never seen or heard anything like it. I felt as if I were stepping into the Red Sea, surrounded not by tumultuous walls of water but by waves of explosive female prisoners—all angry and about to pounce. I was determined not to let them see my fear. Showing fear in the world behind the razor wire results in a loss of respect— something I couldn't risk when walking into a life-threatening situation.

Moments before, Officer Miller had issued a call for assistance over the radio, and a number of us had come running to J-Dorm. The dorms were lower security than the towers. Inmates were housed in large rectangular dorm rooms with bunk beds stacked two high that were bolted to the cement floors, and a large common area with tables in the center was used for dining, card games, reading, and leisure. Sarge arrived first and entered the dorm. I was right behind him, followed by a handful of other officers. Miller, standing in the center of the dorm, was in a screaming match with the inmates.

Evidently, an inmate who'd been feeling ill had not lined up promptly with the others when Miller had called them to come for chow. A few moments later the inmate made it to the line where her friends were waiting to squeeze her in. Miller was incensed by her tardiness and ordered her to the end of the line. Her friends protested, saying they were more than willing to step back for her, but Miller would have none of it. She heatedly reprimanded the women for disrespecting her, which set off angry responses. Things quickly escalated. Miller insulted them, they yelled louder, and soon the entire dorm had been engulfed in angry screams—all evidence of how severely Miller was disliked and how poorly she managed discord.

Sarge quickly assessed the situation and ordered all the women into their bunks. Physically they complied, but Miller, nearly hysterical, kept screaming at them so they screamed back. The sergeant turned to calm her down, but the women yelled out their complaints against Miller, attempting to explain the situation, and again the entire room exploded in rage and frustration. We faced a dangerous situation. My mouth went dry, my palms were sweating, and I trembled inside. It would only take one or two angry inmates leaping from their bunks and lunging for Miller for an all-out riot to begin.

"Miller," Sarge bellowed. "I want you out of here. Take a walk and don't return for at least twenty minutes!" The inmates started clapping, so Miller screamed again about their lack of respect for her, forcing the sergeant to repeat himself. "Go! Now!"

As Miller turned to leave, Sarge addressed the inmates. "I want you all to calm down, or you will be put on lockdown for three days," he yelled. "No visitations! No classes! You will stay on your bunks for all three days. Do not make me have to come back into this dorm tonight. Do not make me call the special response team. Do you all understand?" As the level of noise reduced to a dull hum of grumbling, simmering females, Sarge looked at me. "Moerke, you have the dorm until I send Miller back. The rest of you officers, out!"

Did I hear him right? Me? Why me? But there was no mistaking his direct order. "Calm them down, Moerke."

Before closing the locked door behind him, Sarge barked his final warning to the inmates, "You give Officer Moerke any problems and you *will* be on lockdown."

The minute the door slammed behind him, the inmates' fury ignited again, as their adrenaline was still pumping. It didn't matter that Miller was gone. Now I was the only uniformed person in their territory—representing every authority that had ever wronged them. So they were venting their rage at their jailers, at the system, at life—all at me.

I knew I couldn't show my fear though my entire body was flooded with panic responses. I realized they didn't see Debra, the caring (and frightened) officer desperate to restore peace and order before officers in riot gear stormed the room. They didn't see my compassionate heart, nor did they know that inside I was far more of a dorm mom than a jail guard, a prayer warrior than a security officer. No. They needed to see Officer Moerke looking cool, calm, confident, in charge.

I did my best to look in control in every way as I took slow steps through the dorm. Thankfully, they couldn't hear my desperate silent prayer. *Oh God, please give me the wisdom I need to calm them. Give me the words because I haven't got a clue. Please keep us all safe—them and me. Defuse this ticking time bomb.*

I did the only thing that came to mind—the opposite of what they'd expect. I didn't bellow orders or threats as I'd seen other officers do. I strolled, silently. Hands clasped behind my back, I took small, rhythmic strides, as if I had all the time in the world—more the pace of a wedding march than a near-riot response. I made eye contact wherever I could—an act of bestowing value, to let them know that I saw them as individual women with names, not voices in a screaming mob. Fortunately, all the women stayed in their bunks.

I was on stage in the heart of the room. My audience was angry beyond words. I pressed forward thinking, *If I perish, I perish.*

What a bizarre contrast to when I had glided across the pageant stage in my elegant gown and three-inch heels. That audience had been dressed in stylish attire, admiring the contestants, politely applauding. All the men in black-and-white tuxedos and women dressed to the nines. This audience was decked out in black-and-white striped scrubs, and they were anything but polite—they were spewing venom, and I was the handy target.

Still, it was an audience, and my job was to win them over before conditions escalated and people got hurt or, worse yet, lives were lost. The stakes were high. So I didn't focus on their words or threatening gestures. I focused on their faces, their eyes, one woman at a time.

Finally, one woman held my gaze.

"I have a question to ask," I said to her quietly. So quietly that I could barely hear myself. How could she possibly hear me? But she was curious to know what I'd said. I was curious, too—why had I said that? I'd just said what popped into my mind. *God, what's my question?* I shot my prayer heavenward with no small amount of desperation.

"What?" she yelled.

"I have a question to ask," I repeated, no louder, still clueless as to what question I had for her. Now several of the women noticed our dialogue and were tuning in. Several others stopped yelling and turned to each other.

"What'd she say?"

"Couldn't hear her."

"I said, 'I have a question to ask,'" I repeated a tad louder, searching for eyes to meet.

"I think she said she has a question," I heard one say to another.

"What's going on? What does she want?" The curiosity was

spreading until a small group of them started shouting to the others, "Shut up. Moerke wants to ask us a question." It had taken many months, but I had managed to gain some respect from many of the inmates. They were willing to hear me out.

My stomach tightened, and my knees felt like Jell-O. No question was coming to mind.

I prayed again, feeling more than a little anxious that my mind was still a complete blank, yet as I prayed I watched with amazement as the screaming mob of inmates began to slowly transform into an attentive audience. I resumed my rhythmic pacing, looking to my left and right, making eye contact and pausing with each connection, willing each woman to simmer down and listen. The silence was spreading.

"Shhhh," I heard all around me. "Quiet. Moerke's gonna ask something. Go ahead, Moerke. What's the question?" But they weren't all quiet yet.

"No, I'm not asking . . ." I drew out a long pause—I was buying more time, waiting on God for the question, right along with my audience. I decided to look casual, so in spite of my quivering muscles I hopped up to sit on one of the metal tables in the center of the room. "I am not asking you the question until it's completely quiet." Another pause. "It's a very important question, by the way."

My heart was rising in my throat. *A very important question? What am I saying? Hello, God! What's your plan here? That's my question to you!* I felt the pressure in me build. *Lord, I haven't got a clue what question to ask.*

That's what was happening internally, while on the outside I scanned the room and nodded, trying to look every bit like the all-knowing schoolmarm who had total control and all the time in the world. "This place has got to be quiet," I said softly. *God, you are so clever! The unspoken question is working. They've calmed down. Please . . . fill me in on the question to ask!* I started swinging my legs as if I were relaxed and patient.

A few voices spoke out, "Okay Moerke, okay. We're quiet now. Everyone's quiet." Some of them were still whispering, "Be quiet!" The miracle was we could all hear the whispers.

Okay, God. Any time now. We've got their attention. I felt like John Wayne whose grand entrance into the rowdy saloon made the room fall silent, but I was still wondering, *What's the question?*

"Okay. This is the question . . ." I was afraid my stalling technique was looking too transparent. "This is my question to all of you." A thought came to mind, and immediately I heard myself saying, "How many of you are mothers?"

As soon as it came out of my mouth I thought, *That's it? What? Where do I take this line?* But I just sat there, still acting like I had a clue.

"What did you say, Moerke?" a few voices called out.

I repeated myself. "How many of you are mothers?" My confidence began to build. They were as surprised by my question as I was, but I was far more surprised by the response. First a few hands went up, then more, and as I sat, astounded, about 90 percent raised their hands. I'd had no idea. And as they raised their hands, their faces softened, for in that act they were remembering their own identities before they were prisoners. My heart stirred for them.

"Okay," I said, and I raised my hand with them. "I'm a mother too."

At that moment, an unspeakable bond was formed.

"Why are you asking us that?" one girl asked softly. And from that point on, God gave me all the words.

"The reason I'm asking is this. Do you see all those windows?" I pointed to the wall of security windows through which we could see the pale-yellow cinder block wall of the hallway. "Look at the windows." (And they did!) "What if your kids were standing right now behind those windows, watching what was going on in this dorm?"

You have to understand. When God is giving you a word-for-word message, he's teaching you something. I thought of Courtney at home and her imprisoned birth mom back in Wyoming. I sensed God's presence, the importance of this moment for myself as well as for them, and my heart leapt. I was deeply moved by this common bond. Motherhood united us. They were dead silent. Then, to my amazement, some of them started weeping.

"If your children were standing there watching, who would they see? I think many of you know me. I call you ladies, do I not? I don't call you sluts or other vulgar names. I say, 'Ladies, time to lock down.' 'Ladies, time for chow.' Because you are ladies first. God has created you to be that. So, if your kids were looking in here, who would they be seeing? What kind of mom would they see? What are you demonstrating? You know what you were demonstrating a few minutes ago? You were demonstrating that you were allowing yourselves to be provoked and put on temporary lockdown tonight. You nearly let Miller get you to start a riot. You allowed another person to do that to you.

"So what kind of message do you want to teach your children? You have an opportunity, right now, that when that officer comes back in, you can choose to be who she thinks you are or who you *really* are. Don't let her dictate who you are! Don't let anyone determine that for you. You choose. You can choose to be respectful and self-controlled." I paused again, not because the words weren't coming, but for effect. I was on a roll and could now see clearly where God was taking this.

"I want you to do something with me. Everybody sit up on your bunks." Nearly all the inmates began sitting up! I was amazed.

"What now, Moerke?"

"I want everybody to do this with me." I jumped off the table and took in a big exaggerated breath, then slowly blew it out. "Come on! Do this with me!" I coaxed. I smiled and saw smiles in return. I took another exaggerated deep breath, and now nearly the whole dorm of women was breathing in sync with me.

"I want you to breathe deeply. That reminds you that you are in control of yourselves. Now when Miller comes back in, I'm going to leave. You ladies can have self-control. And if you have self-control, you will not get out of control. You will not let some officer get you in a riotous state and unleash consequences on you. Therefore, you will not miss visitations, because remember, ladies, that tomorrow is women's visitation day."

I paused to let them think about the loved ones they'd be seeing the next day if they stayed self-controlled. "You will not miss your visits. Are we good?"

"We're good, Moerke. We're good."

Suddenly, I could see their eyes shifting to look behind me. I followed their gazes to see Miller through the windows marching toward the door. As she stepped inside the dorm, I backed up. We could all see the shock and confusion on her face, my fellow mothers and I. They remained quiet as she looked slowly around the room. I watched little smiles appear on many faces. Miller didn't know why they were smiling, but they knew, and I knew with them. God, in his wisdom and through the words he had given me, had given them peace.

I confess, it was funny to watch the expression on Miller's face. She turned to me and said, "What did you do to them?"

I said, "Nothing. We just had a little talk about respect—right, ladies?"

"Right, Moerke," many answered.

"And with that respect you'll all be fine."

Miller kept looking at me quizzically, then looking at them, and looking back at me. Her expression clearly asking, *What did you do?*

As I walked out, I went slowly by the windows and saw Miller staring at me. I stood in the hallway for a few moments, looking at 150 calm, smiling women who were looking back at me. I took a few deep, exaggerated breaths, and they all started laughing. Miller was clearly baffled. It was awesome! Minutes before I'd stepped through that door thinking, *If I perish, I perish.* I had never seen them so out of control.

Now look at them, Lord. I've never seen them all laughing. I've never seen them as a room full of mothers.

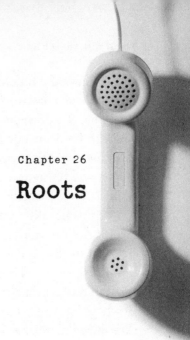

Chapter 26

Roots

LIFE IN THE DESERT, we discovered over time, could be as rich and filled with meaning as our life in Casper had been. I could see how God was using our time in this new place to bring some rest to our souls. As always, my roles of wife and mother brought me deep satisfaction. We could see that we were thriving as a family. My role at Estrella kept me focused on watching God at work in mysterious ways, much as my ministries at the crisis pregnancy center and rescue mission had done. I was exercising my gifts and growing in my comprehension of God's boundless grace. And Al and I found that in spite of our very full schedules, we were at a place in life when we could focus more intently on each other, especially as Helen and Charles grew more independent. Yet, as rich as all of these blessings were, we couldn't deny the simple fact that we missed home in Wyoming.

So, each summer the five of us returned to Wyoming for a week. Al, Courtney, and I went to Pathfinder Ranch during branding season where Al and I worked as cooks with John and Chris. Helen and Charles stayed in Casper visiting friends. It was great fun and a highlight of our summers. While there, I would always take a day to visit Karen. She and I talked about the Lord together. We prayed together. Both of us grew in our faith, trusting the Lord for our futures. We talked about our children and how and what they were doing in life. I shared what Courtney was doing and funny stories that would make Karen laugh. We never talked about Hannah. Never. Her name was not mentioned. The crime was not discussed. Only the consequences.

One of the saddest consequences is that, at times, Karen didn't see that she had much of a future. I reminded her that she did. As long as she was still breathing, God had a plan for her life, even in prison. Karen brought up what she had been learning in her Bible study group and I marveled at the miracle of her spiritual growth. We talked about her life in prison. She shared how some of the women who knew her crime could be very cruel.

Each time I visited, we shared tears. Our tears said more than our words ever could. It was as if we both wanted to talk about Hannah, but neither of us brought her up. Would we ever? The prison visitation room didn't seem like the best place to talk about her. We spoke about what was comfortable and left our tears and ending prayers to speak our hearts.

In June 2004, the cool Rocky Mountain temperatures in Wyoming welcomed us back to another Pathfinder Ranch branding. We had arrived at John and Chris's home and stayed the night before heading to the ranch the next day.

In the morning, Chris made an announcement.

"I heard that the Natrona County Sheriff's office is hiring. Just sayin'," she added with a big smile. "Deb, you could call for an interview while you're here."

Al and I looked at each other. "That might be a way back to Casper. Should I call?"

Al raised his eyebrows and said, "Sure. Can't hurt."

I made the call and set up an interview for the middle of the week. I would be elbow deep in cooking at the ranch, but Al, John, and Chris said they would cover for me. Chris and John wanted us to move back to Casper as much as we wanted to make the move.

On Wednesday I made the familiar drive to town on Highway 220 for the interview. After an hour and a half interview, I was asked how soon I could move back to Casper and step into a position at the jail!

When I returned to the ranch and shared the good news, there were cheers and tears of joy. Chris and John invited Courtney and me to stay with them until we found a place to live.

Our family returned to Surprise, and I gave my notice with the Maricopa County sheriff's office. Within days I packed our van, and then six-year-old Courtney and I headed for Wyoming. Al would put the Arizona house on the market and planned to join Courtney and me in Casper as soon as it sold. Then he'd hunt for a job in Casper.

Charles had just graduated high school and was planning to stay in Phoenix with a friend. Helen and her best friend, Tricia, were living in a two-bedroom apartment in Casper while they attended the local college together. But Tricia had plans to move to her aunt's home to save money, so Helen, Courtney, and I would live together in her apartment until our Arizona house sold and we found a place to live in Casper.

The other children were settled in their own lives. Sadie had graduated from the University of Wyoming and was living in Laramie. Jason had returned from Germany to complete his education and was accepted into the flight school program in Wichita Falls, Texas. Elizabeth had married a wonderful guy, Wes, and was living in Atlanta, Georgia. Finally, Al and I were on our way home to Casper. Everything seemed to be working out perfectly.

As Courtney and I drove to Wyoming, I was surprised by the waves of anxiety rising within my chest. Our decision to return to Casper stirred up pain and fear. In Surprise, Courtney and our family had been protected from *the story*, speculation, and rumors. Did potential turmoil await us in Casper? Would people remember the murder case? Were we about to head back into the line of fire, or had Casper moved on? When people saw Courtney with me, would they question me about the adoption, Karen, or Hannah? Would Courtney be followed by gossip about her birth mother's crime? We hadn't thought much about what we would face once we arrived.

I wrote to Karen to tell her about our return. Happy to know we would be closer and I could visit more often, she asked if her family was going to be notified and be able to see Courtney. I told her we would wait until Courtney was older and she could make that decision for herself. I longed for Courtney to grow up as a normal, healthy child without having to be caught up in the tragedy that her biological siblings had experienced years before. I would have to explain that to Karen's parents and hope they understood.

Within a week I had registered Courtney for kindergarten, then started my new job at the Natrona County Detention Center, where I'd served as a chaplain and had visited Karen. Adjusting to working twelve-hour days after the eight-hour shifts I worked in Arizona left me exhausted. I had to depend on Chris and Helen to help with Courtney. I contacted Starla, our former babysitter, letting her know we'd moved back to Casper and asking if she had room in her day care for Courtney after school. She welcomed her back with enthusiasm.

Everything seemed to be working out until they scheduled me to work graveyard shifts, allowing me little time to be with Courtney. My being gone evenings and nights left her confused and sad. It seemed that my new position with the sheriff's office had added unforeseen stressors to our family's life.

I did, however, find a little house for us to rent. Then good news arrived. Al had sold the house in Arizona!

December came quickly. Our house in Surprise closed, and Al and Charles drove from Arizona to Casper. Helen and Sadie joined us for a traditional Moerke Christmas, complete with snow and a fir tree decorated with lights and our old-fashioned ornaments. We all felt we were truly home again.

While in college, Helen had been dating a wonderful young man named Matt. He came to our home to spend a few days with us and asked for Helen's hand in marriage—to which we gave our full blessing. After a yearlong engagement, they planned to marry in July of 2006.

Months before the big day, I stopped at the wedding shop where Helen had bought her dress to make a quick payment on the flower girl dress. Seven-year-old Courtney was standing next to me at the counter when I heard someone call my name. I looked around to see DeAnn, Karen's oldest daughter. Surprised to see her after so many years, I gave her a hug. She had grown up into a pretty young woman who was getting married as well.

We chatted for a moment when, suddenly, she moved closer to Courtney and said, "Hi, Courtney, do you know who I am?"

I gently moved Courtney behind me and leaned toward DeAnn, shaking my head to get her to stop talking. "No. She doesn't know, and this is not the time or place to share that information," I said quietly.

I was shocked that DeAnn had approached Courtney like she did. I knew DeAnn was young and wanted to know the biological sibling she had missed growing up with, but Courtney knew nothing more than that she had been adopted. Although she knew I would answer any questions about her adoption, she hadn't asked many. I had not mentioned to Courtney that she had any other siblings, and the wedding shop was not the time or place to introduce a biological sister.

DeAnn appeared upset. She stepped back with a startled look and simply said, "Okay."

Days later, DeAnn called me. She asked why we wouldn't let the family be in Courtney's life. Why couldn't they get to know her?

I tried, as kindly as I could, to explain that we needed to protect Courtney from things she wasn't old enough to understand.

"There isn't anyone here who wants to hurt her," DeAnn said.

"I realize that none of you would hurt her physically. But she is too young to know the whole tragic story of her family history."

I knew that if she were united with family in Casper, someone would share the horrible truth with her. Courtney had been shielded from the harsh reality of her mother's crime. I begged DeAnn to give Courtney time to grow up before she learned about her biological family.

I felt bad for DeAnn. She told me that she and her grandparents didn't understand, but they would respect our wishes.

While we still lived at the rental house, the city hired Al for his old position at the Casper Events Center and we celebrated. I resigned from the sheriff's office and enrolled in real estate school with Chris. We loved being back in Casper with close friends and our church family, though living there did give me reason to look over my shoulder everywhere we went. I didn't want another meeting like the one at the wedding shop.

That same spring Courtney and her little girlfriend from next door were playing on the sidewalk. When I looked out later to check on them, I saw four children I hadn't seen before talking with the girls. Two of the children looked familiar to me, and when Courtney came into the house for dinner, I asked whom she had been talking to.

"They live four houses down from us. They asked me what my name was and when I told them, they asked me my last name. Then they asked if you knew their mom. Her name is Renee."

Shrugging her shoulders as if to say, *I don't know why*, she sat down at the table to eat and didn't say anything more about the new playmates.

Renee—Karen's former friend. She was the one who'd asked me to take care of Karen's belongings. I fought to keep calm and not change my tone or expression. Now I knew who two of the children were. Renee had adopted Ally and Steven, Karen's youngest. All the time I spent looking over my shoulder at the mall and grocery stores, and two of the Bower children were living four doors down from us! It was time to move.

I told Al what had happened, and we went house shopping immediately. Within a few weeks we found the home we live in today.

Helen and Matt married that summer of 2006, and Courtney served as a flower girl as she had in our daughter Elizabeth's wedding. The newlyweds settled into their little home in Green River, Wyoming, three hours southwest of us. Chris and I started our real estate business. I liked the flexible hours that allowed me to pick up Courtney and go to her school events and programs. With Chris as a partner, I could rest assured that business would be taken care of. Life back in Casper was turning out beautifully.

Over the next few years, we never seemed to run into any of Karen's family in town. Finally, I began to relax in public.

One evening, Al, Courtney (now ten years old), and I were dining at a restaurant with friends. During our meal, Courtney asked to go to the restroom. It was close by, so I let her go by herself. When she returned, she looked pale and stayed quiet for the rest of dinner. I asked if she felt okay, and she said yes.

That night, Courtney began to cry as I tucked her into bed and was about to start our bedtime prayers.

"Why are you crying?" I wrapped my arms around her. "What's wrong? Tell me what you are thinking."

"I'm scared. I didn't want to talk to her. I just wanted to leave and go back to the table with you."

"Who are you talking about?" I asked.

"When I went into the bathroom, a lady came up to me and said she was my sister."

"What did the lady look like?"

When Courtney described her, I knew it was DeAnn. Anger burned in my heart as I remembered the incident at the wedding shop. When she and I talked on the phone afterward, DeAnn had agreed to get our approval before saying anything to Courtney. She must have been at the restaurant and followed Courtney into the restroom.

"Does she know where we live? What if she comes to our house and breaks in?" Courtney continued to sob and asked for me to sleep with her that night. I had lost all confidence in DeAnn's promise not to approach Courtney without our permission. I knew I needed to do something. I thought of the agent in our office who was also an attorney and decided I needed to call her.

She advised going forward with a court hearing seeking a ruling to keep DeAnn from approaching Courtney again. I felt empathy for DeAnn. I had no idea of the trauma she had suffered before and after her mother's crime. But she was now an adult and was trying to initiate a reunion with Courtney before Courtney was ready. DeAnn had to know we were serious about protecting our daughter.

DeAnn was summoned, and she and I went before a judge.

The judge was compassionate toward our situation and though he was kind in hearing out DeAnn's desire to know her sibling, he reminded her that she needed to honor our wishes. Courtney was our daughter, and DeAnn could not force a relationship on a young child without her parents' permission. DeAnn agreed to stay away and not approach Courtney until we invited her to do so.

On my next visit to Karen, I explained what had happened and talked with her about the reasons Courtney needed to be kept separate from her biological family until the right time. Fortunately, we had built a relationship of trust—a trust that allowed us to openly share our hearts about our families and what was best for Courtney.

I visited Karen at the prison at least once a year, sometimes more. We had developed a routine for our conversations. First, we talked about what was going on in her life in prison. It was getting better for Karen once she stopped getting into trouble. In her earlier prison years her anger, attitude, and tongue would get her sent into lockdown or moved to an area where she had little contact with others. Though it took a number of years, I began to see softness in Karen as well as maturity. She realized that she was doing herself no favors fighting with others and trying to be in control. At one point, she suffered deep depression and didn't want to live anymore. Counseling, praying, and reading the Bible were her only hope. She and I talked about stories in the Bible and prayed God would teach her and continue to change her heart as she looked to him to guide her life.

At times we discussed prison administration changes. New wardens meant new policies that affected many areas of her life. After talking about policies, administrators, and the different jobs Karen worked, we moved to reports about family members. Karen knew little about how her children were doing. Few people communicated with her, and the people who had adopted her children did not want any communication. Karen got some details from her parents in occasional phone calls with them. Of course, I kept her up-to-date on Courtney's life through my visits and the photos and letters I sent.

After we had exhausted all the information, I would ask Karen how she was doing with the Lord. She shared times of wrestling with him and asked questions about what certain verses meant or asked me to explain some of the history in the Bible. She also shared things she was learning in the Bible studies she attended. She could see that some fellow inmates were allowing God to change them while others were not ready to give up control of their lives to the Savior. Karen was growing and changing. She was not the same person I had known years before. She could see that God loved her even though she had taken the life of her child. As always, we cried together. But the tears we shared were expressing thankfulness and gratitude for what God was doing in both of our hearts.

The one statement she made to me while visiting one summer, reflected not only who she was becoming but also the miracle of the Holy Spirit's work in her heart. She said, "I would rather be in prison for life with Jesus than living my life in Casper without him."

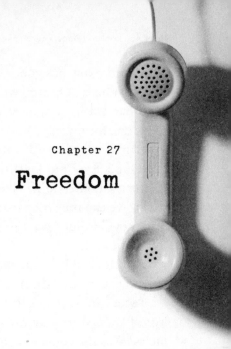

Chapter 27

Freedom

As TECHNOLOGY ADVANCED through the years, communication with Karen increased. For a time, she could call and leave a message at my real estate office. Then along came cell phones. If I couldn't answer, she would leave a voice mail telling me when she could call next. We had a system, and it worked well for us.

One day in 2011, Karen called me in tears, asking if I'd come visit. Her oldest son, Kyle, had died in a motorcycle accident. He was only twenty-one. I hadn't seen him since he was a little boy. His life cut short brought another tragedy to the Bower family.

I went to see her a few days later. Tears streamed down both of our faces as Karen shared the information she had received from her parents. Once again, she would not be able to attend one of her children's funerals. The talk of loss and heartache brought Karen to a place of sober personal reflection and spiritual inventory.

"I have cried and thought a lot about Kyle dying before I was able to see him again. He was so young when I went to prison. I'd hoped that once he was grown, he would come to visit me. He never did. Now he's gone. All I can do is pray that he knew Jesus and that he is in heaven with God."

I handed her a wad of tissues from a box on the table, then took one for myself.

"From what I heard years ago," I said, "the family who adopted Kyle and Kyra are Christians. I believe they were raised in a Christian home. So it's likely that Jesus made himself known to Kyle. We can only pray that Kyle came to know Jesus and is with him now." I didn't want to sound preachy, but I did want to give her hope.

"With all this happening, there is something I've wanted to talk to you about," Karen said as she blotted her tears with tissues.

I scooted my chair a little closer so others couldn't hear. I wasn't sure I wanted to hear what she had to say. Was there more bad news? Was she going to confess to something she hadn't before?

"What is it?" I asked, in spite of my reservations.

"Since I heard of Kyle's death, I wondered if I would see him in heaven. I wondered if he would know me and if he has seen Hannah."

It was the first time she'd ever mentioned Hannah by name since her confession to me thirteen years ago. In a rush of awe, I thanked God for the miraculous changes in this woman since that horrendous day. I remembered how emotionless she'd been as she'd recounted her vicious attack on that precious child and marveled now at the tender, spiritually searching believer who sat before me. I smiled as fresh tears filled my eyes. Tears of hope. Tears of joy. Tears filled with the good news and promises of Jesus.

"If the Word of God is true, and I believe it is, Hannah and Kyle have already embraced in heaven. If you believe the Bible is God's Word, you can have peace in his promises." I reached over and rested my hand on Karen's arm.

"I want to believe," she said. "I want to believe that Kyle has forgiven me for all I did—especially for Hannah's death. What I did broke up our whole family and caused all my children to be separated and raised by different families. It caused them to be angry and to hate."

I shook my head and said, "God knew you and your children were in a bad place before Hannah's death. If God had not intervened, there would have been more abuse and you would have continued down the same road, if not worse. I believe the night Hannah died, Jesus, in his grace, took her home with him the moment she breathed her last breath. He loves her. He loves Kyle, and . . . he loves you."

"Do you really believe that?" There was such hope in her voice.

"Yes. God does not lie. He is truth, and so he is true to his Word."

"I have something more to ask you. It's about forgiveness," Karen said.

"Forgiveness? We haven't talked much about that."

"I want you to know I did ask God to forgive me for taking Hannah's life."

A wave of joy swept through me, and my heart leapt.

"And do you believe he has forgiven you?"

"Yes. I do." She answered with conviction. "I asked Hannah to forgive me as well."

"And do you believe she has?"

"Yes." Karen's eyes, now dried from her tears, glistened, a soft smile gracing her face.

"That's wonderful to hear. It has taken many years for you to come to this place. Do you have some sense of peace now?"

"I do. And . . . I asked my parents for forgiveness as well."

"What did they say?"

"My mother said yes, she forgave me, though it took her a long time to be able to do so. My father said, 'It's in the past now.' I think that's his way of forgiving me. I'm not sure. He never used the word *forgive*. I still have to ask forgiveness from my other children though. That may take longer. They have a lot to work out in their hearts. I believe God has told me that will come in time. I'll have to wait and see."

"God has been working on your heart for the past thirteen years. I am so happy for you. God is good. He will never leave you nor forsake you. You are experiencing the power of forgiveness. It frees you from hate, anger, sorrow, and guilt. It can bring joy where only heartache, and perhaps bitterness, lived before." I hugged her, and she returned the embrace with a long, firm hug.

"There is one other person I need to ask forgiveness from," Karen whispered.

"Who is that?" I asked, also in a whisper.

Our eyes locked, as they often did when truth was being spoken. It seemed to be our way of looking into each other's souls.

"You."

"Me?" I sat up, stunned.

"Yes. You loved Hannah. You asked me twice if she could stay with you until I got my life in order. If I hadn't been so selfish and had let her go with you, she would be alive today, I would have my children with me, and I wouldn't be serving a life sentence. So, I am asking you now. Will you forgive me?"

Taken aback at her question, I drew in a deep breath and moved closer to her.

Tears pooled in her eyes. She looked hopeful as she chewed on her bottom lip, anticipating my response.

"I already have," I whispered, looking directly into her eyes.

Karen buried her face in her hands and wept while sweet tears of gratefulness for what the Lord had done in her heart rolled down my face.

So many tears at one visit. Tears of sorrow and loss, of regret, and of forgiveness.

"Thank you." Karen nodded, receiving what she had waited to hear.

We had both come a long way. How different our lives could have been. Where would we both be if I hadn't surrendered to the

Spirit challenging me to accept the call from Karen on the yellow phone all those years ago? What if I hadn't been obedient to the Lord's prompting to visit her? What if I hadn't shared God's love and hope with her, the promise of a new life in him? Who would she have become?

Who would I have become? If I hadn't chosen to surrender to God, what path might I have taken?

I noticed the clock. Karen and I had been visiting for more than two hours. I needed to leave to get home before dark.

"Before you go, I have something else I want to ask you." Karen moved closer to me again, twisting her fingers as she always did when she was nervous.

What possibly could be harder to ask me than what she had just asked?

"I have a number of pictures of the kids that you have sent to me over the years, but I don't have any pictures of Hannah. I can't ask my parents. There isn't anyone I could ask other than you. I know you have some pictures of her. I'm asking because I am beginning to forget what she looked like. I don't want to forget her." Karen appeared humble and sincere.

I understood her need to see Hannah's little face and remember the child whose life she had cut short. I folded my arms and leaned back against my chair, studying Karen's eyes again. She looked at me, then looked down at her hands. I needed to ask God how to respond. I hadn't expected her to ask me for forgiveness or to provide her with a picture of Hannah. It was a lot to process. With so many years of us not speaking about Hannah, this visit seemed to be opening a whole new level of communication.

Neither of us spoke. A few minutes passed as Karen squirmed in her chair and I waited for God's wisdom.

Unfolding my arms, I felt ready to share my thoughts.

I nodded and said, "Okay, this is the deal I will make with you. For the next few weeks, I want you to think and pray about receiving a picture of Hannah. Then, if you feel you still want me to send one, I want you to write me a letter and request it. I want you to write in your letter that *you* asked me for it and that you have prayed about it and feel you are ready to receive it. I don't want you to get a picture of her, see it, then get overwhelmed with sorrow and have a breakdown. If you do, and you need to see a counselor or get medical help because of it, the first question those people are going to ask is, 'Why would some cruel person send a picture of Hannah to you? What a mean thing to do.' I want to make sure you have taken the time to prepare yourself. A letter would show me, and perhaps someone else who may need to know, that you thought it through and it was a request on your part."

Karen smiled and gave a little chuckle. Her stiff posture relaxed as I explained my reasoning. "I'll write a letter. I understand why you would be concerned. I think I'm ready to have a picture of her. I don't want to forget her. I want to be able to see her face."

Karen had grown to a place of not only natural maturity but spiritual maturity. Our level of communication and honesty exceeded my expectations. God truly had been with us during our visits through the years, and he was certainly with us this day.

We ended our visit with prayer, as we usually did. This time, we prayed a special prayer for each one of our children. We prayed as two mothers with the heart of God for our children. We had moved far beyond foster mom and abuser mom. Forgiveness had been spoken. Forgiveness had been given and received. In that forgiveness, healing and hope filled our hearts.

At various points over the past thirteen years, especially in the early ones, I had left my visits with Karen feeling a profound mixture of confusion, being overwhelmed, and questioning God. Why did he call *me* into her story? Could he possibly have a plan and a purpose for Karen after what she had done? Hurting a child was never acceptable. There was no argument. No legitimate excuse. No mother is perfect, but what redemption could there be for a woman who kicked her child to death? Initially, I stood in judgment. I know God says in Romans 3:23, "For *all* have sinned and fall short of the glory of God" (italics added). But . . . this crime went beyond sin, in the eyes of most people. How could *this* sin be forgiven? And yet . . . it had been. By God, and by me.

Freedom in prison sounds contradictory. Can one really be free in a secured facility with guards watching your every move? And this freedom . . . . what did that mean? Free from the consequences of a crime? No. Free from the eternal destructive consequences of sin? Yes. Free to reflect and demonstrate what freedom in Christ really means? Yes.

Will everyone choose that freedom to respond to God's invitation to surrender to him? Sadly, no.

So Karen and I walk in freedom, where others may still walk in bondage, in prisons where the bars are invisible. Where unforgiveness, bitterness, and judgment restrict them.

What, I wondered, did God have in store for Courtney? She hadn't yet even learned her family's story, but when she did, she, too, would suffer its consequences. I prayed for her journey through it and that she, too, would surrender to the lordship of Jesus Christ and one day walk in the freedom and power of forgiveness.

Chapter 28

The Revelation

COURTNEY WAS THIRTEEN THAT pivotal day when I picked her up from the mall and saw the two youngest Bower children, Ally and Steven, with her. It was the summer of 2012, and while I didn't feel personally ready to disclose the story behind her adoption, by the time we'd come home, changed into our pajamas, and crawled up on my bed with our pillows and tissues, I realized that God had known the timing of this moment all along. Courtney was ready, and God had prepared me as much as he needed to. I needed to surrender to God's timing.

We both sat cross-legged on the bed facing each other, hugging pillows to our chests. On the way home, I had decided I would invite Courtney to ask all the questions she had and I would answer them as honestly as possible.

"I have always told you that when you are ready and you have questions, I will answer them truthfully. What is it you want to know?" I smiled and spoke softly, wanting her to feel comfortable.

"How many biological sisters and brothers do I have?" she asked. "And what are their names?"

"There are seven. Their names are DeAnn, Kyle, Kyra, Hannah, Andrew, Ally, and Steven."

"Where do they all live?"

"Five of them live in Wyoming," I answered.

"And what about the other two?" she asked.

"The other two are with the Lord." I answered her question without changing my tone or expression.

Pausing, Courtney looked at me as if waiting for more to the answer. When I shared nothing more, she continued her questioning. I could see that she was processing my answers, thinking about what they meant.

"Why are two with the Lord? Which ones? What are their names? How did they die?" The questions fired from her lips.

"Kyle died about a year ago in a motorcycle accident. He was twenty-one. Hannah died many years ago, when she was five." I knew what was coming next. I braced myself and prayed.

"How did Hannah die?" Courtney scooted closer to me on the bed and searched my face.

"She was beaten to death." The words were always hard for me to say. They were especially hard to say to Courtney. Taking in a deep breath, I looked directly into Courtney's eyes, wanting to be prepared for her response. I had no idea how she might react. I prayed that God would be with us as I knew what her next question would be.

"Who beat her to death?" Courtney cried out.

Pausing for a second, I whispered, "Her mother."

Stiffening, Courtney seemed to be holding her breath as she looked away and then back at me. I said nothing more. She needed to process the answer I had given to her. She sat up straight and then blurted out her conclusion. "Her mother is *my* birth mother, right?" She scrunched her face trying to connect the relationship.

"Yes," I answered.

"What's her name?"

"Karen."

Silence. For the longest time, only silence.

The only sound was the slight ticking of the clock on my bed stand. Frozen, we didn't move. The chilling words that had come out of my mouth seemed surreal. *Was this the right timing?* I wondered. Now I wasn't so sure.

"Is she the person you have gone to visit all these years? The one you didn't tell anyone you were going to see? Is that the Karen we have prayed for since I was little?" The puzzle pieces were starting to fall into place for her. The truth was hard.

"Yes. She is the person."

"Where is she now?"

"She's in Lusk, at the women's prison." I responded softly, though there was no way to soften the story.

"What happened? How did Hannah die? What did Karen do to her?" The questions I had feared were coming at me so quickly. *How do I answer? How far do I go with the details and truth?* Her questions were the ones I had dreaded for so many years.

"Courtney, Karen was a different person then. She used drugs and alcohol and was making wrong choices for her life. She was with bad people. She wasn't a nice person to a few of her children. One night, she lost her temper. I don't want to say any more. When you are older I may tell you more, but not now. Not tonight."

I didn't want to have to tell Courtney about Hannah being placed in a garbage bag and stored in the garage for nine months until the police found her body. I only wanted to answer the questions she asked. But there was more she needed to know about Karen.

"Karen has changed through the years. She has received Jesus and he has changed her. I go to see her and pray for her because God has called me to do so. As I have watched her change over the years, I have come to love her and forgive her."

I knew there was more truth to be shared even though Courtney didn't know to ask. I wanted her to know her birth mother was now a follower of Christ and that over the years she had found forgiveness. I hoped hearing this would help to prepare Courtney's own heart to forgive her mother one day. I had come to believe that was one of God's main purposes in allowing me to be Courtney's mother. He wanted me to teach her to live a life of surrender and to know the power of forgiveness. But this would take time. I'd have to be patient.

"Does she know about me?" Courtney asked.

I chuckled. "Of course, she knows about you. She gave birth to you."

We both let out a little laugh.

"Oh, yeah. That's true."

"I have written to her and sent pictures of you throughout the years. She knows all about you. She prays for you."

Breaking down in tears again, Courtney blurted out, "This means I was never planned or wanted."

"Yes, you were. Many children aren't exactly planned by their parents. They come as a surprise when the mother finds out she's pregnant. Not all of my other children were *planned*. They were wonderful surprise gifts from God. Only God can create, and he created you. You were planned by his will and for his purpose. Karen wanted you as well. Her circumstances wouldn't allow her to keep you. Her gift to us was gracious. Her gift to us was you."

Tears flowed down our faces. She rocked forward and sobbed. What sad news for a young girl to learn. How does a teenager process such devastating information? I rubbed her back and let her cry. Handing her more tissues, I gave her a hug and boldly said, "I . . . love . . . you."

"I love you too," she said through her sobs.

Moments passed. We sat silently again, both our eyes red and wet.

"When do you go to the prison to see Karen again?" Courtney asked.

"I had planned to go this coming Friday."

"Can I go with you?"

I was taken aback. Really? She wanted to meet Karen? Wanting to meet her birth mother was one thing, but knowing what Karen had done to Hannah, I was surprised that she wanted to meet her. Perhaps she needed to see for herself who this woman was.

"Yes. If I can arrange it, you can go with me." I smiled and gave her another hug.

"What do you think she will say if I go to see her?"

"I think she will be so happy to meet you. Your visit would bring her great joy. She has suffered much for what she did. Being able to meet you will be an amazing gift of grace." I pushed hair from Courtney's wet face as I spoke.

"I want to go," she said.

"Okay then," I said. "I will call the prison to see what we need to do to get you a pass and write Karen to let her know. Are you sure you want to go?" I still wanted to protect Courtney from the whole story even though much of it had now been laid before her.

"And I want to meet the rest of my biological sisters and brothers. Can I do that?" she asked hesitatingly.

"Yes. And you have grandparents who would love to meet you as well. Do you want to meet them?" Was I offering too much too soon?

"I want to meet all of them. Do you think that's okay?"

"If that's what you want to do, I will contact them as well." I didn't know if I should make that decision or leave it up to Courtney. There had been many unanswered questions in her life. She seemed to want them all answered at once. I began retreating a little as I shifted on the bed, squeezing the pillow I held against my chest.

Courtney looked at me, then scooted up next to me. "You are my mom," she said. "I love you. *You* are my mom."

We both began to cry again.

"I know. I'm concerned for you to take on so much so quickly." I wiped away the tears that continued to roll down my cheeks.

We held hands as I thanked God aloud for his grace. We thanked him for working in Karen's life and in our own. We asked him to prepare the Bower children and the grandparents for my call.

The next day, I let Al know all that had happened the night before. I called the prison regarding a pass for Courtney, then I wrote a letter to Karen sharing everything with her and telling her that Courtney planned to come with me on the next visit.

Friday morning arrived. Courtney and I set off for Lusk. Music on the car radio helped to fill what would have been a silent two-hour drive. As the miles drew us closer to the prison, I became more and more aware of how desperately I wanted this to be a positive experience for Courtney and Karen. But I also knew this was beyond my control. I could not orchestrate the visit, and I had to surrender any desire to do so. My job was to bring Courtney to her birth mother, then step back and allow the two of them to find their own way of relating. As I drove, I prayed, entrusting their hearts and hopes to the Lord.

Once we arrived, parked, and began our walk up to the prison, Courtney slowed her pace as she scanned the fences with their barbed wire and the exterior walls of the prison. "This is it? Wow. It's big."

I announced our presence at the security gate speaker box. The lock clicked, I pushed the gate open, and Courtney experienced for the first time the checking-in process that I knew so well. I thought back to my own nervousness when I'd first visited Karen here. *Surely, Courtney's feelings must be just as intense or even more so than mine had been*, I thought. I longed to make it easier for her but knew that was beyond my control.

When we reached the visitation room, we stood off to one side, our gaze focused on the security door. One by one, female prisoners were searched and cleared to enter the room through a security door. We could see them through the large glass window. Each time a woman approached the security door to come into the visitation room, Courtney asked, "Is that her?"

After a handful of women entered the room, I could see Karen at the window.

"There she is," I whispered to Courtney.

Karen appeared a little anxious, but I had never seen such a big smile. When she reached us, I said, "Karen, this is Courtney. Courtney, this is Karen."

They gave each other a tentative hug. I wrapped my arms around both of them. Although there was more healing to come, this one act allowed for healing to begin. Tears flowed as we moved to an area where we could all sit and talk. As I watched Karen and Courtney talk to each other, I couldn't help thinking that Karen knew so much about Courtney, while Courtney actually knew nothing about Karen.

I appreciated it when Karen said, "Your mom has told me so much about you." It was kind and respectful.

What could Karen share? She wouldn't want to share her daily life in prison with the child she had only seen as a five-week-old infant. So small talk filled the hour visit. But that was okay. Deeper conversations might come in time. Courtney had met her birth mother. Many unanswered questions had been answered. This was only the beginning.

Time was up. Karen and I hugged, then Karen hugged Courtney.

"Thank you for coming," Karen said. "I am so happy I could meet you. I hope you come again."

The drive home wasn't as quiet as the drive to the prison. More questions flowed from Courtney. Our talk was less emotional than the one in the bedroom, though. Courtney's first visit with Karen had satisfied her initial curiosity about her birth mother.

There were other people in her family line to meet, so we talked about setting up a visit with DeAnn and the grandparents. Where should we meet with them that would be comfortable for everyone? Always thinking about food, Courtney said, "How about Dairy Queen?" Dairy Queen it was! Just enough time for an ice cream and a little chat.

I was nervous to contact the grandparents. I knew they were not happy that I had kept Courtney from them for so many years. I left a message on their phone saying that their granddaughter would like to meet them.

Within hours I received a call from DeAnn. She was calling on behalf of her grandparents. They were all excited to meet with Courtney and me at the Dairy Queen that weekend. When I told Courtney the news, she said she was nervous to meet them. DeAnn had frightened her when she had approached Courtney in the restaurant bathroom. Now that they were both older, maybe they could start over. Maybe they could even have a relationship.

The biggest hurdles seemed to be over. Courtney had met Ally and Steven at the mall and learned they were biological siblings. She knew the truth about her birth mother and her family. She'd visited Karen at the prison. Now, we were about to walk into the Dairy Queen to meet her oldest sister and the grandparents she had never known.

Entering the fast-food restaurant, I scanned the tables for the Bowers. DeAnn and a man I thought might be her husband sat next to the grandparents at a large table. Their smiles welcomed us, making us more comfortable.

"Hi, Courtney," Grandpa Bower said. "I'm your grandfather, and this is your grandmother. We are so happy to meet you."

Courtney responded with a shy, "Hi."

"I'm DeAnn, and this is my husband, Trey. We're happy you came."

We all ordered ice cream, and each of us found a little security in the comfort of food before us. Light talk about trivial things filled our short time together.

"I understand you are on the girls' hockey team. We would love to come and watch you sometime," DeAnn said. "When are your games?"

Talk of hockey and game schedules ended when our ice cream was eaten, signaling a unanimous end to the visit. I stood back as each family member hugged Courtney, wanting them to have their special time with her. I wanted her to take in all the attention from them that she deserved.

Grandpa Bower broke away from the small group and walked toward me. I wasn't sure what was about to happen and stiffened a little.

He stretched out his arms, then wrapped them around me. With soft sobs, he said, "Thank you. She is wonderful. Thank you."

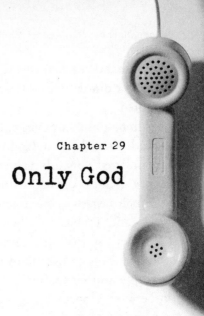

Chapter 29

Only God

AFTER THEIR FIRST VISIT, Karen wrote to Courtney a few times and sent her little gifts she made in prison. Courtney wrote back. One of her biggest questions for Karen was, *Who is my biological father?* Courtney had already asked me, and I'd told her, as Karen had told me, that Karen didn't know. She hadn't even known if Courtney would be born white, part Hispanic, or part African American, and even after she was born with very fair skin, Karen still couldn't be sure who the father was. When Karen was unable to identify the father, Courtney understandably felt disappointed. It can be a hard thing for anyone to learn that some of life's big questions must remain unanswered, but perhaps hardest of all for a young adopted adolescent.

After several months, Courtney decided to stop writing Karen and didn't want to go with me to see her. When I would visit, she simply asked how Karen was doing. That seemed to satisfy Courtney's need for connection with Karen throughout the rest of her final middle-school year. Her interest in her halfsister DeAnn, however, began to grow during this same period. DeAnn and her husband reached out to Courtney with invitations to their home for dinner with them and their children. Courtney eagerly accepted.

After a number of visits, I began to see a change in Courtney's attitude toward Karen. Courtney had many questions, and DeAnn remembered a disturbing history with her mother. As the oldest of all the siblings, she had witnessed more of their mother's choices and their negative consequences on all of her siblings.

Al and I began to be concerned about a subtle shift in Courtney's spirits. She seemed a bit more withdrawn than usual and her energy lower than normal. We did our best to remain available and close, but ever so slowly a distance was creeping in between Courtney and us, and an undercurrent of anger and resentment toward Karen was beginning to grow in her.

When Courtney entered high school, I hoped she would excel as she had in middle school. She was smart and had potential to do well. But her wounded heart seemed to quench her motivation. Her anger was beginning to surface more and spill out not only in her attitude toward Karen, but in her overall demeanor. This had been one of the things I had feared in exposing Courtney to her story and birth family, but there was no going back now. By the time she turned fifteen she was struggling in school and was choosing to hang out with some friends who were less than ideal in terms of their influence on her. Her attitude became rebellious and unkind. She had lost interest in ice hockey and decided to quit. At times, I found her being sneaky and dishonest. Al and I continued our efforts for healthy conversations with her, but it felt like she'd stopped communicating.

I wondered how much of her pervasive negative mood had to do with adjustments to being fifteen and how much might have to do with her feelings surrounding the circumstances of her adoption. So one day, I asked if she would like to speak to a counselor about all the information she had discovered concerning her biological family. She agreed, and I set up an appointment with a counselor. She and Courtney connected, and after a handful of visits, Courtney seemed to be doing better and felt she didn't need to see the counselor anymore.

In spite of the counseling, however, going to church as a family of three only seemed to push our daughter into more rebellion. She would slump down in the seat with her arms folded or want to put her head on my lap and sleep. I constantly nudged her to sit up, and Al let her know she was to be respectful and not to rest her head on my lap in church. I worried over her apparent disinterest in her spiritual life. Eventually, I had to realize I'd hit another point of surrender. Courtney would need to grow into her own personal relationship with the Lord—I couldn't make it happen. Instead, I needed to trust the Holy Spirit to do his work in the heart of my precious daughter.

Our frustration grew as Courtney continued to withdraw from school, us, and church. She even acted jealous of our older children. One day during a visit to see Karen, I shared with her, mother to mother, my concerns.

"It's really all my fault," Karen said. "Because of me, she has so many unanswered questions. And the answers she does get are not the ones she wants to hear." Karen was sincere in her concern. She told me that a few of her other children had written to her over the past few years, asking her questions as well. They, too, struggled, even though the families who adopted and raised them were loving Christian families. I could see that she had been maturing as a mother even though she had not been able to parent her children since they were young.

I knew from my own experience that there are wounds that no person can heal. Only God can bring real healing to a torn heart and a confused spirit. Knowing the devil is the father of confusion, I could only pray that God would intervene and bring truth and healing to our daughter. More surrender.

One evening, just before I was about to turn off my light and go to sleep, there was a soft knocking on my bedroom door. Slowly, the door opened and Courtney whispered through the crack, "Are you going to sleep, Mom?"

"I was about to. Do you need something?"

"Can I talk to you for a minute?"

"Sure. Come in."

She crawled onto my bed and reached for Al's pillow. He was watching the late news downstairs and wouldn't be up for some time. Watching Courtney hug the pillow, I could see our talk wouldn't be short. I scooted upright and fluffed my pillow behind me. "What's up?"

Courtney tried to conjure up a hint of a smile, then looked down at the bedcovers. I waited. Whatever it was, I sensed I needed to brace myself. Over many years, I had learned to be still and ready for whatever the Lord was going to allow into my life, but now fear slowly began to rise in my chest as I folded my hands and rested them in my lap, readying myself for what was about to come.

"I'm pregnant." Courtney began to cry.

I didn't move. I couldn't. I could barely breathe. This was not something I was ready for. As Courtney sobbed, all I knew to do was to hold her. I said nothing. I gave myself an internal slap and told myself to toughen up. *Use your head, Deb, not your heart.* I couldn't speak from my heart; it was breaking all over again.

In a state of shock I asked, "Who is the father?" I was not surprised at the answer. I had warned Courtney, and I had set rules and guidelines that the two of them were not to be alone at our home. But, like many of us, she didn't heed the warnings or follow the rules. And now she was expecting a baby.

How much more, Lord? How much more is there before there is no more heartache in our family? My silent prayer reached toward heaven in desperation. Would I ever be able to say "I'm done"?

And in an instant I knew the answer.

No.

Life this side of heaven continues on with its challenges and ups and downs whether we feel ready for them or not. Surrender isn't a lesson learned all at once. It is a choice to be practiced time and time again until it becomes our automatic response—and that may take a lifetime of practice. We don't graduate from life's trials, nor do we retire from spiritual growth. I knew that this wasn't because God was heartless or cruel—just the opposite. God was still about the business of conforming me to the image of his Son. As God's Word says in Philippians 1:6, "being confident of this, that he who began a good work in you will carry it on to completion until the day of Christ Jesus."

God is still committed to completing his work in me—a work he will not complete until I step into eternity. Continually calling me to surrender my will to his will is his plan for the rest of my life. The choice to do so willingly, not begrudgingly, with thanks in my heart, is the opportunity to watch his grace at work in breathtaking ways.

The question to ask was not, *How much, Lord?* The only question to ask was which direction we should look to find the help we need to face our challenges. I knew that answer already. There was nowhere else to look but to my Lord. So in this new challenge with Courtney, Al and I would ask God what to do, surrender to his leading, and leave it in his hands. I knew it wouldn't be easy, but it was the only way forward.

I let Courtney cry until she stopped long enough to look at me. She kept saying, "I'm sorry, Mom. I'm so sorry."

"I know." It was all I could say.

"I asked God to forgive me. Can you forgive me?" she said through her tears.

"I know God will forgive you. And yes, I do as well."

But forgiveness doesn't eliminate consequences. And I knew that my daughter now had life consequences to face. This meant consequences for Al and me as well. And soon! A few questions to Courtney revealed that this baby was likely to be born in only about two months! Courtney had hidden her growing belly from us well by wearing her oversized baggy hoodies. My spirit felt heavy. It was late. We were both tired, and the next morning was a school day. We agreed to get some sleep and talk to Dad the next evening.

The news crushed Al when Courtney told him. I cried when I saw the expression on his face. We'd had such hope for our daughter. We'd done everything in our power to raise her right, raise her with love, support, and the knowledge of God who loves her and has a plan for her life. I had told my children as they were growing up not to put all their faith in us as their parents. We would fail them. We wouldn't want to, but we would. Instead, I urged them to put their faith in Jesus. He would never fail them. Did we fail Courtney?

Isn't that the first thing parents think? *What did we do wrong?*

I praised God later that day when Courtney told us that she'd made the choice early not to abort. I told her I was proud of her that she had decided to choose life and had not made the same mistake I had to abort at the age of seventeen. We agreed that we would discuss parenting or adoption. I felt adoption would be the best choice, but I knew that Courtney needed someone to talk to, other than Al and me, about this critical decision. This was a lifetime decision that only she could make, and I surrendered it to the Lord immediately. The child she carried was her child. I didn't believe I, or anyone else, could or should make the decision for her. She was the one who would have to live with her choices.

When we gave our older children the news of the expected child, they had a complex mix of responses—love, disappointment, grief, anger, tenderness, and concern. They were all distressed, and tension and resentment wrapped their ugly selves around the ones we loved. What Courtney would decide about adoption versus parenting would make a huge difference in the relationships with our other children. I found myself shrinking into depression and an intense sense of sorrow and loss. My grief was so severe it was as if Hannah had died all over again. Something within me had died.

There was turmoil in my family, and the dreams I had for saving Courtney from a terrible life felt as if they all came crashing down.

I thought back to when I was a young girl growing up in southern California. I loved spending time at the beach. One day I'd spent hours building a great sand castle when out of nowhere, some mean kids came and kicked it down, laughing as they destroyed my hard work. I felt overpowered and intimidated. Now it felt as though the evil one had kicked down the castle I had worked so hard to build. Not only with Courtney, but with the rest of my family. The family discord broke my heart.

One very difficult call I had to make was to Terry Winship at True Care crisis pregnancy center, formerly The Caring Center where I had been the executive director. Terry had been a volunteer counselor during my tenure, and now she was the director of the center. During the ten years I had been the director, I had counseled, supported, and loved on many women and teens in our community through a crisis pregnancy. Now, humbly, it was my turn to be the recipient of such support. It was my daughter facing this difficult path. I was so thankful for Terry's loving encouragement. I made an appointment for Courtney to confirm her pregnancy with a test and ultrasound.

On the day of the appointment, as I watched the well-developed unborn baby moving around in the womb of my young daughter, the reality of the life in her hit me like an unexpected tidal wave. Courtney looked up at me, reflecting my own devastation. Then, while my young daughter dressed, I was escorted by the counselor toward a waiting room. Though a volcano of emotions wanted to erupt, I remained expressionless. The woman walking alongside me commented, "You are amazingly calm for just finding all of this out."

I slowly looked over at her and said, "This is my expression of shock and heartbreak. It is a mask I have created for such times like this. I have had much practice."

A few days later, I took off work so Courtney and I could

drive an hour and a half across Wyoming to meet with an adoption counselor from Bethany Christian Services. She drove up from Cheyenne to meet with us halfway at a coffee shop. I told Courtney she could meet with the woman alone, and I would wait outside. She needed to ask all the questions she wanted and find out all the information she needed without feeling pressure from me. An hour later, Courtney came out and got into the car. We drove home in silence as tears poured uncontrollably down my cheeks.

I hated that I couldn't keep from crying. My internal slap was not working. I couldn't find the muster to toughen up. I was broken again. I couldn't fix it, and I had no idea how God would. The dreams of Courtney finishing high school, going on to college, meeting Mr. Wonderful, marrying, and then having precious little children were gone. Was she following in her birth mother's footsteps? As much as I had come to love Karen, my prayer had always been to remove Courtney as far as possible from the lifestyle of drugs, alcohol, and promiscuity Karen had chosen to live. I grieved and mourned the death of what I had hoped for my daughter.

I asked a friend of ours if she would visit with Courtney as well. She had relinquished her baby when she was a young teen. She was now married and had three children. I knew Courtney could talk to her about the pros and cons of her decision. I drove Courtney to her home, two hours away, and let the two visit for a few hours. When I picked Courtney up to head back to Casper, I could see a new resolve in her eyes, though she didn't share what she was thinking.

Weeks passed. Pamphlets arrived in the mail from adoption agencies that were meant to educate Courtney so she could make an informed decision about either adoption or parenting. But I knew. She'd made her decision long before all of the counseling. She wanted to parent her child. Though still a child herself at fifteen, she didn't want her baby raised by someone other than its mother. I understood. So Al and I accepted Courtney's choice. We would go through the pregnancy with her and then help her to be the best mother she could be. We surrendered whatever dreams we'd had of soon entering our empty nest years. Parenting our daughter through this critical time in her life became our highest priority.

As a family, we talked about a plan for future education and work. Courtney would remain in school to the middle of her sophomore year, then leave and get her GED. College classes would come later. She would find part-time work for the short time until the baby was born. After a month off she would go back to work. Since we were still raising her, we'd cover her medical expenses. Now that she would be a mother, the baby's expenses would be covered by her. Those expenses would be formula, diapers, clothes, and whatever else the baby needed. This would give her the responsibility she needed to take care of her child. She agreed.

I made a special trip to Lusk to tell Karen about the baby face-to-face. We wept together as Karen expressed how she hoped that Courtney would not make many of the same life choices that she had made. I was touched that Karen asked how my older kids were handling the news, and she was saddened to hear about the tension it was causing, though she understood. Karen told me that she was grateful to God for the love and support we were giving Courtney. In our touching exchange, mother to mother, we comforted each other, and I once again marveled at the growth of the bond the two of us shared.

One evening, I passed Courtney's room carrying an armful of folded laundry. Courtney sat on her bed sorting through clothes.

"Mom! Can you come here a minute?" she called.

"Sure. What's up?" I entered her room and sat down on the bed next to her.

"I want to thank you for supporting me in my decision to keep the baby," she said, giving me a hug.

I hugged her in return. "I want you to understand that it's a big responsibility. You will need help to be a good mom." I smiled back at her. "You need to think about what kind of a mom you are going to be." I wanted to encourage her to be praying and planning on how she would parent her little one.

"I know what kind of a mom I want to be," she said. "I want to be like you."

I bowed my head as tears fell from my eyes. My heart was full. Full of loss, sorrow, and what I thought were shattered dreams. But full of love as well. Life was not over yet. I'd been down difficult roads before and knew the Lord would be my strength, even through the storm of my negative emotions.

Motherhood can be the hardest job a woman will ever experience. Joy. Yes, there is joy. Heartbreak? Definitely. Some heartbreaks feel as if they will never heal. Only God can bring healing. Only in God would there be hope.

"Mom, I think I'm going into labor."

I checked the clock. 8:00 p.m. on January 15, 2015. Al and I were surprised at how nervous we felt as we quickly packed a little bag for her, and the three of us headed for the hospital. In the birthing room, as the nurses prepared Courtney, I hovered, while Al turned on the TV. It would be a while before the baby would come. We all needed to settle in and wait. I was surprised how well sixteen-year-old Courtney was handling it. She actually slept between labor pains. Al watched the TV, and I paced and marveled at both of them as they remained calm and ready for the birth.

I watched my young daughter lying in the hospital bed on the same floor of the same hospital where so much had taken place. It was here that baby Ally had been born and I'd picked her up to take her home. It was here I'd first met Karen. It was here I'd sat anxiously in the hallway with the two DFS workers and their police escort, awaiting Courtney's birth, not knowing if we'd be allowed to adopt her. Now Courtney's baby would be born.

I will soon have brought all three home from the time of their birth and, as with the first two, a new chapter of life will begin to unfold. Dear Lord, make me ready for this new chapter.

For much of the evening, I walked the floor of the labor room taking in the wonder of motherhood, my own as well as that of two of my other daughters who had grown up, married, and become mothers. I pondered the lifetime commitment of motherhood, and I prayed God would give me the wisdom to be close enough to be available to my own daughters when needed yet offer enough distance to allow them to be the mothers God had called them to be.

It must have been close to two in the morning when Courtney felt she needed to push.

"The doctor went home to sleep for a while," the nurse said, "believing the baby wouldn't come for hours yet." Obviously, the baby had different plans. Watching three nurses run in and out of the birthing room didn't give us much confidence. Would the doctor make it in time? Would the head nurse be delivering? We hoped not.

Nearly twenty minutes passed before the doctor arrived. He rushed into the room with a big smile and said, "Let's do this!"

We were more than ready.

I held Courtney's hand as she pushed, reminding her that she was doing a great job and the baby would come soon. Then with one big push, lil Miss Mary made her debut. Nurses rushed to receive the newborn from the doctor, ready to weigh her and clean her up for her mommy to hold. Within minutes, Mary was wrapped in a pale green-and-white receiving blanket, just as Courtney had been sixteen years before, and placed on Courtney's chest. I cuddled close to both of them and watched mother and child connect. Tears of joy rolled down our cheeks as we witnessed precious new life. It was then that, deep in my spirit, I sensed God speaking to me in a way I had never heard before.

"It is through heartache, heartbreak, and pain that I grow you, Deb. But I have given you a free will so that you can choose. Will you live, or become bitter and die? Will you allow me to work in your life in the way I see best to encourage the most positive possible outcome, or will you be satisfied to live small and crippled within your own limited borders?"

The Lord brought Deuteronomy 30:19 to my mind.

This day I call the heavens and the earth as witnesses against you that I have set before you life and death, blessings and curses. Now choose life, so that you and your children may live.

Then he continued speaking to me. *"All I have allowed into your world is not only for your good, but for the good of others. I didn't create the world to revolve around you. I created the world and created you to become more of the image of me. The face of this newborn baby is the face of me. The only way I become life in you is through pain and laboring. I know it hurts. I know you feel lonely and separated from those you love when you choose to follow me rather than what others want you to do. I know there are times when you feel like giving up and that life seems hopeless and you feel helpless. I know. I know.*

"But my mercies are new every day. My grace is made fresh every morning. My love is never-ending, and the depth of my love for you goes far beyond what you could begin to imagine. My love is not limited like yours. My love is everlasting. I break you because I love you. I disappoint you to show you that it's your own appointments that are dis-appointed—they are not my appointments for you.

"You can never give the way I give. You cannot see as I see. You cannot love as I love, until, like my Son, you have entered this world, been broken by it, and then, love through it. Only I can fill you with my power of forgiveness. Only I can take the sorrow and turn it into something beautiful."

In the sweet face of new life, God spoke truth into my heart. And I knew beyond a doubt that only God could do that.

Only God could create Mary and place her in loving arms.

Only God could have put Hannah, a child who was going to be murdered, into the hands of a family who would truly love her and show her Jesus.

Only God could bring forth a forgiveness that goes beyond just saying the words.

Only God could lead me to become a lay chaplain in a jail, knowing that I'd be able to hear the murderer's confession and lead her to Christ.

Only God could put me in a Mrs. International pageant at a time when I was broken beyond repair and bring eternal truth and beauty from the event.

Only God could blossom in the heart of a woman serving a life sentence and fill her with new purpose and his love.

Only God could take down the giants of bitterness and hatred, of broken lives and desperate circumstances, and craft new lives that live for him.

Only God could lead me to the depths of sacrificial obedience and repeated surrender.

Only God could use a murder and the calling of motherhood to demonstrate his miraculous grace!

Interview with Debra Moerke

How did your story come to be a book?

Years ago, as I saw God's hand move in my and Karen's hearts, I recognized that the hearts of many others were not moving forward toward healing. I sensed God encouraging me to share what he was doing, believing that healing could take place in others if they knew the love, forgiveness, and hope he could bring to those who sought him. The pressure to tell the story became more intense as the years passed, until I realized I needed help to accomplish the task. I knew God would have to bring the right people into my life to write the book. And he did!

Was it difficult for you and your family to relive the events?

Yes. Writing the book prompted discussions that my husband, children, and I had never had before. It brought out feelings many of them didn't want to feel again. A few didn't want to talk about the story at all, while others opened up and poured out all they felt after the events took place. For some, feelings of anger, unforgiveness, and pain hadn't changed over the years. For others, talking about and sharing the hope and healing the story might bring to those who read the book caused them to rethink, evaluate their hearts, and recognize how God can forgive and bring good out of evil.

Why did it feel important for you to write the book, and what do you hope readers will take away from it?

I didn't doubt that God was urging me to write it. I believe he wants others to know the growth and freedom I went through, as well as what Karen went through, to bring healing and truth to their own lives. I hope that readers—no matter where they are coming from—will walk away with a better understanding of how God can work in our lives; how trusting him for direction, healing, and hope can offer us freedom and peace; and how following him can lead others to that freedom and hope.

Do you still visit Karen or stay in contact with her in any way? Has her faith continued to grow?

Yes. I talk to Karen on the phone a few times a month, and I visit her three to four times a year at the prison. She is more at peace with God. She has acknowledged to me that she knows he has forgiven her, and she reads her Bible and devotionals daily. She ministers to other women when they are open to listening to her. Her countenance has changed dramatically over the years as God has been working in her life.

Did you consult with Karen during the process of writing the book?

Yes. She knew years ago that I felt called to write the book. She and I both had our fears in doing so. It was another level of growth for both of us, and we prayed for each other as we decided to move forward with me writing the book. Karen read the manuscript, and that process seemed to bring about even more growth and healing.

Has the aftermath of what happened affected your feelings about the foster care system?

It has helped me to understand that no organization, company, group, or system is without fault. People are involved and people are flawed. We can do our best in serving others, but we cannot cover every need of every person. The intent of social service organizations is to serve and help children and families. They are overloaded with cases, and even though they want to do the best they can, they will fall short in areas, as we all do. Grace has to be shown to others if we want grace to be shown to us when we fall short. Just before the book was released, out of respect for the Department of Family Services in Casper, I met with the current director and his wife to explain that my heart's desire in bringing this story to light was to encourage hope and healing to family members, our community, and every person who might read the book.

How did Courtney participate in the writing of this book, and how did she feel when reading it for the first time?

When I first told Courtney that I was going to move forward in writing the book, I said it would be under one condition: I needed to have her support and blessing. She thought for a moment and then said, "If you promise to tell the whole truth, you have my support and blessing." We agreed! Once the entire manuscript was completed, I let Courtney read it. She cried at many parts of the book. She laughed at a few. She had questions for me. We talked about them, and then she said, "I'm proud of you, Mom," and she hugged me very tightly. I asked her to tell me why she was proud of me, so she wrote me a note that said, "I am proud to call you my mom and to stand by your book because of the hardships you dealt with in everything. In the end, Hannah and God were typing your story, helping you to create it. I believe Hannah was tapping you on the shoulder and pushing you, saying, 'It's time to tell my story and your story.'"

How are Courtney and Mary doing today? What are Courtney's plans and hopes for the future?

Courtney is a loving and protective mommy, completely committed to Mary. As I write this, Mary is four years old and goes to preschool. She is a happy little girl with a sweet heart. The two of them live with my husband and me. Courtney is finishing her schooling in medical billing and coding to pursue a career that would bring future financial security for Mary and herself. Providing for Mary and raising her to be a healthy, happy, well-adjusted young lady is of the utmost importance to her mother.

Are you or Courtney still in touch with anyone from Hannah's biological family? Are there any updates you're at liberty to share?

Yes. Courtney touches base with a few of her brothers and sisters now and then. A few times a year, two of her siblings stop by our home. Courtney and Mary have dinner with Karen's father every so often. About once a week, he comes to the restaurant where Courtney works to have a meal and see her. She and her grandfather have a good relationship. After Karen's mother passed away, I began visiting him, too, bringing him a meal or dessert. A special blessing is that Karen's father and I have gone to the prison together to visit Karen. That is an amazing gift.

You share in the book that your past includes an abortion. Was that a difficult part of your story to relate?

Somewhat. I knew that before I could minister to others, especially publicly, I had to confess the truth to my extended family. (My immediate family already knew.) I have shared my story for years in order to minister to others, but it is not an easy confession to make.

How has it influenced your life decisions such as fostering, working at a pregnancy crisis center, and adopting?

Ever since I chose to follow Jesus, I have found that he uses all my past sins and even my failures to open my eyes and heart to the needs of others. Whether to people in pain from a past event or to those struggling with decisions today, I believe God has called me and uses me to share his love and forgiveness with them. When I was a young girl of seventeen, I believed a baby in the womb was just tissue. Not until science and the medical field said, "No, this is a human life from conception" did I understand why there would be such a feeling of guilt over just tissue. It was hard to get counsel for something that was considered a nonissue. Decades later I read *Aborting America* by Dr. Bernard Nathanson, one of our nation's top abortionists in the 1960s. In the 1970s he had a complete change of heart. His conviction—that we were killing babies—became my conviction as well, and I began to understand where and why God was calling me into a world of protecting children while loving their parents. My heart is for the innocent children, born and unborn. I believe God gave me a heart for them.

What message is on your heart to share with other women who have abortion as part of their story?

Women today have a wide spectrum of opinions and experiences when it comes to abortion. For some, it is not a matter of *if* the unborn baby is human or not, or alive or not, but that there are laws that give us the right to abort. While the latter is true, each of us needs to decide who gave us that right. Was this a God-given right or a government-given right? That would be my question to anyone considering abortion. Each of us needs to answer that question according to our own conscience and heart.

Then there are those who wrestle with the decision, knowing or believing it is wrong but feeling trapped in their circumstances. They believe the lie that they have no choice but to abort. They believe they can live with the regret better than living with an unwanted baby.

There are also those who choose abortion and then live their lives with such guilt that they can't function. Their shame and secret eats at them every day of their lives.

Only God can change our hearts. Only God can forgive and heal those who were deceived in believing they didn't have a choice. Only God can restore life to the woman who is eaten up with shame and guilt. I choose to love all of them with the help and love I receive from Jesus.

What advice would you give readers who have children in their lives and are struggling, not sure where to find help?

When Karen and I committed to sharing this story, her hope was that it would prevent someone else from doing what she did. She knew she had been too prideful and stubborn to accept help. She regrets that now, and she and I have prayed that if there is a struggling parent out there who needs help with his or her children or his or her own pain, that he or she would seek help. Counselors, churches, and social services can help.

What's next for you, Al, and the rest of your family?

We have no idea! We will see what the Lord brings and remain committed to surrendering to his leading.

Acknowledgments

I am filled with gratitude to my incredible prayer team whose faithful prayers saw me through every phase of writing this book: Helen Vaughn, Ron Kirkegaard, Dale Hampton, Lauree Benson, Shauna Letellier, Jewel Saunders, Pam Bartosh, and Chris Larramendy.

I thank those who gave me such generous support and prayer throughout this project: Thom and Marla Johnson, Angela Heigler, Leebett Calar, Jamie Barbe, Darcie Gudger, Jackie Brown, John and Chris Larramendy, Tom and Charlene Bichel, and Sandy Meyerson.

Publishing a book was even more of a team effort than I ever imagined. Thank you to the Tyndale House Publishers team who so graciously contributed their skills and creativity: Jan Long Harris, executive publisher; Sarah Atkinson, associate publisher; Bonne Steffen, senior editor; Julie Chen, senior designer; Sarah Kelley, associate editor; Jillian Schlossberg, acquisitions editor; Kara Leonino, acquisitions editor; Maria Eriksen, marketing; and Amanda Woods and Katie Dodillet, public relations.

Lissa Halls Johnson also invested her keen editorial insight. I thank you.

I am grateful to Wes Yoder, my agent, who believed the story had to be told, and to Cindy Lambert, my collaborative writer. Cindy, without you hearing my story and feeling called to using your expertise and gifts to bring it to life, this story may not have been written.

How can I possibly express to my daughter Courtney and my husband, Al, what it meant to me to have their support and encouragement through every step of this adventure? There were many days they had to fend for themselves. I love you both and appreciate you so very much.

And finally, I give special thanks to "Karen" for reading the entire manuscript for accuracy. Karen, your support throughout the process meant more than words can say.

About the Authors

Debra Moerke and her husband, Al, were foster parents for eighteen years, taking in more than 140 children. Debra has served as the director of women's and children's ministries of the Central Wyoming Rescue Mission; the executive director of a Christian crisis pregnancy and counseling center; a jail guard; and a jail chaplain. In 2017 she graduated from Gateway Seminary in California with a certificate in Christian ministries. She is currently an associate real estate broker and owner of Stratton Real Estate. Debra and Al live in Casper, Wyoming, and have six children and seven grandchildren.

Cindy Lambert, a freelance writer and editor, is a veteran of the bookselling industry. For nearly two decades she owned an award-winning bookstore before expanding into leadership roles in such companies as Ingram, Simon & Schuster, and Zondervan, where she served as vice president and associate publisher. She and her husband, Dave, have six children and nine grandchildren and live in Michigan.